What if Culture was Nature all Along?

New Materialisms
Series editors: Iris van der Tuin and Rosi Braidotti

New Materialisms asks how materiality permits representation, actualises ethical subjectivities and innovates the political. The series will provide a discursive hub and an institutional home to this vibrant emerging field and open it up to a wider readership.

Editorial Advisory board
Marie-Luise Angerer, Karen Barad, Corinna Bath, Barbara Bolt, Felicity Colman, Manuel DeLanda, Richard Grusin, Vicki Kirby, Gregg Lambert, Nina Lykke, Brian Massumi, Henk Oosterling, Arun Saldanha

Books available
What if Culture was Nature all Along?
Edited by Vicki Kirby

Critical and Clinical Cartographies: Architecture, Robotics, Medicine, Philosophy
Edited by Andrej Radman and Heidi Sohn

Books forthcoming
Architectural Materialisms: Non-Human Creativity
Edited by Maria Voyatzaki

What if Culture was Nature all Along?

Edited by Vicki Kirby

EDINBURGH
University Press

Edinburgh University Press is one of the leading university presses in the UK. We publish academic books and journals in our selected subject areas across the humanities and social sciences, combining cutting-edge scholarship with high editorial and production values to produce academic works of lasting importance. For more information visit our website: edinburghuniversitypress.com

Edinburgh University Press Ltd
The Tun – Holyrood Road, 12(2f) Jackson's Entry, Edinburgh EH8 8PJ

Typeset in 11/13 Adobe Sabon by
IDSUK (DataConnection) Ltd

A CIP record for this book is available from the British Library

ISBN 978 1 4744 1929 1 (hardback)
ISBN 978 1 4744 1930 7 (webready PDF)
ISBN 978 1 4744 1931 4 (epub)

Contents

Acknowledgements

A big thank you to Iris van der Tuin for her early appreciation of our collective efforts and her vision and encouragement in helping us to realise this project. I would also like to thank those participants in *Mull*, our regular reading group, who did not make it into the book. The conversations and general good cheer of several 'floating' Mull members over several years of the book's gestation have been invaluable; Naama Carlin, Holi Birman, Jasmin Kelaita, Suzi Hayes, Sophie Robinson, André Etiamby, Nayana Bibile and James Banwell. And one thing we can agree upon is that The Cricketers Arms and Strawberry Hills Hotels have never let us down.

The University of New South Wales, School of Social Sciences, has provided welcome support with a small grant towards the indexing of the book, which is much appreciated.

Foreword

Where to Begin?

A visit to Sydney by Iris van der Tuin, one of the editors of the New Materialisms Series with Edinburgh University Press, first alerted most of the contributors to this collection that we were doing something unusual. The 'doing' involved our participation in a regular research workshop that we affectionately called 'Mull', and it was here that we committed to reading the most challenging texts in our individual research areas. We weren't too fussed about the subject matter or whether we all shared an interest in a particular author; the agreement was to read together and to encourage an environment of curiosity. I have mentored all of the contributors in one way or another over many years, and as a result we have all become comfortable with our differences. Looking back however, I can see that in the beginning we were especially satisfied with the outcome of these get-togethers – we could spot an argument's logical misstep and follow its repetitions with reasonable ease, enjoying the advantage of a group hunt. But as cornering and despatching our quarry with increasing alacrity began to disappoint I think it was only then that the more difficult task of learning *how* to read *with* an author – how to find the value that might be hidden in faltering hesitations and contradictions, how a weak spot might be an opportunity to be mined rather than a flaw to be condemned – became our main objective.

My own view is that we were learning how to read grammatologically, and yet this description tells us very little. Deconstruction is the methodology that eschews methodology, indeed, its paradoxical identity is a mirror maze of confusion for the novice. Not surprisingly, its linguistic reductionism and hermeticism have drawn criticism, and in the main, deconstruction has appeared peripheral and even redundant in relation to contemporary political and sociological concerns. Although I have never accepted this reading it has been popular nevertheless; a ready excuse for dismissal without the bother of actual engagement. However this perspective appears to be shifting, and in regard to this particular project, scholars such as Claire Colebrook, Cary Wolfe, David Wood, Michael Marder and Timothy Morton argue that deconstruction might ventilate current debates in posthumanism and deep ecology, and complicate the impasse between the humanities and the sciences. Although this book's collective argument is not an 'application' of deconstruction – Derrida's name is rarely mentioned – many essays deploy deconstructive strategies to explore what might be called 'natural sociologies'.

To explain this; a conventional reading of Derrida's well-known axiom, 'no outside text', is usually interpreted to mean 'no outside culture'. However, my own revision of this apparent enclosure to read, 'no outside nature', discovers a comprehensive landscape where nature is literate, numerate and social, and where the exceptional status and identity of the human is one of quantum dis/location. Importantly, we have not left the text in this revision, nor privileged nature instead of culture, because, quite simply, there is no outside, no remainder that is not already involved and evolving *as* text. Inevitably, the very notion, 'text', assumes the status of a question in this reading. As a result, matters of methodology take centre stage because the separation of subject from object, or even one position from another, becomes uncertain. This in turn complicates the triumphalism of negative critique and dismissal that can too easily motor and justify new materialisms – 'not epistemology but ontology', 'not the subject but the object', 'not language but matter' – instead, refracting individual positions through tangled intimacies. Rather than rely on these blunt and censoring adjudications our collective commitment is to enable and encourage curiosity through an ethics of generosity, one that refuses to refuse an argument outright, or too quickly. We may well fall over in the attempt to re-read through complicities, but we may also achieve a less predictable outcome by attempting such an exercise.

A signature ingredient in all these contributions is the question, 'where to begin?', and for this reason there is heavy reliance on feminist and critical theories whose sustained scrutiny of the nature/culture division and its conservative legacies have proven transformative. Although there is healthy scepticism about all oppositional logic that rests on an unquestioned a priori, the aim is to shift the temperament of these logics rather than to discount them automatically. A powerful intervention, for example, is to search for the usefulness in arguments we might otherwise denounce by rendering certain words and their meanings more pliable, even delinquent.

'Biologism' and 'naturalism' tend to be terms of accusation in critical analysis and commentary: they describe relatively static determinations whose causal prescriptions can seem timeless and irrevocable. All too predictably the reliance on these terms is answered with calls for '*de*-naturalisation', a gesture that focuses on the productive intervention of cultural interpretation and the difference that context makes. This reversal from natural to cultural explanations brings a sense of dynamism and political possibility – in short, no need for despair if we can change things. Yet such interventions also carry the message that nature/biology/*physis* is, indeed, the 'other' of culture, the static and primordial benchmark against which human be-ing and its agential imagination secures its exceptional status. But if the capacity to think stretches across an entire ecological landscape, what then? If nature is plastic, agential and inventive, then need we equate biologism and naturalism with a conservative agenda, a return to prescription and the resignation of political quietism? Many of these arguments offer suggestive evidence for why culture (ideation, agency, mobility) is an inherent expression of nature (biology, matter, *physis*), and this manoeuvre discovers that initial conditions can be intrinsically mobile, dispersed and contemporary. In sum, the aim is to highjack conservative certainties by rerouting and redeploying their assumptions rather than simply rejecting their terms of reference.

This sort of work leaves us with riddles that are as awkward and persistent as they are bewildering and exhilarating. What happens, for example, if the very stuff of 'matter' is ubiquitous and chameleon and 'the natural order' is essentially sociological, errant, and always 'out of place', or 'out of sync' with itself? With this as a grounding assumption, the self-conscious attempt to rethink the puzzle of mediation is of crucial importance. The task risks misssteps and slip-ups at every turn, and for this reason such exploratory endeavours are as experimental as they are statements of conviction.

The sense of evidence in this volume presumes intra-disciplinary purchase, and perhaps because contributors hail from the social sciences where evidence-based research is the mantra of best practice we need to ask, again and again, what determines that something is 'evident'? The specific aim will be to show how allergic reaction, hormonal, neuronal, genetic and perceptual plasticities, climate, time, indeed, even the behaviour of the simplest organisms, are all intrinsically social matters. And this, not because biology and physical reality are interpreted *through* a cultural lens that will misrecognise culture as nature, but because those properties and capacities that we understand as properly cultural have always been in the nature of nature to have, to do and to be. For this reason there can be no founding blueprint, no absolute, prescriptive determination. Indeed, it would be fair to suggest that even nature's 'essential humanity' is explored in these contributions – its literacy, agency, technological innovation, but also its murderousness, duplicity, racialisations and stubborn refusals. Within this reconfigured vitalism, albeit one whose internal 'machinery' is comprehensive, even the fact of death as something final, the absolute and definitive cut that divides time into separate packets and guarantees there will be no haunting, no afterlife – even this truth is put into question.

The implications of a 'natural sociology' certainly muddle received understandings of what belongs where, and for this reason the narrative order of chapters is intended to assist in orienting the reader. Chapters 1 and 2, Vicki Kirby and Ashley Barnwell respectively, are companion pieces. They bring coherence to the arguments by outlining the legacy and consequences of oppositional logic such as the nature/culture division, or the imperative to determine right from wrong, especially for political debate and critique. They also provide a contemporary take on how this difference is currently being managed. Bookending these introductory chapters are three contributions whose subjects assume grand dimensions, namely, nature, time and death. Astrida Neimanis casts nature as subject/author, the writer/librarian of its own living literatures. Will Johncock argues that time's spacings are relative, appearing as individual and separate instantiations that must nevertheless commune as intra-active 'moments'. These meditations on the general and the particular return us to old questions, here refashioned and reinvigorated for a new materialist analysis. Importantly, political and ethical concerns about human exceptionalism aren't put aside but reworked and reimagined by these writers. The humanist subject, for example, is displaced, dispersed, and uncannily recuperated in a very different guise. If no-thing can be excluded from this enlarged scene of intra-ference, a sort of vitalism revisited, then it is not surprising that Peta Hinton's exploration of death, absence, lack and loss, closes the volume.

The middle tranche of chapters, six in all, takes us into the familiar terrain of the body. However, this is not a body that is 'spoken about' in Cartesian terms, the mere object of our inquiries and one to which we concede our 'attachment'. Here, it is the body/biology/nature that reflexively speaks of itself. In Chapter 3, Florence Chiew argues that perception is not the primordial substrate of cognition but a site where the eye/I (the Subject) is constantly renegotiated through, and as, diffracted sensory modalities. Descartes is significantly displaced as we consider recent evidence about the intelligent synaesthesia of biology where, for example, the ear can see and cognise. Similarly, Chapters 4 to 8 show how information from the biological sciences can be brought into productive conversation with cultural constructionism. These arguments – Michelle Jamieson on allergic reaction, Rebecca Oxley on the sociality of hormonal behaviours, and Noela Davis on the social nature of gene expression – complicate cultural explanation and challenge the latter's explanatory circumscriptions. Xin Liu explores the question of race in terms of biological comportment and Jacqueline Dalziell takes us into the world of slime mould where social life, agential and complex decision-making behaviours, are strangely in evidence.

As a concluding remark I want to underline that the aim of these arguments is not to trump previous analysis but to revisit the complicity with which critics of the nature/culture division and its cognates can remain caught in its iterative tic, a repetition that inevitably returns nature, matter, the body, biology (the feminine and the racialised other, or what is broken and lacking by default) to a position of passivity, inherent threat, original purity or brute animality. *What if Culture was Nature All Along?* undermines this predictable narrative by asking, what if there is no 'before the social', no prior and unchanging 'given' that can adjudicate what can and can't be changed? No prelapsarian space of goodness before the fall into culture's corruption? Or its inverse, no unthinking and programmatic adaptation before the chance rupture of intelligence, agency and decision? What if the drive for change is as natural as the desire to prohibit, refuse and conserve?

Vicki Kirby

CHAPTER 1

Matter out of Place: 'New Materialism' in Review

Vicki Kirby

Background to a Problem

There once was a time, a time that includes the present, when scientific observation was equated with objectivity, when perception was thought to be a transparent and neutral act, and when the identification of mind and reason as incorporeal and transcendent over nature was pre-requisite to the determination of truth. Although a plethora of research in the sciences actually contests such ill-informed assertions, this cartoon representation of science fundamentals is widely held. Many science practitioners continue to explain their goals and achievements in such terms, and perhaps ironically, even cultural and social analysts who reject them may require this caricature as their interventionary departure point. But whether we hail from the humanities, the social sciences or the sciences, and however we image or represent our opinions and observations, we are all caught in the business of knowledge notation. This is a shared human practice regardless of disciplinary commitments. Consequently, a major concern in cultural and social analysis is to understand how symbolic systems actually connect to, or reflect, what they purportedly re-present. And yet the question is not unknown in the sciences.

Theoretical physicist and mathematician, Eugene Wigner, acknowledges the conundrum of representation in 'The Unreasonable Effectiveness of Mathematics in the Natural Sciences' (1960). Aiming to capture a riddle whose mysteries are almost invisible because commonplace, he contrives a scene where two old school chums are catching up and chatting about their respective occupations. One of them, a statistician working on population trends, illustrates what his work involves by showing his friend the Gaussian distribution tables that symbolise specific aspects of a particular demographic. However, as the statistician dilates on the implications of the diagrams his friend becomes 'incredulous'.

> 'How can you know that?' was his query. 'And what is this symbol here?' 'Oh', said the statistician, 'this is π'. 'What is that?' 'The ratio of the circumference of the circle to its diameter'. 'Well, now you are pushing your joke too far', said the classmate, 'surely the population has nothing to do with the circumference of the circle'. (Wigner 1960: 1)

Although Wigner concedes, 'we are inclined to smile about the simplicity of the classmate's approach' (1960: 1) the tale's purpose is to register something extremely complex about applied mathematics, namely, the wonder of its translative powers. In sum, Wigner is exercised by the ability of representation, here, mathematical signs, to conjure a material world out of what is routinely described as arbitrary abstraction. Indeed, Wigner's genuine sense of puzzlement leads him to admit that this naïf is in some way an honest version of himself. And yet, although 'bewildered' by the ability of symbols to re-present, or capture a world that is not inherently symbolic, the physicist-mathematician remains content to live with this riddle whose difficulty can be appreciated but not answered. Gesturing towards a theological force that supersedes the human capacity to comprehend it, Wigner concludes that the language of mathematics 'is a wonderful gift which we neither understand nor deserve' (1960: 14).

However, if the mystery of how a symbol can *effectively* jump the gap of mediation is acknowledged by some on one side of 'the two cultures' divide[1] only then to be set aside as pragmatically inconsequential, the humanities and much of the social sciences tend to adopt a very different view. Whereas Wigner wonders how a symbol, or ideational figure, can function as if it is the world it represents, an accepted doxa within cultural and social analysis today is that the world is inherently symbolic. However, the meaning of this assertion isn't straightforward and its tricky convolutions can generate very different assumptions and radically different conclusions. As a way into this slippery slope of contention we might begin by suggesting that the world we experience is made meaningful through the cross-referencing of cultural and social webs of signification, and that these symbolic and representational systems of meaning-making induce a 'worlding' effect. Importantly, this process of 'real-ising' will prove so operationally persuasive that its effects actively produce the only world we humans can actually comprehend. A corollary of this, and a rather troubling one now that academic research is increasingly exercised by ecological concerns, is that what makes human species-being special, indeed, exceptional, is our self-definition as *un*-natural.

But let's unpack this claim a little more so that the equation of being human with being cut adrift, or radically segregated from the natural world is better understood. If it is true that we invent a world through a refractive hall of mirrors from which there is no escape, no substantive appeal to an extra-linguistic or causal origin, then it makes sense to assume that culture's hermetic self-capture discovers a 'second nature' (which is really culture in disguise) as the ground and explanation of who we are and how we should live. Of course, this needn't mean that what we might call a 'first nature' – what exists before the arrival of human species-being – can have no existential reality. More accurately, according to this view it can have no *directly perceived*, or substantive facticity because the very act of making sense of a world is necessarily an interpretive makeover. In other words, what appears as that which precedes the arrival of the human remains a cultural back-projection with no unmediated presence, and this then implies that cultural signs *of* nature overlay a now inaccessible and unknowable *nature as such*.

If we return to Wigner and for heuristic purposes consider his perspective representative of scientific endeavour as it is commonly understood within a classical, pre-quantum framework, then we can appreciate why pragmatic success militates against thinking too much about questions of mediation and measurement. Admittedly, there are social rules of compliance that will distinguish the scientific method *as* scientific if the reproducibility of results can be confirmed. And yet little attention is given to the normative structures of observation that actually shape what can, and even, what should be seen. This particular exercise in repetition aims to define objectivity and accuracy against the contamination of subjective judgement and the vagaries of reading/interpreting. Consequently, the replication of experimental results, if successful, has the effect of conflating models, representations and measurements with the facticity of the natural order. In short, if the science is deemed valid then the mediating role of the investigative apparatus is erased and reality appears self-evident.

We could liken this need to discount questions about perception, models and mediation to the sleight of hand of a shell game. The punter naïvely assumes that the 'shuffling' of the three shells will not distract his unwavering focus on the shell that hides the pea. He is watching intently! However, the trickster easily relieves him of his money because she knows that what is taking place right before our eyes can escape observation: ironically, the trickster's repeated success

proves that observation can be deceptive, subjective, and yet predictable (repeatable) in its results. Returning to the question of symbolic
mediation and its self-evident success, Wigner certainly questions the
process of translation that turns what is abstract into what is substantive; indeed, he marvels that the difference disappears because the
ideational effectively becomes material. And yet his 'answer' is more
of a caveat against pursuing the matter further, because if we persist
in asking questions we assume the role of the naïf, and who wants to
draw attention to themselves as the know-nothing ninny who fails to
understand what seems perfectly apparent to everyone else? Although
it may well be a case of the emperor's new clothes, challenging an
accepted response, especially when it invites personal derision, is difficult to sustain. But where does this leave us as we try to appreciate 'the
how' of scientific claims to rigour and evidence in light of this mystery?

What seems especially odd about Wigner's disarmingly honest
admission that the efficacy of representation is a genuine puzzle is that
his explanation of why it works is unashamedly unscientific. If mathematics is a 'gift' whose divine origin decrees that it must exceed our
comprehension, then Wigner's argument effectively censors inquiry, or
deems it pointless, because the imperative now is the call to believe.
Mathematics works! It just does! Don't ask why! We are reminded here
of Louis Althusser's famous scene of ideological interpellation when he
tries to account for how we humans become enculturated. Importantly,
Althusser cannot explain that causal moment of transfer when ideology
is first taken up. However, this is not a failure on Althusser's part for
this is precisely his point: it can't be explained because how we perceive
the 'real conditions of existence' (1971: 163), or what makes sense to
us, is so fundamental to our being, so *always/already* (1971: 172) in
train, that its fabrication is existential – there can be no 'before'. Thus,
if ideology is a performative pragmatism that grounds the very possibility of being in the world then we can understand why Althusser evokes
Pascal's tautological explanation of the origins of religion to illustrate
the riddle: 'Kneel down, move your lips in prayer, and you will believe'
(1971: 168).

But it is precisely here that the difference that separates the humanities and social sciences from the sciences may seem like no difference at
all. Both perspectives conflate representation, reproducibility (often re-
theorised as performativity in social analysis) with the materiality of the
real world. 'It just is!' And yet on closer examination the commitments
that underpin this seemingly common claim couldn't be more contested,
indeed, even incommensurable. In the sciences, a methodology involves

an instrument of measurement and observation, a tool that bridges the purported gap that separates the interpreter (subject) from the interpreted (object). The impact, or interference factor of epistemological frames of reference and modelling decisions can seem relatively inconsequential in a classical science approach that rests on the possibility of truth and precision. However, a cultural, interpretive model discovers its object *within* the productive force of the representation process itself, which means that the object of investigation will always, and necessarily, gather its legibility, or meaningfulness, through webs of subjective and cultural significance. Judith Butler's work is exemplary of this latter position and clearly illustrates the point for us.

In her influential book, *Bodies that Matter: On the Discursive Limits of 'Sex'* (1993), the title anticipates her argument by placing the word sex in inverted commas. In what operates as an effective qualification, the presumptive and enduring truth of sex is displaced, indeed, a precultural, or extra-linguistic appeal to what we might term the reality of sex is not just impossible to grasp because access is denied; more profoundly, it is rendered unthinkable because it is only with/in language and discourse that the world appears sensible. As a consequence, 'sex' becomes a specific historical and social artefact, and this more complicated understanding of what constitutes the thingness of an object, or what appears as inherent to a particular act, must discount the stability, persistence and facticity of a reality that science claims to measure.

In an interview with Butler, which in part explores how evidence in the sciences might be deployed in the humanities, she explains that all data, regardless of their disciplinary provenance, are interpreted through a cultural lens. In my role as interlocutor I am especially interested in the evidentiary leverage attributed to these different ways of knowing. My question concerns the routine assumption in social analysis that signs (or what we mean by language and representation) are confined to the arena of cultural production, even as certain breakthroughs in the sciences purport to discover languages in nature. Given this incongruity I asked the following question.[2] 'There is a serious suggestion that "life itself" is creative encryption. Does your understanding of language and discourse extend to the workings of biological codes and their apparent intelligence?' (Kirby 2011: 73). What motivated my inquiry was evidence that bacteria have code-cracking capacities inasmuch as they decipher the chemical encryption of antibiotic data. This particular example has an extra fascination because what constitutes an apparent epistemological skill by bacteria is at the same time an ontological process of reinvention: in the act of reading and decipherment (knowing) bacteria re-engineer themselves and evolve accordingly (being). Given this remarkable collapse of epistemology with/in ontology, I wondered why such an achievement could not be regarded as a language skill. Rejecting this suggestion, Butler's response is a cautionary warning that illuminates what is at stake in cultural constructionist commitments and why they are so fiercely defended.

> There are models according to which we might try to understand biology, and models by which we might try to understand how genes function. And in some cases the models are taken to be inherent to the phenomena that is [*sic*] being explained . . . I worry that a notion like 'biological code', on the face of it, runs the risk of that sort of conflation. I am sure that encryption can be used as a metaphor or model by which to understand biological processes, especially cell reproduction, but do we then make the move to render what is useful as an explanatory model into the ontology of biology itself? This worries me, especially when it is mechanistic models which lay discursive claims on biological life. What of life exceeds the model? When does the discourse claim to become the very life it purports to explain? I am not sure it is possible to say 'life itself' is creative encryption unless we make the mistake of thinking that the model is the ontology of life. Indeed we might need to think first about the relation of any definition of life to life itself, and whether it must, by virtue of its very task, fail. (Butler in Kirby 2011: 73–4)

We could describe the difference between the two cultures in terms of illusion versus fact, fantasy versus reality, or ideation versus physical or material substance, and many theorists subscribe to a version of this view, albeit one whose details are complicated, politically nuanced, and elaborated in myriad and even competing ways.[3] However, the worth of a cultural constructionist approach is entirely lost if we equate this way of thinking with a reductionist and glib refusal to acknowledge the perceived insistence of the world around us. A constructionist perspective appreciates that the weight of reality is experienced through the force field of the political, where sociocultural grids of understanding are active in producing our most intimate sense of self, our dearest moral and ethical convictions, the rationale and felt compulsions for why we love or hate, or why we live our gender, race and sexuality in ways that are historically and socially legible.[4] In other words, if pleasures, perceptions and experiences resonate with political possibility and discrimination then these quite specific cultural forces are intrinsic to who we are, how we perceive ourselves and what makes reality liveable . . . or not. Importantly, if this is an illusion of sorts then it isn't clear how its material effects could easily be corrected or put aside. What matters for constructionists, then, and this is the real leverage in this position, is the conviction that social and political forces are comparatively mobile because they are not subject to natural decree. Without a foundational, prescriptive, universal constant – at least, none that escapes the vagaries of interpretation – it makes sense that the lability of culture's agencies should receive special analytical attention. Cross-cultural and historical evidence offers further proof that inherited ways of being and knowing morph over time and are open to change; in short, if the ingredients of injustice can be challenged then things can be otherwise.

And yet, what was once an almost hegemonic explanation about culture's comprehensive ability to make a world in its own interpretive terms has suffered an assault. The origin of this assault is hard to date, probably because it has been mounted on several fronts for many years and its logics and implications are unevenly aligned and appreciated. The accelerating pace of innovation in technological and medical research has certainly challenged what it means to be human. And further to this, ecological degradation, species loss and global warming, now conveniently wrapped up in the pejorative term, 'the Anthropocene' (Zalasiewicz: 2010), have brought a political urgency to these debates, aggregating different forces into a critical mass that feels both immediate and incontestable. But here is the rub: these most pressing questions about the achievements of science or about environmental dramas that threaten species diversity and human survival require stories that are heavily reliant on scientific evidence for their political credibility and *gravitas*.

A further consequence of this turn to the sciences is the related critique of anthropocentrism. Cultural constructionism installs human species being as sole author and reader of its world, thereby emphasising human exceptionalism as the incontrovertible ground of these arguments. And yet this need to corral the human against its others because we are profoundly *in*capable of knowing and appreciating the ecology writ large feels increasingly bankrupt and just plain wrong. First, constructionist arguments have worked hard to make us wary about identitatarian politics that rest on the atomic integrity and separation of entities, indeed, the very notion of 'otherness' as straightforwardly outside and foreign – conventionally a denigrated and negative version of the privileged referent – has been thoroughly problematised. Nevertheless and despite this, the certainty that human identity is circumscribed and proper to itself grounds the constructionist critique of identity. Second and not unrelated, a growing appreciation that the ecology, in its broadest sense, appears as an intimate and involved sociality of sorts, casts the hermeticism of the linguistic turn in a very different light. Given this, the stubborn focus on the political aspects of representation and language are increasingly seen as a mistake, or at least, an histori-cal moment of over-reach. It seems that the linguistic turn must now be 'turned' as we are encouraged to get back to basics, to more physical, pragmatic and pressing matters. Enter 'new materialism'!

New Materialism, a Problem Resolved or Displaced?

I want to sidestep a definition of what is loosely recognisable as 'new materialism' because its identity is often contradictory and its cross-disciplinary rationalisations and commitments quite muddled. But as we need to begin, we might start with Stacy Alaimo's and Susan Hekman's edited collection of essays, *Material Feminisms* (2008), which suggests that an obsession with discourse and language has effectively hijacked our ability to engage reality. As Hekman notes,

> many commentators have argued [that] the linguistic turn in philosophy and critical theory has entailed an almost exclusive emphasis on epistemology . . . [which] necessarily skews philosophical discussions in the direction of words rather than matter; the real takes a backseat to the discursive. (2008: 97–8)

Hekman endorses Linda Alcoff's bid to correct the imbalance by add-ing ontology to the mix because 'ontological theories are about mat-ter; unlike epistemological theories, they cannot "lose" the real – it is their subject matter' (Alaimo and Hekman 2008: 98). But if confusion threatens to cloud the distinction here – after all, words and writing are the stuff of both – Hekman clarifies that, 'for the new ontology, our language structures how we apprehend the ontological but it does not constitute it' (2008: 98).

This insistence that representation (culture/epistemology) mediates reality (nature/ontology), that the ideational is not 'material realism', and that some sort of aggregation or managed 'rapprochement' between the two is now required (2010: 6), is reiterated in another seminal text, Diana Coole's and Samantha Frost's edited collection, *New Materialisms: Ontology, Agency and Politics* (2010). In 'Introducing the New Materialisms', the editors offer a nuanced meditation on the failures of constructionist arguments while nevertheless refusing to downplay their ongoing importance. This is an informative and thoughtful summation, an acknowledgment of the juggling act that a 'reprisal of materialism' (Coole and Frost 2010: 3) must undertake if it is to avoid a simple reversal of the previous inattention. As they state, 'our material lives are always culturally mediated, but they are not only cultural' (2010: 27). The strategy, in the main, is to repair the oversight and supplement the privileging of subjectivity with an almost celebratory focus on science and what we mean by objectivity; indeed, we now encounter objects, biology, affect, animals and plants and all things ecological, geological, climatic – the list is long and diverse.

However, because this is a turn from, or minimally, an intervention against, the hegemony of cultural, discursive and textual methodologies, the special signature of new materialist concerns can be surprisingly predictable. It is as if we have grown tired of our previous self-absorption and can admit to a fascination with science, with the non-human and post-human and with the technological revolution and the natural world around us. Described in this way, the special marker of new materialism can seem comparatively more generous, more inclusive and outward looking, and certainly more self-critical about the narcissistic self-congratulation of human exceptionalism.

Another important and influential work that now operates as a foundational guide in this emerging field is Rick Dolphijn's and Iris van der Tuin's *New Materialism: Interviews & Cartographies* (2012).[5] The book is divided between analytical commentary by the authors and a series of interviews with prominent scholars. Importantly, the book's overview is a prism of diffracted perspectives rather than a unified position. The authors, for example, favour a monist approach and are suspicious of the primariness of mind, whereas several contributors take a different stance. The interview titles of Manuel DeLanda's and Quentin Meillassoux's contributions, respectively, argue that the linguistic turn and the analytical focus on culture and subjectivity has been displaced by a turn outward and away from what now appears as human solipsism: 'Any materialist philosophy must take as its point of departure the existence of a material world that is independent of our minds' (DeLanda in Dolphijn and van der Tuin 2012: 38); and 'There is contingent being independent of us, and this contingent being has no reason to be of a subjective nature' (Meillassoux in Dolphijn and van der Tuin 2012: 71). So far so good, yet already we could complicate the issue by insisting that Judith Butler would be in complete agreement if we simply left it at that. Because despite their differences, all three thinkers attribute a subjectivity, or complex cognitive interiority, to the human and each regards this 'property' as circumscribed and, surely, exceptional for that! It seems that the human mind and its special ability to think and *do* 'materialist philosophy' somehow proves this 'independence' from what is not human, or more pointedly, what is not mind. And if our very biology is in a contingent relationship to mind, as Descartes' meditations conclude, then have we moved all that far?

If the difference that new materialism might make feels unclear at this early stage, things get even more puzzling when we read Karen Barad's argument in this same collection of interviews. We might assume that this particle physicist turned critical theorist would set us straight; surely the physical sciences, as the name suggests, will bring hard definitional contours to clarify the ambiguity. However, Barad's 'Matter feels, converses, suffers, desires, yearns and remembers' (in Dolphijn and van der Tuin 2012: 48) is entirely at odds with the previous titles. How could matter *be* subjective? How could it remember, and by implication, cognise? Is the unapologetic anthropomorphism in Barad's intervention a glaring mistake? Has Butler's insistence that signification 'matters', an argument reliant on ideational efficacy, been endorsed in this description, or somehow re-routed? Or again, is a certain affect theory, a popular expression of new materialism, affirmed in this claim because corporeal matter's pre-symbolic behaviour is thoroughly and differently agential before it is pressed into discursive regimes of comparative compliance?

Perhaps we need to take stock of why Barad's intervention understands representation and language as thoroughly ontological, or why the sense of language as a specific entity *in* a particular (cultural) location that shapes the epistemology of the observer is at the same time non-local; appearing as the ontology of the object.[6] Interestingly, and as we will see, this chiasmatic muddle, or transformative capacity whereby identities blur, is not unidirectional – from human interpretation/culture to nature as impassive and material support of a constitutive misrecognition; anthropomorphism's error no less. The latter presumes that human beings author an interpretation, and that cultural constructionism produces the 'fact' (always in inverted commas) of the object in this process. However, something counter-intuitive and quite threatening to humanism and human exceptionalism begins to make its appearance if we suggest that the object is also the subject 'who' interprets, which in turn implies that authorship of the model/ interpretation is an involvement wherein epistemology was always inherently ontological.[7] Indeed, the translation, metamorphosis, or even transubstantiation *between* these apparent differences, call it what you will, appears to *involve no transition through a passage of time or a gap in space*. In other words, this is not a simple recuperation of Butler's assertion that language mediates a reality that resists its translation, a language that is doomed to misrepresent because intercourse between nature and culture, matter and ideation, object and subject is literally barred. And yet nor does it follow the emerging conventions of many new materialist arguments that struggle to shift the terms of these debates by including matter and objects into the mix while acknowledging the latter's *own* agentic resistance and independence.

If an accommodation of what appears oppositional in these arguments is required because *relationality is not mediation; it is not an in-between entities*, then the difference/same, correct or mistaken adjudication that is so appealing to all of us will assume the status of a conundrum. The dimensions of this difficulty are especially pertinent because Barad finds diffractive resonance in the work of 'philosopher-physicist' Niels Bohr, but also in the philosophy of Jacques Derrida, even though the latter's 'no outside text' is for many the error against which new materialism takes its leverage.[8] How, then, should we explain the interventionary relevance of an emerging intellectual perspective – new materialism and its cognates – if its cacophony of arguments can take such shape-shifting form that the difference between the linguistic and materialist turns is confusing, and at times, even confounded?[9]

The general direction of new materialist arguments has certainly shaken up the rigidity of our received wisdoms and encouraged a more science-friendly exploration of what will count as evidence. This is a timely and much needed intervention that is changing the scope of the humanities and social sciences in unexpected and exciting ways. And yet stubborn questions about what to do with the efficacy and ubiquity of language, especially when its communicative complexities appear as the lingua franca of an adaptive and exquisitely involved non-human ecological 'socius', routinely end up in Wigner's too hard basket. Forensic investigation, for example, rests on our ability to bring soil samples, the flesh and secretions of bodies, insects, plants, graphology, psychology, demographics, climate data, even astronomy, into one implicated concretion, a sort of superpositional punctum, or condensation of evidence. The philosopher, Quentin Meillassoux, provides an interesting explanation of how this might be possible when he suggests that the language of mathematics translates these differences, even allowing us to eavesdrop on the chatter of a primordial 'ancestrality' before the arrival of humans.[10] Meillassoux's impatience with cultural constructionism's inability to consider a world without or before humans is certainly understandable. Meillassoux explains this impasse as one of 'correlationism [which] consists in disqualifying the claim that it is possible to consider the realms of subjectivity and objectivity independently of one another' (2008: 5). Sometimes called speculative realism or object-oriented ontology, this exercise in rethinking the analytical routine of correlationism refuses what Meillassoux calls,

the modern philosopher's 'two-step' [which] consists in this belief in the primacy
of the relation over the related terms; a belief in the constitutive power of recip-
rocal relation. The 'co-' (of co-givenness, of co-relation, of the co-originary, of
co-presence, etc.) is the grammatical particle that dominates modern philosophy,
its veritable 'chemical formula'. (2008: 5–6)

However, the foundational positing of the human as an entity, or
individual, *among* others, arriving later in a linear narrative of independent moments in time and space, appears as the shared conviction
of cultural constructionists, new materialists of various and competing stripes, and even most scientists. Although Meillassoux comes at
these questions from a very different tack, his solution to the riddle
of re-presentation actually underscores why it remains a riddle. When
Meillassoux argues that mathematics binds the world's differences
together such that science has access to reality – and we might assume
this for the same reasons of representational efficacy that Wigner
describes – we are forced to conclude that reality must be inherently
mathematical. And yet Meillassoux gives little attention to how this
model of mathematical notation can operate as if it is the world to
which it refers. Nor does Meillassoux explain why parts of the world
(subjectivity/culture) are positioned outside the reach of this universal language, and this exclusion begs further questions. Meillassoux
separates the human from the non-human, arguing that correlationism's needy pairing must be broken. And yet we are left to wonder
how, or why, the ubiquity of mathematics as the world's working
ciphertext has no purchase on natural languages, the study of affect
and psychology (subjectivity) and cultural behaviours more generally. If mathematics is manifestly shape-shifting with comprehensive
reach, does the need to establish an inside (objectivity) versus outside
(subjectivity) mathematics actually make sense? Further, is correlationism broken if we replace similarity between apparent differences
(nature *as* culture), with an apparent dissimilarity between these
same differences? Surely the question that endures despite our every
attempt to answer or ignore it is what, exactly, is being compared?
How is difference – which already assumes the existence of identities
and their separation – determined?

Of course, these are very old questions that continue to hold our
attention, and perhaps for this reason a small detour into this strange
and yet familiar terrain is warranted. As we have been thinking about
mathematics, and recall our earlier discussion of life as cryptography, it seems appropriate to briefly return to the vexing question of
translation. Cryptography is an exercise in code cracking that can use

algorithms to find an unknown; and importantly for this argument, that unknown must also exhibit algorithmic habits. For example, when a team of linguists, mathematicians and cryptic-crossword boffins gather at Bletchley Park in England to crack the Enigma Code during World War II, they are intent on accessing the deadly secrets that the clunk and glow of moving keys, lamps and rotor drives might reveal. A cipher code involves pure reference: every sign conjures another, and another, and another, sliding along a chain of associational possibilities. However, the very process of this sliding transformativity that appears straightforwardly linear is at the same time a punctum, wherein radical alterity (another language in this case) is already 'present' in the point of departure and arrival.

To explain this, the Enigma Code originally presents as a meaning-less 'pattern', or more accurately, a configuration whose significance, or coherence *as* a pattern has yet to be revealed. What is worth pondering is how the pattern of this particular mathematical algorithm can also *be* the pattern of a natural language – in this case, German. How can a superposition of recognisably different codes, an essential de/coherence, nevertheless appear as *one* language? How can any individual language have myriad manifestations, or translations *within* it? The point here isn't to prove that Meillassoux's understanding of mathematics as a universal cipher key is correct, although his argument certainly presents us with an exciting escape route from the dead end of cultural solip-sism. More pressing is a further question about the identity of math-ematics as such. How can this particular language be so ontologically ubiquitous and morphologically diverse that it includes everything it is defined against?

Derrida's counter-intuitive notion of a 'general text' helps us here because it evokes a sort of dynamic tower of babel whose cross refer-ence animates each and every language, and yet not as an aggrega-tion of differences as we see in Meillassoux's sense that mathematics can supplement and resolve correlationism's error. Derrida dilates on this riddle with specific reference to algebra, whose etymology from the Arabic, *al jebr*, means 'the reunion of broken parts'. This language with no centre or foundational referent can be looked at in two ways according to Derrida. 'One thinks of algebra as a field of ideal objects, produced by the activity of what we call a subject, or man, or history, and thus, we recover the possibility of algebra in the field of classical thought' (1970: 268). This reading understands mathematics as a tool of access, a model of measurement authored by a subject. However, Derrida's alternative, 'or else we consider [algebra] as a disquieting mirror of a world which is algebraic through and through' (1970: 268) misplaces the humanist subject – the author/interpreter/origin of this language – because suddenly she is radically dispersed, fractured, broken into and out of. If we work with the latter deconstructive reading then we can affirm the spirit and necessity of Meillassoux's need to break out of culture's self-enclosure, and yet without the need to corral the subject from the object, or culture from nature, as if the difference is clear and the problem is answered in terms of dependence or independence; correlation or the lack of it.

Importantly, it is not just mathematics that has no foundational referent, or centre. And this matters, because the progressivism in new materialism – the hope that we can separate ourselves from earlier errors – is something we might want to reconfigure if the need to narrativise tends to denigrate and devalue what came before. The difference that new materialism might make can feel liberating, as if we are at last given access to material reality and all those objects that were previously barred to us – biology, geology, climate, animals, plants, objects; the list is infinite and the intervention seductive. But whether constructionist or new materialist, ontology or epistemology, object or subject, this tendency to posit two separate entities or systems leaves their respective identities intact. Can we work with a sense of 'materiality' that is more surprising, involved and, dare I say, scientifically leveraged, by contesting the actual identity of these terms and their respective contents, circumscriptions and capacities?

Matter Misplaced

One way into this question is via the canonical work of anthropologist, Mary Douglas. In *Purity and Danger* she argues that all human societies are preoccupied with 'chasing dirt' (2001: 2). While the actual identity of this 'dirt' proves elusive when compared across cultures and histories, the specific need for its removal and the amelioration of its contaminating effects remain compelling. Although the particular definitions and circumstances vary widely and can be individually and idiosyncratically manifest, even within the same culture, what binds this diversity of what we might call compulsive tidying behaviours is the need for clear structures and legible borders. Ironically, even the deliberate flouting of rules, regulations and normative patterns of propriety are oriented in terms of the very structures they eschew, so for this reason the need to return things to their rightful place or to disobey the demand to conform is the stuff of the political. According to Douglas, every society will monitor its boundaries, margins and sites of ambiguity in the hope of reproducing the existential values that make it work. Consequently, a perceived breach in a society's organisational integrity, or how it understands itself, represents a potential threat to its collective identity.

Douglas's notion of 'matter out of place' helps us to appreciate the antics of critique and the inevitable turf wars between new materialism, 'old' materialism, the linguistic turn, the affective turn, the pragmatic turn and so on. Our need to identify materiality oppositionally involves us in an agonistic wrangle over right or wrong adjudications that necessarily censors mystery, contradiction and surprise. While I can't recuse myself from this imperative to decide, locate and identify, I can at least register, as many have done,[11] that such forms of critique can be more intent on managing a threat than exploring a question. For this reason my focus is on the confusions and paradoxes that leave us wondering; ambiguities that can't be resolved and made proper; riddles that defy and complicate our dearest convictions about the natural order of things and what it means to be human.

My assumption is that matter and its cognates are morphologically plastic and that these transubstantiations are myriad, appearing as words, as plants and objects, as blood and belief. Of course, things get weird if we assert 'there is no outside matter', or 'no outside nature', because the identity of matter – what it means and how it does what it does – will appear misshapen, multiple, treacherous and even monstrous. And yet, this is not an attempt to legitimate reductionism, where the importance of the cultural is rejected and the self-evidence of material realism accepted. If what appears to come second is conventionally regarded as more evolved, more intelligent and complex – a hierarchy of subject over object, human over non-human and culture over nature – then discovering that 'firstness' already involves forces and capacities that purportedly have yet to arrive provokes us to question what a reduction actually means. Rosi Braidotti's interview in *New Materialism: Interviews & Cartographies* captures this well, as we see in her title, 'The notion of the univocity of Being or single matter positions difference as a verb or process of becoming at the heart of the matter' (Braidotti in Dolphijn and van der Tuin 2012: 16). However, we can certainly feel stymied about what to do if the processual nature of differentiation isn't strictly *against* anything. How are physics and literature ontologically entangled? How is biology social, and what will this call for the last to be first, an 'originary humanicity'[12] no less, involve?

The point that concerns us is that if the spatio/temporal order of things is truly muddled and any one thing (e.g. photon, person, concept) is inseparable from another, then what we mean by mediation and identity require review. Karen Barad invents the neologism 'intra-action' to complicate the assumption that entities pre-exist their relations, and this manoeuvre breaks the equation of mediation with an 'in-between', a dead space, a gap, nothing or absence. More brutally, we might say that there is no distance or space in between things because there are no 'things', no *givens*. A corollary of this riddle of becoming atomic, or becoming-thing is that conjunction and aggregation are not synonyms for inseparability. Given this apparent contradiction it is not surprising that the challenge in Barad's contribution is poorly understood and rarely explored, even by those who acknowledge her work as path-finding. For this reason we need to move 'forward' with due care, as the problematic we are exploring is counter-intuitive and mind-bendingly strange.

An example of a too-quick translation of Barad's thesis can be seen in Gill Jagger's recent article in *Signs*, 'The New Materialism and Sexual Difference' (2015). Making a comparison between my own work, that of Elizabeth Grosz and Karen Barad, Jagger praises Barad's interventions and finds them exemplary of how new materialism might reconfigure the political landscape. I concur with Jagger in her positive regard for Barad's vision, however her need to disambiguate what is most perplexing and truly marvellous in Barad's manoeuvring, namely, that matter is always 'out of place' and its agentic capacity ubiquitous, is unfortunate. Jagger never questions that there are two entities or ontologies (culture and nature, ideation and matter, mind and body), and even manages to recuperate a humanist author who retains 'responsibility and accountability in determining which practices are in intra-action with which bodies' (2015: 339). Jagger prefers to aggregate identity rather than to question the enigma of univocity, as we see in her summation; 'Barad's account of the material-discursive relation involves the active participation of both sides . . . the interimplication of the discursive and the material' (2015: 340). But if the discursive *is* the material? If there is no aggregation, no 'both'? And if 'no outside nature' is comprehensive, excluding nothing, not even nothing, what then?[13]

If we allow the question of matter to remain untidy and unruly – open – for as long as possible, then we will not resolve this confounding riddle of mediation in a hurry. Barad offers us a provocative invitation in her magnum opus, *Meeting the Universe Halfway: quantum physics and the entanglement of matter and meaning*.

Rather blasphemously, agential realism denies the suggestion that our access to the world is mediated, whether by consciousness, experience, language, or any other alleged medium . . . Rather like the special theory of relativity, agential realism calls into question the presumption that a medium – an 'ether' – is even necessary. (2007: 409)

It is fascinating to consider that this call to think again about the how and what of Being comes from a physicist, but also from a philosopher, Jacques Derrida. And importantly for our discussion, neither thinker understands the problematic of entanglement/*différance* as 'the active participation of both sides', as Jagger would have it. In his unpublished seminar, *La Vie La Mort* (1975) for example, Derrida ponders the relationship between information transfer and instruction in the language of the gene in François Jacob's *The Logic of Life* (1993), and he compares this with the pedagogical instructions and rules in institutional and cultural life. Derrida asks, in all seriousness, if there is any discernible difference between these operational involvements, and this in turn opens the broader question of how we segregate nature from culture and what is exceptional about being human. The routine management of such a question – the tidying reflex that answers the suggestion that matter is very much out of place here – is to remind us that a model is not the reality to which it refers, as we saw earlier in Butler's attempt to prohibit my own question about biological cryptography and literacy skills. However, just as Barad has done, Derrida also contests this appeal to an in-between, a third term or model that mediates the relationship between subject and object.

That which we, men [*sic*], claim to accept in culture as model, that is to say discursive texts or calculators and all that we believe to understand familiarly under the name of text, that which we pretend then to accept as model, comparison, analogy with the view of understanding the basic living entity; this itself is a complex product of life, of the living, and the claimed model is exterior neither to the knowing subject nor to the known object . . . The text is not a third term in the relation between the biologist and the living, it is the very structure of the living as shared structure of the biologist – as living – of science as a production of life, and the living itself. (Derrida 1975: Seminar 4, 5)

The importance for new materialism of deliberately engaging the confusion within conventional co-ordinates of time, place and identity is that it allows us to reassess the perverse agility of the political, yet in a way that is not entirely alien to previous strategies and familiar commitments. We are not lost in a soup of homogeneity or sameness when we explore the intimacies of differentiation. On the contrary, limits will still appear as prohibitive and censoring; however their rigidity and uncompromising status will also reveal brittleness and vulnerability. It should be emphasised that in denying the routine understanding of mediation, neither Barad nor Derrida are offering us an 'access all areas' corrective. The intervention is more perplexing than this because if being is a diffracted, non-local manifestation *of* the world's Being itself, it is nevertheless, and at the same time, a local and very specific punctum, or concrescence, *of* that same world: although the individual is not in opposition to the universal or general in this account, individuation is always and necessarily unique.

There are intriguing implications in the warp effect of these distortions of logic that remain uncannily and surprisingly faithful to that same logic.[14] For example, for those of us interested in new materialism's broader reach into the realm of objects, technological change and insights from the sciences, there is no reason why the lessons learned from social inquiry, which are also experiments that explore and transform reality, should not be regarded as intrinsically scientific and technologically transformative. Admittedly, the words 'scientific' and 'technological' suffer considerable alteration in such a claim, just as the subject who inquires is no longer 'one' among others in the classical sense. Hidden onto-epistemological transitivities will pervert and entangle the difference between thinkers and thinkers, objects and objects and thinkers and objects. Indeed, if the critique of critique within new materialism means anything at all, then the difference in a corrective will at times appear as the error it hopes to repair. We get some insight into the why of this muddle when Derrida discovers that biology is cultural and vice versa. To accommodate and explain this blurring of apparently different identities he suggests that the author of a reading, any reading/writing, is life itself. And yet this needn't mean that we humans are somehow excluded from this process, or that our myriad and competing perceptions of what the world is and how it works are diminished or marginalised when compared with life's seemingly superior and transcendent overview. If what appears as an aggregation of different and separable entities *in* the world is a chiasmatic mangle of the world's own individual perceptions of itself, then our very becoming is articulated through the intricate and comprehensive refractions of this processual inquiring/perceiving. In other words, life's self-reflexivity is a working science, a *dispositif*, whose myriad methodologies/perceptions confound subject with/in object in the will to be/other.

How we might write from a position that tries to acknowledge its immersion in/as an 'in-between' no-*thing* can seem infuriatingly impossible, and yet all around and within us opportunities for such investigations and experiments present themselves. A recent example of how one of the most enduring questions in feminism – the mind/ body, culture/nature distinction – might be broken open and how a whole cacophony of competing feminist work on the body can be kept alive, is offered by Elizabeth Wilson in *Gut Feminism* (2015).[15] Wilson explores the complexity of the body as so many have done before her. And yet her admission that there is something in her research that feels elusive, experimental and even maddening is salutary for a new materialism that questions both its defining terms. Wilson asks a disarmingly simple question: how can we talk *about* the body's interiority when our argument chafes at the routine segregation of meat from mind, object from subject and inside from outside? How do we affirm cultural constructionism's important critique of Cartesianism and the conservative implications of the latter's divisive political legacy when that same critique recuperates its oppositional and hierarchical logic even more forcefully? What can be done when biology becomes an embarrassment, a matter to be eschewed and removed from what we understand as the political? More explicitly and bizarrely, a large part of Wilson's argument answers these questions by getting down and dirty, asking how the enteric system is invested with, and responsive to, words and images, psychological states, glances and memories. As Wilson is a thinker who persists in asking if Freud's 'mysterious leap from the mind to the body' is any leap at all, or more specifically, how biology can 'comply' in cases of conversion hysteria where cultural significance is said to be somatised, her questions are instructive for how a new materialist approach, or any other for that matter, might find value in 'dirt'.

In sum, what Wilson is determined to explore when she refuses the routine separation of nature from the social, or matter from ide-ation, is the question of what, precisely, biology involves. The riddle is frustratingly banal and inescapable, despite our every attempt to flee its self-evidence, and it is this. How should we, indeed, how can we, comprehend the goop and spill of corporeal interiority, the bone, muscle and sinewy connections, the colons, tracts, membranous pouches and bags of provisional containment, the greens, reds, yellows and browns that pulse and ooze just under our skin? How to reconcile the knowledge that a severe body blow might reveal the liquid seep of selfhood? Wilson delivers a *coup de grâce* to the humanist subject who sees herself as a pilot within the mere container of her body when she asks us to consider if the latter is abruptly different from the former. In all seriousness, we need to consider if a discursive analysis *of* the body is authored *by* that same goop and spill, the liquid ooze, electric field, peristaltic jerks and synaptic leaps that seem to utterly confound our very dearest sense of personhood.

How might we approach this internal, corporeal landscape whose apparent mess Wilson describes as thoroughly political, and can we do it without becoming paralysed with fear, or even rage, at the very horror of being ... *that*? Wilson's skill in this is to wrangle feminist and related political insights and axioms into a different shape without abandoning their wisdoms altogether and without leaving us entirely disoriented. Her 'conclusions' are indebted to scientific evidence, and yet this evidence is as curious as it is baffling. How, for example, could a placebo, a little bit of 'nothing', disrupt the pharmaceutical industry's ability to secure a clear distinction between the effects of anti-depressant drugs and mere suggestion? What difference does it make to think of the enteric system as thoroughly psychological, or to ask if certain organs are transferentially 'alive' to each other's moods and reasonings? Is the gut already social, psychological, cognitive, mindful, and not just because it contains the human biome and its cross-species ecology? Wilson's exploration of how cognition might be operative 'below the neck' (2015: 172) opens a battery of investigative puzzles that make no sense in terms of the nature/culture distinction.

Can we embark on a political physics if the only constant in our rules of measurement and valuation is their provisional status? Or to put this in a way that might be more familiar to us, can we risk the suggestion that nature, in essence, is 'under construction'?

Notes

1. 'The two cultures' was a phrase coined by C. P. Snow in the 1959 Rede Lecture. Snow was bothered by the pomposity with which literary scholars justified their ignorance about such things as The Second Law of Thermodynamics, and this self-congratulatory ignorance lead him to conclude that 'the majority of the cleverest people in the western world have about as much insight into it as their neolithic ancestors would have had' (1998: 15). Scientists were in turn disparaged for their ignorance of the literary canon and the works of Shakespeare. However, the phrase now carries the extra complication of how these different enterprises might be reconciled, given the difference between scientific endeavour, which aims for truth and objectivity, and the interpretive enterprise in the humanities that underlines the subjective and situated aspect of any explanation.
2. The interview was originally published in Breen et al. (2001).

3. To take just one example, in cultural and social analysis the work of French philosopher and psychoanalyst, Jacques Lacan, has been of crucial importance. Lacan's contribution was to theorise the unique genesis of the human subject into the sovereign coherence of an 'I am' by way of desire, self-deception and illusion (Lacan 1977). Indeed, much structuralist and poststructuralist thinking relies heavily on some version of this story that understands the human condition as one that must break from nature/the origin. In sum, to be human is to be de-natured and reborn into a world already mapped by cultural and social significations, and importantly, this process inaugurates the political. For an introduction to the history and relevance of this style of thinking see Descombes (1982); Silverman (1984); Coward and Ellis (1977). Thinkers such as Louis Althusser, Chantalle Mouffe, Ernesto Laclau, Judith Butler, Slavoj Žižek and Fredric Jameson are just some of the scholars whose work is indebted to Lacan.

4. A pertinent reference that surely makes the point is Michel Foucault's well-known claim about the interpretive vagaries that surround 'homosexual acts' across history.

> The nineteenth-century homosexual became a personage, a past, a case history, and a childhood, in addition to being a type of life, a life form, and a morphology, with an indiscreet anatomy and possibly a mysterious physiology. Nothing that went into his total composition was unaffected by his sexuality . . . The sodomite had been a temporary aberration; the homosexual was now a species. (1980: 43)

What needs to be underlined is that sensation, pleasure and desire are consequent to this, which explains Foucault's insistence that, '*homosexuality* is a notion that dates from the nineteenth century, and thus it's very recent' (2011: 386).

5. I am being a little cheeky in the following discussion when I reduce the content of several interviews to their one-line titles. While I have no wish to denigrate these particular efforts *in toto*, far from it, I do wish to question their foundational premise, which the titles effectively capture.

6. In this regard, it is important to also acknowledge the pioneering work of Iris van der Tuin on the transformative political physics of new materialism. Her sustained insistence that ontological questions already reside with/in the accepted and apparently circumscribed identity of epistemology have been pathfinding. See, for example 2015 and 2013.

7. The apparent misuse of the pronoun 'who' is reminiscent of Eduardo Cadava et al. (eds), *Who Comes After The Subject* (1991), where several essays, including Jacques Derrida's, entertain the possibility of the subject before and after the purported arrival of human being.

8. I have also argued that Derrida's work could productively be read through the better-known quandaries of quantum mechanics (1997, 2011), and Arkady Plotnitsky has written at length on the subject, although from a very different perspective (1994).

9. An interesting moment of proprietorial hussling about the accurate representation of feminism's history and the error of new materialist claims appears in Sara Ahmed's 'Imaginary Prohibitions: Some Preliminary Remarks on the Founding Gestures of the "New Materialism"' (2008), and what reads like a companion piece, Nikki Sullivan's 'The somatechnics of perception and the matter of the non/human: A critical response to new materialism' (2012). Among other criticisms, Ahmed reprimands new materialism for its misguided attempt to leverage the value of its insights against the purported biophobia of previous feminisms, and Sullivan is disappointed by new materialism's inadvertent return to the nature/culture split that it claims to escape. Although space prevents me from responding in detail to all of Sullivan's concerns, I can at least question her need to homogenise new materialism into a common set of commitments, and to this end, to decontextualise citations in order to make the claim stick. Barad's laboriously detailed intervention, for example, is not mounted against language and representation. As this brief introduction to new materialism attests, it is extremely difficult to find common ground, and where it seems to appear as a division between nature and culture, writers such as myself, Karen Barad and Elizabeth Wilson would support Sullivan's disquiet. Similarly, Ahmed's assertion that new materialists forget the legacy of feminist research on biology misses the related and more vexing point. If the body/biology isn't a mere object about which we inquire, if it is the 'who' that inquires (of itself), then the Cartesian reflex of thinking 'about' (subject versus object) is what is at stake here. However, the argument I want to further is even more difficult to manage because it recuperates what at first seems like an error. If biology, for example, is capable of bifurcating itself into the apparent error of Cartesian separation, then it is also capable of *agonising* over its own identity, differentiating Ahmed and Sullivan from Barad and Wilson while at the same time confusing and confounding their differences. To this end we are all of us in the mangle of materiality's schizoid methodologies of self-inquiry, which includes disavowal, repression and denial. How we negotiate this shared dilemma of difference *within* univocity is a question we can't get around with correctives, although we are surely compelled to try. For further discussion of this difficult issue, see van der Tuin (2008) and several contributors in this collection; Davis (2009), Hinton and Xin Liu (2015).

10. Apart from the interview with Meillassoux already mentioned, see Meillassoux (2008) for a detailed elaboration of this position.

11. See, for example, Latour (2004), Butler (2001), Braidotti (2006), Badiou (2014).

12. I entertain the neologism 'originary humanicity' in order to reconsider what it means to be human. If we linger over the question of cognition and survival smarts for example, those capacities whose clear superiority defines human being, we would have to ask broad questions that include

why the transition from a prokaryotic to a eukaryotic cell (the development of a nucleus) isn't the creative and technological equivalent of various human achievements. Of course, the shift in the former case is explained in terms of mindless adaptation, whereas human technological innovation is evidence of intelligence and decision. Originary humanicity asks us to justify what has become automatic in this reasoning (2011).

13. See Barad (2012), who dilates on the unexpected busy-ness of nothingness.
14. See Hinton & Xin Liu (2015), 'The Im/Possibility of Abandonment in New Materialist Ontologies' for an interesting meditation on how this tethering of old with/in new might unfold.
15. For a longer discussion of *Gut Feminism*, see Kirby (2015).

References

Ahmed, S. (2008), 'Imaginary Prohibitions: Some Preliminary Remarks on the Founding Gestures of the "New Materialism"', *European Journal of Women's Studies,* 15: 1, pp. 23–39.

Alaimo, S., and S. Hekman (eds) (2008), *Material Feminisms*, Bloomington and Indianapolis: Indiana University Press.

Althusser, L. (1971), 'Ideology and Ideological State Apparatuses', in *Lenin and Philosophy and other Essays*, trans. B. Brewster, New York: Monthly Review Press, pp. 127–86.

Badiou, A. (2014), 'The Critique of Critique: Critical Theory as a New Access to the Real', lecture at the Global Center for Advanced Studies, *Dingpolitik*, 9 January 2014, available at <https://dingpolitik.wordpress.com/2014/01/09/the-critique-of-critique-critical-theory-as-a-new-access-to-the-real/> (last accessed 21 February 2016).

Barad, K. (2007), *Meeting the Universe Halfway: quantum physics and the entanglement of matter and meaning*, Durham, NC: Duke University Press.

Barad, K. (2012), *What is the Measure of Nothingness: Infinity, Virtuality, Justice*, Documenta 13, 099, Berlin: Hatje Cantz.

Braidotti, R. (2005/2006), 'Affirming the Affirmative: On Nomadic Affectivity', *Rhizomes: Cultural Studies in Emerging Knowledge*, 11/12, available at <http://www.rhizomes.net/issue11/braidotti.html> (last accessed 21 February 2016).

Breen, M. Soenser et al. (2001), '"There Is A Person Here": An Interview with Judith Butler', *International Journal of Sexuality and Gender Studies*, April 2001, 6: 1/2, pp. 7–23.

Butler, J. (1993), *Bodies that Matter: On the Discursive Limits of 'Sex'*, New York and London: Routledge.

Butler, J. (2001), 'What is Critique? An Essay on Foucault's Virtue', in D. Ingram (ed.), *The Political*, Oxford: Blackwell, pp. 212–28.

Cadava, E., P. Connor and J-L Nancy (eds) (1991), *Who Comes After The Subject*, New York: Routledge.

Coole, D., and S. Frost (eds) (2010), *New Materialisms: Ontology, Agency, and Politics*, Durham, NC: Duke University Press.

Coward, R., and J. Ellis (1977), *Language and Materialism: Developments in Semiology and the Theory of the Subject*, London: Routledge & Kegan Paul.

Davis, N. (2009), 'New Materialism and Feminism's Anti-Biologism: A Response to Sara Ahmed', *European Journal of Women's Studies,* 16: 1, pp. 67–80.

Derrida, J. (1970), 'Structure, Sign, and Play in the Discourse of the Human Sciences', and 'Discussion', in *The Languages of Criticism and the Sciences of Man: The Structuralist Controversy*, in R. Macksey and E. Donato (eds), Baltimore: Johns Hopkins University Press, pp. 247–65; 265–72.

Derrida, J. (1975), *La Vie La Mort*, trans. A. Pont. Jacques Derrida Papers, MS-CO1. Special Collections and Archives, University of California – Irvine Libraries, Irvine. Private copy.

Descombes, V. (1982), *Modern French Philosophy*, trans. L. Scott-Fox and J. M. Harding, Cambridge: Cambridge University Press.

Dolphijn, R., and I. van der Tuin (2012), *New Materialism: Interviews & Cartographies*, Open Humanities Press. An imprint of MPublishing, Ann Arbor: University of Michigan Library.

Douglas, M. (2001), *Purity and Danger: an analysis of concepts of purity and taboo*, London and New York: Routledge.

Foucault, M. (1980), *The History of Sexuality: Volume 1: An Introduction*, trans. R. Hurley, London and New York: Vintage Books.

Foucault, M. (2011), 'The Gay Science', trans. N. Morar and D. W. Smith, *Critical Inquiry*, 37: 3, pp. 385–403.

Hinton, P., and Xin Liu (2015), 'The Im/Possibility of Abandonment in New Materialist Ontologies, *Australian Feminist Studies*, 30: 84, pp. 128–45.

Jacob, F. ([1976] 1993), *The Logic of Life,* trans. B. E. Spillmann, Princeton: Princeton University Press.

Jagger, G. (2015), 'The New Materialism and Sexual Difference', *Signs: Journal of Women in Culture and Society*, 14: 2, pp. 321–42.

Kirby, V. (1997), *Telling Flesh: The Subject of the Corporeal*, New York and London: Routledge.

Kirby, V. (2011), *Quantum Anthropologies: Life at Large*, Durham, NC: Duke University Press.

Kirby, V. (2015), 'Visceral politics: an oxymoron?' Review of Elizabeth Wilson's *Gut Feminism*, Durham, NC: Duke University Press, *BioSocieties*, 10: 4, pp. 499–502.

Lacan, J. ([1949] 1977), 'The mirror stage as formative of the function of the *I* as revealed in psychoanalytic experience', *Écrits: A Selection,* trans. A. Sheridan, New York: Norton, pp. 1–7.

Latour, B. (2004), 'Why Has Critique Run Out of Steam? From Matters of Fact to Matters of Concern', *Critical Inquiry*, 30: 2, pp. 225–48.

Meillassoux, Q. (2008), *After Finitude: An Essay on the Necessity of Contingency*, London and New York: Continuum.

Plotnitsky, A. (1994), *Complementarity: Anti-Epistemology after Bohr and Derrida*, Durham, NC: Duke University Press.

Silverman, K. (1984), *The Subject of Semiotics*, Oxford: Oxford University Press.

Snow, C. P. ([1959] 1998), *The Two Cultures*, London: Cambridge University Press.

Sullivan, N. (2012), 'The somatechnics of perception and the matter of the non/human: A critical response to the new materialism', *European Journal of Women's Studies*, 19: 3, pp. 299–313.

van der Tuin, I. (2008), 'Deflationary Logic: Response to Sara Ahmed's "Imaginary Prohibitions: Some Preliminary Remarks on the Founding Gestures of the "New Materialism"', *European Journal of Women's Studies*, 15: 4, pp. 411–16.

van der Tuin, I. (2013), 'Non-Reductive Continental Naturalism in the Contemporary Humanities: Working with Hélène Metzger's Philosophical Reflections', *History of the Human Sciences*, 26: 2, pp. 88–105.

van der Tuin, I. (2015), *Generational Feminism: New Materialist Introduction to a Generative Approach*, Lanham, MD: Rowman & Littlefield (Lexington Books).

Wigner, E. P. (1960), 'The Unreasonable Effectiveness of Mathematics in the Natural Sciences', *Communications on Pure and Applied Mathematics*, 13: 1, pp. 1–14.

Wilson, E. (2015), *Gut Feminism*, Durham, NC: Duke University Press.

Zalasiewicz, Z. et al. (2010), 'The New World of the Anthropocene', *Environmental Science & Technology*, 44: 7, pp. 2228–31.

CHAPTER 2

Method Matters:
The Ethics of Exclusion

Ashley Barnwell

Intellectual movements have often forged an identity via generational rebellion, positioning their current interventions against their precursors, in both name and stated intention. In recent times, furthermore, the softer 'neo' has given way to the radical 'post', which implies a starker sense of graduation and progress. Modernism becomes postmodernism, structuralism becomes poststructuralism, and so on. However, the informed observer of these intellectual shifts will know that this prefix rarely marks a clean break. Just as, on a social level, one generation tries to make sense of its parents – on the one hand recoiling from their values and beliefs, and on the other, conditioned into these same commitments (even when the overwhelming need is to reject them) – a 'post' school of thought remains mired in, rather than departs from, its inheritance. Postcolonialism, for example, does not arrive in a world without colonialism: it grapples to understand the effects of colonialism as a lingering social force with real and enduring effects. Postcolonial theorists, therefore, are not wholly indoctrinated by imperial ideology, but then neither are they free of its legacy. Although an intellectual regime may seek to radically sever itself from the past in the hope of redefining its future purpose, this history remains vital to its very constitution, legibility, value and political leverage.

There is an agonism, therefore, that drives a corrective, particularly the kind that aims to repair past errors. It is faced with a necessary contradiction: it must exclude those who are condemned for their own practice of previous exclusions. In other words, to qualify as 'post', or to chasten the oversights of the past generation, the 'new' school must ignore the ways in which its own endeavours are enabled by the very heritage it is defined against. As such, novel interventions often describe the value of the intellectual past, or older methods, as stale and static, when a close reading of this legacy may reveal quite lively and enduring complications. Indeed, it is often the very oversights, provocations and unresolved queries of precedents, already pushed to the point of unravelling or dissemblance, that inspire and inform the present zeitgeist. In a counter-intuitive way, therefore, the next generation can exhibit the very life and potential of old ideas and questions, albeit in a somewhat different guise than is conventionally acknowledged, opening them to new contexts and incarnations. The agonism, in this context, is not a stalemate, but a living dialectic embodied in the very emergence of the 'new' form.

If we acknowledge the co-dependant nature of these generational rifts, the question arises as to whether we can ever truly dissociate ourselves from past methods and ideologies. It is worth considering, furthermore, if the leverage of an assumed differentiation, a troubled identification with a previous 'other', may well be vital to the very progress of intellectual work itself. When we think about how to approach this paradox there is, inevitably, also a question about reflexivity and method lurking nearby: a question of consciousness or cognisance. To what extent is an assumed divorce from the past an error that we can actually acknowledge or correct? Is it at all possible to wage an intellectual turn that can account for its own exclusions, or address the chafing familiarity, the necessity, or even the creative potential, of its antecedents?

Questions of intellectual inheritance are particularly pertinent to this chapter as it is concerned with a specific generational shift: the current turn from humanism to posthumanism. In general terms, the posthuman project could be described as a shift from human-centred to ecological models of agency. Two major aims of this intellectual current are, firstly, to move away from notions of human mastery or centrism, and secondly, to encourage a radical inclusion of all agencies in life's constitution, both human and non-human. Because such inclusive intentions are often highlighted, posthuman arguments are in an apposite position to consider how they negotiate with, or accommodate, the past – both its methods and values. While this 'post' movement's aims have more recently been directed towards the politics of ontology, the stakes of posthumanism also beg interesting questions about the ethics of methodology more generally. For instance, how might a critical intervention differentiate itself from competing modes of analysis without the usual masterful inference of graduating to a higher form of intellectual consciousness: an assumed progress that often casts alternatives aside? Furthermore, are posthuman arguments across the sciences, social sciences and humanities in a position to decentre human mastery, not only by acknowledging the sentience or agency of non-humans, but by exploring the agential role that existing ideologies and social currents play in structuring the very terms of these same interventions? In other words, might more traditional sociological questions be extended, rather than superseded, by this turn?[1]

To explore the politics of intellectual progress, this chapter examines the methodological claims of several arguments that are comfortable within the category of posthumanism, and whose aim is to distribute agency beyond the human realm. After a brief overview of several current trends within this interdisciplinary field, specifically the shift away from critique, I focus upon two recent arguments against human-centred ways of knowing in the social sciences and humanities: Jane Bennett's *Vibrant Matter: A Political Ecology of Things* (2010) and Brian Massumi's theorisation of affect (Massumi 1995 and 2002). Although their projects are quite different, these two theorists have been selected for attention because they are influential and often cited, but perhaps more importantly, because they both explicitly grapple with how to position their current intervention in relation to past and existing intellectual trends. In short, the initial terms of both Bennett's and Massumi's proposals offer fertile ground from which to consider the ethics of exclusion, and particularly, from where and how an argument's leverage might be derived.

It is vital to acknowledge here that posthuman-oriented arguments are heterogeneous: theorists draw from a variety of disciplines and political positions. However, while posthumanism is a dissonant field in some respects – for example, it would be difficult to reconcile some new materialists' insistence on the sentience of matter with many affect theorists' arguments that bodily instinct is precognitive – there are, nevertheless, also shared commitments and aims. A generational or collective spirit loosely unites them, namely, a timely anxiety about human exceptionalism. Calls for posthuman approaches aim to reconfigure our understandings of the world – what constitutes an actor, and what we mean by participation. In this more inclusive vision, humans recognise non-human animals and things as fellow agents in the living creation of a broader social ecology. This intellectual movement has given rise to an energised and evolving reassessment of life's complex fabric. Schools as relationally and internally diverse as new materialism, actor network theory, speculative realism, object oriented ontology, affect theory, non-representational theory and ecocriticism all seek to change the parameters of how scholars engage their environment. In different ways these arguments seek to disrupt ideas about how and by whom life is animated, and of course, what is deemed *living*. If we can risk generalising here, in the main, the scene attempts to include the entanglement of all matter in the action, or, as Karen Barad has termed it, 'intra-action', of life (2007: 140).

However, even for a shift that is so explicitly about inclusion, the question of how to deal with an intellectual inheritance remains problematic. To the reader of posthuman theory, exciting questions about context, ecology and agency are clearly opened up, but sometimes it seems that this explosion of provocative and unforeseen possibilities may be won at the expense of existing methods and concerns. The questions of subjectivity, language and structure that were the focus of last century's key critical movements, namely, poststructuralism, new historicism, deconstruction, postcolonialism and psychoanalytic theory, are often explicitly put aside in posthuman arguments, seemingly on the basis that they are too human-centred. Ontology (being) is favoured over epistemology (knowing), and, perhaps above all else, the method of critique – particularly the close scrutiny of ideology, or how norms of thinking are generated and become entrenched – is thought to have been exhausted of its intellectual value. This marginalisation is of concern, not only because it seems discordant in stated arguments about inclusion, but also because some of the methods thought to be outmoded are still used to valuable effect within these very same interventions. Might certain intellectual nuances and tensions – the kinds of contradictions that, if included and explored further, can lead to insight and complexity – be lost, or unnecessarily denigrated, in this generational backlash? What is at stake, for instance, in the current shift away from critical modes of reading and writing?

The sense that critique has become a perfunctory reflex, ill-suited to our times, echoes across recent arguments about the value of existing methods. For instance, in an interview in Rick Dolphijn's and Iris van der Tuin's field-defining book, *New Materialism: Interviews & Cartographies* (2012), Karen Barad explains that,

> I am not interested in critique. In my opinion, critique is over-rated, over-emphasized, and over-utilized, to the detriment of feminism. As Bruno Latour signals in an article entitled 'Why has critique run out of steam? From Matters of Fact to Matters of Concern' (2004), critique is a tool that keeps getting used out of habit perhaps, but it is no longer the tool needed for the kinds of situations we now face. (2012: 49)

As Barad gestures here, Latour's work has been a major impetus for the turn against critique, and given this, there is good reason to pause and look carefully at his characterisation of critique and its failures.

According to Latour, critique is much too negatively conceived and geared toward the revelation of human false consciousness. Indeed, in his 'Compositionist Manifesto' (2010), Latour argues that critique's utility and value has expired.

> To be sure, critique did a wonderful job of debunking prejudices, enlightening nations, prodding minds, but, as I have argued elsewhere, it 'ran out of steam' because it was predicated on the discovery of a true world of realities lying behind a veil of appearances. (Latour 2010: 4)

Marking critique as essentially limited and destructive, Latour explains (summoning Friedrich Nietzsche's *Twilight of the Idols, Or, How to Philosophise with a Hammer*, (1968)) that, 'with a hammer (or a sledge hammer) in hand you can do a lot of things: break down walls, destroy idols, ridicule prejudices, but you cannot repair, take care, assemble, reassemble, stitch together' (Latour 2010: 4). He argues that '*what can be critiqued cannot be composed*' (2010: 4). But perhaps it is worth asking if critique – and methods in general – are as fixed and predictable in their uses, indeed, even expendable in their potential and application. This either/or division of creative versus destructive capacities is surely troubled by such obvious examples as the demolition of the Berlin Wall, which was, for some, the first step both in assembling peace and stitching Europe back together. Yet even more prosaically, hammers create and build homes, repair cars after panel beating . . . the list is endless: destruction from one perspective is hope and restoration from another. Nonetheless, Latour deems it 'necessary to move from iconoclasm' to 'the *suspension* of the critical impulse' (2010: 5, emphasis added).

This fatigue with critique as a method of reading, and as the routine that guarantees political efficacy, also extends to the humanities. It appears in arguments that are not specifically posthuman but are more generally sympathetic to a turn toward analyses of 'real' experience, rather than rhetoric, semiotics or representation. In their editorial opening to the *Representations* special edition 'The Way We Read Now', Stephen Best and Sharon Marcus, for instance, argue that 'symptomatic reading', 'popularised by the linguistic turn of the 1970s' and 'the acceptance of psychoanalysis and Marxism as metalanguages', is no longer relevant to contemporary political realities, but rather has come to seem 'nostalgic, even utopian' (2009: 1–2). Justifying this waning relevance, they contend that,

> those of us who cut our intellectual teeth on deconstruction, ideology critique, and the hermeneutics of suspicion have often found those demystifying proto-cols superfluous in an era when images of torture at Abu Ghraib and elsewhere were immediately circulated on the internet; the real-time coverage of Hurricane Katrina showed in ways that required little explication the state's abandonment of its African American citizens; and many people instantly recognized as lies political statements such as 'mission accomplished'. (2009: 2)

In *Uses of Literature* (2008), Rita Felski similarly argues that there is 'a dawning sense among literary and cultural critics that a shape of thought has grown old' (2008: 1). With the same collective, genera-tional certainty as Marcus and Best, Felski argues that de-mystification is outdated.

> We know only too well the well-oiled machine of ideology critique, the x-ray gaze of symptomatic-reading, the smoothly rehearsed moves that add up to a hermeneutics of suspicion. Ideas that seemed revelatory thirty years ago – the decentered subject! The social construction of reality! – have dwindled into shopworn slogans [. . .] what virtue remains in unmasking when we know full well what lies beneath the mask? (2008: 1)

Felski claims that critique divides the scholar from social reality, and further, that scholars who practice critique are not truly concerned with revealing the nature of everyday experience, being more interested in the ease and satisfaction drawn from using the well-rehearsed method of revelation itself.[2] The political relevance and efficacy of critical anal-ysis is thought to be outmoded across this interdisciplinary collection of arguments.

To better understand what is going on here, it appears that the method of critique is positioned outside and above the fact and vitality of current experience, becoming an emblem of humanist hubris, or an over-confidence in human knowledge as revelation. Against this, there is a desire to get back to the real matter of life – the in-itself of reality, and specifically to try and know the world from beyond, or outside of, our limited human perspective. Quentin Meillassoux argues that the pre-human focus of speculative realism aims 'to achieve what modern philosophy has been telling us for the past two centuries is impossibil-ity itself: *to get out of ourselves*, to grasp the in-itself, to know what is whether we are or not' (2008: 27).[3] Nigel Thrift similarly explains

that non-representational theory aims 'to be resolutely anti-biograph-
ical and pre-individual, to trade in modes of perception which are not
subject-based' (2007: 7). To counter critique, and what he perceives as
its pathological paranoia, Bruno Latour also calls for 'a realist attitude'
(2004: 245), or a renewed faith in material facts. Such stated preferences are not uniform, and at times the various formulations contradict
each other. Nevertheless, the same leitmotif recurs enough to create a
critical and unifying impact; a consensus that past critical methods, in
their self-certainty and distrust of human perception, actually burden
and circumscribe life's natural dynamism. There is a further suggestion
that new methods will be the key to correcting this error and liberating
as yet unexplored possibilities. Projects often marked as the domain
of critique, such as the desire to examine sociological structures, or
to decipher the mercurial nature of semiotic meaning, are explicitly
set aside as the somewhat foolish and even pompous anthropocentric
concerns of a generation past. But is such a narrowing of focus really
helpful to the project of challenging exclusion? To explore this question, I turn now to a discussion of 'scope setting', specifically in regard
to method and focus as outlined in Jane Bennett's *Vibrant Matter*, and
then to Brian Massumi's work on affect.

In her popular book, *Vibrant Matter* (2010), Jane Bennett argues for
more 'intelligent and sustainable engagements with vibrant matter and
lively things' (2010: viii). She is interested in how a perspective of political arrangements that includes non-human participants would change
the way we value, view and practise politics. 'How would political
responses to public problems' she asks, 'change were we to take seriously
the vitality of (non-human) bodies?' (2010: viii). Bennett's case studies
primarily focus on public health and environmental issues – obesity, stem
cell research, landfill and electricity consumption. For example, in regard
to electricity, she asks, 'what difference would it make to the course of
energy policy were electricity to be figured not simply as a resource, com-
modity, or instrumentality but also and more radically as an "actant"?'
(2010: viii). Her questions in regard to these cases are focused on an
examination of what could be gained by recasting the agential distribution between humans and non-humans.

The leverage and innovation of Bennett's argument is based
partly upon this shift from the oversights of humanist politics to
posthuman determinations and concerns. Setting the scope for her
inquiry, Bennett is forthright and honest about her need to navigate
the human/posthuman tension. She argues that to cultivate 'new

determinations' we might need to 'elide the question of the human' and 'the topic of subjectivity' (2010: 120), and choose instead to 'make a meal out of' what has previously been excluded from 'the feast of political theory done in the anthropocentric style' (2010: ix). *Vibrant Matter*, therefore, juggles the paradox of an argument for inclusion, leveraged by a seemingly necessary exclusion; namely, a putting aside of those methods and subjects about which we have already heard enough.

The project then, is reoriented against the zeitgeist of the past. To open up a 'distributive agency', for example, Bennett maintains that it is vital to 'strategically elide' several existing interests and methods because they are human-centred (2010: ix). Those now conventional questions about how we know and think, how we signify and read meaning, and how our subjectivities are formed and performed, are largely irrelevant to a posthuman project and can be given 'short shrift' (2010: ix). Previous concerns of political theory, such as the power of speech acts or the agency of subjects, questions that were foundational for new historicist and postcolonial methods of reading for example, are thought to restrict the very possibility of ecological thinking. 'I will shift from the language of epistemology to that of ontology', Bennett states (2010: 3); from the 'inadequacy of representation' (2010: 14), and the 'fetishisation of the subject, the image, the word' (2010: 19).

Further to this, a social or political science concerned with the dialectic between individual citizens and the larger civil society now becomes inessential to the project of a vital materialism, specifically because it imposes a static structure upon a dynamic ecology. For instance, departing from 'the agency-versus-structure debate in the social sciences', Bennett argues that 'the category of structure is ultimately unable to give the force of things its due: a structure can act only negatively, as a constraint on human agency, or passively, as an enabling background or context for it' (2010: 29). The potential problem that arises from this statement is that it precludes the possible dynamism of structure, and thereby circumscribes what can count as a potential field of agency. There are questions that could be asked here about the nature of structure as something that we might at least consider as not necessarily human-based, constructed or centred, or even essentially constraining and fixed. Could sociological structure, or context, be deemed malleable and responsive; in short, could structure also count as a vital 'actant' in the ecology of political life?

On a methodological level, the value of critique is also called into question, and yet Bennett concedes that it remains valuable to her efforts. Bennett argues that,

> for *this* task, demystification, that most popular of practices in critical theory, should be used with caution and sparingly, because demystification presumes that at the heart of any event or process lies a *human* agency that has illicitly been projected into things. (2010: xiv)

Although it aims to emphasise previously overlooked agencies, this strategic departure from what have been accepted critical concerns and methods risks implementing a different set of limitations, rather than promoting a radically inclusive framework. It unintentionally undercuts the value and importance of the structural and ideological realities that Bennett's argument deploys in order to make her case against the anthropocentric nature of current political discourse. Her argument, one of revelation, relies upon the method of critique to demonstrate that past political theories have overlooked the non-human agencies that structure our society and environment.

Although one can certainly understand Bennett's disquiet when scholars cling to the habitual, and as a direct consequence, struggle to engage with the vitality of 'non-human' actants, it seems unnecessary to cast previous concerns and methods as essentially undynamic, and thus inessential to an inclusive ecology. If we follow Bennett's line of thought, what becomes clear is a certain faith that if a human-imposed structure, in this case, a method or set of guiding intellectual questions is removed, then a natural, 'freethinking' liberty, or agency, will be revealed as it *truly* is. However, this way of thinking introduces new political puzzles for scholars who then need to ascertain *which* agencies are productive and whether certain methods and questions can be declared redundant as agential actants in social and intellectual life.

To exclude, diagnose or denigrate a particular method, social force or political concern as strictly an anthropocentric imposition, a mere social construction, seems to rule out a process by which such concerns, or methods, may well have evolved from *within* the comprehensive and intricate matrix of life that Bennett describes. Indeed in the grammar of Bennett's argument, what are considered humanist 'topics' have their own active verbs and actions, as if the idea itself has agency and force to direct and affect the human. The disquiet, in these terms, is not that method is extraneous, but that method – or the inclination even to ask the very *question* of the human – will inevitably direct and disable the unwitting scholar. Method is not without agency. We will recall that Bennett describes it as a vital, if obstinate, agent in perpetuating anthropocentricism – beyond the authority of the well-meaning critic.

> A way to cultivate this new discernment might be to elide the question of the human. Postpone for a while the topics of subjectivity and the nature of human interiority, or the question of what really distinguishes the human from the animal, plant, and thing. Sooner or later, these topics will *lead* down the anthropocentric garden path, will *insinuate* a hierarchy of subjects over objects, and *obstruct* freethinking about what agency really entails. (2010: 120, emphasis added)

Does the human have ultimate agency in Bennett's account if the critic can be guided, despite their own intentions, by a 'topic' that 'insinuates' and 'obstructs', or a way of thinking that has its own guiding influence and force? In the quotation above, the question of the human is likened to a Medusa that we cannot even look at lest the pursuit of dynamism be turned to stone. But if anthropocentricism, or the self-interest of a particular species, for example, seems destined to evolve or arrive, is it possible that what is judged as opportunistic ambition is ecologically impelled rather than simply erroneous? At least, this should remain a question to be explored before it is summarily dismissed.

If this is the case, anthropocentricism could not be diagnosed away: it would be a puzzle to factor in, even within a posthuman project. To inform such an approach, we might look to Vicki Kirby's concept of originary humanicity (2011), which so thoroughly destabilises the kind of easy temporality, and causality, that is assumed when we conceive of the anthro as a modern parasite on an otherwise balanced, or unhindered, ecos. Reorienting rather than ignoring the insistence of questions about what constitutes subjectivity or the bounds of the human we could follow Kirby in decentring human sentience, intelligence and literacy to ask if perhaps the system, the ecos, interpellates anthropocentrism.

Furthermore, we might qualify the argument that critique has not recognised the vitality of things so as not to obscure the complexity of a social field that involves the volatile, productive materiality of *things* such as language, faith, desire and morality. Indeed, the stated aim of Bennett's project is to change her reader's perspective and political ideology more broadly. In this context, living questions about the ethical, civil and intellectual implications of how humans, particularly knowledge-producers, exist in the world continue to drive the ontological push and leverage that provide Bennett's argument with its interventionary value. Bennett, for instance, explains that her project is impelled by concern for the environment, specifically human attitudes toward it. Indeed, in a rhetorical fashion that again banks on the transformative power of representation, Bennett aims, through her strategic elision of the human, to change 'human culture' (2010: xi), and she hopes to achieve this goal in book form. 'Why advocate the vitality of matter?' she asks.

> Because my hunch is that the image of dead or thoroughly instrumentalized matter feeds human hubris and our earth-destroying fantasies of conquest and consumption. My claims here are motivated by a self-interested or conative concern for *human* survival and happiness: I want to promote greener forms of human culture and more attentive encounters between people-materialities and thing-materialities. (2010: ix–x)

Bennett's argument is animated by environmentalism, and in other chapters of *Vibrant Matter*, her stated commitments are to further elaborate the ethical and political discourses surrounding stem cell research, obesity and health policy, and the consumption and privatised infrastructure of electricity. The contested, political nature of her evaluations of human motivation and intention, or what makes people happy, along with the conviction that her hunch is right, affirm why a formalist analysis of assemblages or networks is not enough. It is one thing to factor in all of the participants in an event – as Bennett attempts to do when she acknowledges even the authorial contribution of the graphite in her pencil – but we are left with a question as to how, or even why, an inclusive ontology might choose to refuse questions of recognition and epistemology – the contested and conflicting interpretations, methods and values, that are, also, material participants in these arrangements. Moreover, if the scholar cannot see these arrangements omnisciently, as if outside and above them, then this surely implies that our humanity, our very biology and what counts for us as a personal and individual identity or subjectivity, is an involved apparatus that cannot be pulled apart or parts elided.

Indeed, the often-underemphasised methodological focus of such proposals implies that human intentions – to acknowledge, appreciate, be modest, and so on – are what will ultimately *matter*. Bennett aims to recognise the agency of non-human things, but to do this she attributes social responsibility to the human, and specifically to the scholar, whom, she argues, must change the methods and scope of their inquiry if such an outcome is to be achieved. Posthumanism, in the present critical moment, expresses, among other things, a broader social, environmentalist project to transform how humans position themselves as resource-demanding fauna in life's ecology (see also Bennett and Chaloupka 1993, Smith 2011, and Morton 2013). The resulting politics is founded on a faith that if humans change how they think, and specifically what they value, then they can halt environmental degradation. Indeed, there is even the suggestion that we humans can transform the Anthropocene, a contested, yet viral definition of our contemporary geological age, where humans are seen as the primary agents of ecological destruction *and* its potential solution. In this context, the productive substance of social norms and habits of thinking remain tangible and crucial 'actants' in the stakes of posthuman arguments, and critique operates as one of our most active methods of detecting, exposing and revising the common assumption that the human species is the sole custodian of the earth.

The turn to ontology, therefore, is interested in the being of non-humans. However, this turn is also steeped in, and responds to, the quixotic history and experience of critical commentary and evaluation, as well as the interrogation of what may seem obvious, namely, what it is to be human. Such interventions remain entangled in lived, epistemological questions about what qualifies as a proper and fair frame of judgment. The human, in these posthuman arguments, scrutinises itself, finds itself wanting, and consequently challenges its own sense of mastery. And yet in other ways it curiously discounts the material force of its own values, uncertainties and confusions; its motivations and methodological struggles to account for the life that it also manifests and embodies. Ways of viewing the world are underlined as important constitutive forces in some respects, even though, at other turns, method is seen as something we can set aside. If we concentrate on the former approach, then a graduation from what are considered strictly humanist questions is troubled because if method itself is *of* the social it seeks to understand, then it cannot be outgrown and shed like an old skin to reveal an unspoiled, new and entirely different perspective – a pure, dynamic manifestation of matter. Method is not an external lens that, if corrected, will comprehend life as it truly is. The human cannot escape its own materiality, its own self-importance and hubris. To engage with the complexity of life we might need to include the very things that will complicate our project; we must include ourselves and our intellectual inheritance, with all its awkward and conflicting desires and the values that inform, and are informed by, our social acts of self-observation.

Perhaps we might concede that materiality contests itself in provocative ways. The very same material in one context might promote climate action, and in another, climate scepticism. This question of method then, as a productive contest of material values and perspectives, arises as a *particular* perspective, from out of the very 'world of vital, cross-cutting currents' that Bennett calls us to confront: a method is not just an instrumental and extraneous means to fix a problem. In this context, the question of what we choose to exclude – critically and methodologically – should come under close scrutiny. Is there a way to rethink rather than retrench the legacy of humanist theory? Could we consider a lingering humanism not as an error to be weeded out, or an anthropocentric hubris that can be reformed, but instead, as a provocation to trace how the social body, in its complexity, can and does overlook, negate and misrecognise itself? Or again, could we explore how different expressions of life, in their myriad manifestations, can project, attribute, imbue and withhold meaning in and from one another? This line of inquiry would trouble the surety, the disavowed hubris, of a generational progression that posits liberation from the errors of the past, the separation of methodology from matter, and observer from observed.

By questioning a particular methodological corrective as the order of a new day, here, the exclusion or sidelining of epistemology, critique and structure – or its assumption that forces of potential and intensity are essentially liberating – the present discussion follows cultural theorist Lauren Berlant's trepidations about the fervent endorsement of 'better methods'. Berlant specifically addresses Eve Kosofsky Sedgwick's call to turn from 'Paranoid Reading', or the hermeneutics of suspicion, to her antidote, 'Reparative Reading', a turn that has been very influential in affect theory (Sedgwick 1997). Berlant argues that while she is sympathetic with Sedgwick's aims, she 'also resist[s] idealising, even implicitly, any program of better thought or reading' (2011: 124). 'How would we know', she asks, 'when the "repair" we intend is not another form of narcissism or smothering will? Just because we sense it to be so?' Berlant suggests that such a proscriptive ideology, albeit self-consciously dissenting, leads back to the very projection of values it hopes to avoid, in this case, an unshaken faith in the acuity of human discernment.

> Those of us who think for a living are too well-positioned to characterise certain virtuous acts of thought as dramatically powerful and right, whether effective or futile; we are set up to overestimate the proper clarity and destiny of an idea's effect and appropriate affects . . . I'm suggesting that the overvaluation of reparative thought is both an occupational hazard and part of a larger overvaluation of a certain mode of virtuously intentional, self-reflective personhood. (2011: 124)

Following Berlant, it is important to retain the possibility of misrecognition, a sense of fallibility, about even those programmes deemed ethical, because we want to explore the queer efficacy of as many theoretical tools and perspectives as possible, including those that seem to fall short.

Presuming to put certain concerns, methods or histories *outside* a circumscribed realm of what matters is perhaps as misguided as putting human experience, automatically, at the centre. In both cases, we assume what remains in question – how we might finally decide upon the most progressive arrangement, as well as who or what will qualify as the most vital actors. Routinely, indeed, everyday, we must make decisions, but is this point of departure truly all that different from the arguments of the past, in that they are driven by our unique worries about, perceptions of, and responses to, the current state of the world? Can we fairly denigrate the critical methods of the past for their perspectivalism (for example, a focus on identity politics and hidden agencies in scholarship that was informed by the civil rights movement and the Cold War), if such emphases and omissions are inherent to, and often blind spots within, all forms of inquiry; inquiries which, if we assume a dispersed authority, are inevitably socially authored?

The question of self-certainty and scope is an important consideration for posthuman arguments because it is on the level of their stated exclusions, not the validity of their contribution to knowledge as such, that several of these arguments have met with criticism. Though the aim of such methodological shifts is to be more inclusive, these interventions are being read in some quarters as needlessly and ironically exclusionary, particularly towards existing political questions and schools.[4] Philosopher Andrew Cole's critique of object-oriented ontology, actor network theory, speculative realism and vitalism, for example, is not driven by a lack of interest in the vitality of objects, but by what he sees as the unhelpful exclusion of certain philosophical histories in puzzling over this vitality. Lamenting this historical censorship, Cole explains,

> The contradictions within each of these new philosophies – it is and it is not anthropocentrism, anthropocentrism is and is not a bad thing – can be resolved, I suggest, when the idealism and mysticism of these fields are acknowledged rather than disavowed in facile critiques of ersatz idealism and pseudosubjectivism. More crucially, a philosophical Middle Ages, which comes into view when generous attention is paid to the richness of premodern thought, presents an opportunity, if not a challenge, to these areas. (2013: 107)

For Cole, the project of Vitalism, in taking an avant-garde stance that pretends to leave behind a certain intellectual complacency, excludes and denies its actual kinship with, and potential nourishment from, those same older schools of thought. The vitality of things is certainly emphasised, but often 'instead of'. . . the efficacy of language and disciplinary histories, the complex and even structural determination of values and received political investments, and all those lingering questions about intention and social responsibility. Cole raises the question of whether the need to appear novel or progressive can actually get in the way of really challenging and innovating the intellectual field.

Similarly, when we look at the response to affect theory, another recognised domain of posthuman thought, it is clear that its critical reception rests firmly on the necessary exclusions of myriad different theories, rather than the intrinsic value and possible provocations heralded by affect theory itself. One of the key circumscriptions to come under question in the field of affect theory is Brian Massumi's separation of affect from emotion, which is based on a division of language from bodily impulse, and structure from dynamism (Papoulias and Callard 2010, Leys 2011 and Hemmings 2005).[5] Massumi characterises emotion as affect that has been 'pinned down' and defined in words, rendered static by structure and thus made redundant in explaining a dynamic world that presumably escapes it. Massumi explains that, 'what [emotions] lose, precisely, is the expression event – in favour of structure' (2002: 27). As an antidote to this rigid understanding of the frame, he suggests that,

> much could be gained by integrating the dimension of intensity [a word he suggests is interchangeable with affect] into cultural theory. The stakes are the new. For structure is the place where nothing ever happens, that explanatory heaven in which all eventual permutations are prefigured in a self-consistent set of invariant generative rules. (2002: 27)

Massumi sees language itself as devoid of affective force; as a debilitating anchor, perpetually fixed and opposed to affect. It follows that affect is seen to operate outside of structure, which Massumi describes as rigid and thus unhelpful to the analysis of affect (although at the same time that he eschews language as oppressive because lacking in dynamism, he must also preserve structure, and specifically linguistic and epistemological categories, in order to register the very specificity of affect as different and separate from language).

In tune with the broader intellectual push to outstrip, overturn or liberate – in sum, to invent something new – Massumi further argues that the structural and intrinsic qualities of affect render critique obsolete, given that '[affect] is not ownable or recognizable, and is thus resistant to critique' (2002: 28). Massumi seems to offer affect theory as an inevitable or logical correction to critique, arguing that '[critique] doesn't allow for other kinds of practices that might not have so much to do with mastery and judgement as with affective connection and abductive participation' (Massumi in Zournazi 2002: 220). Critical methods, crucially, are not just cast as redundant here, but as obstructive. In Massumi's account, it seems that judgement happens 'at a remove' from experience.

> A critical perspective that tries to come to a definitive judgement on something is always in some way a failure, because it is happening at a remove from the process it's judging . . . The process of pinning down and separating out is also a weakness in judgement, because it doesn't allow for these seeds of change, connections in the making that might not be obvious at the moment. In a sense judgemental reason is an extremely weak form of thought, precisely because it is so sure of itself. (Massumi in Zournazi 2002: 220–1)

Judgment, or the act of interpretation – coming to a decision, or making a commitment – is thought to be counter, or external to, the vitality of life here; the method lags sadly and inadequately behind its object. Language, structure and judgement, the critical concerns and methods of poststructuralism, are written out of the equation in this definition of affect; indeed, they are removed entirely from the arena of life's dynamic – its internal machinations. The consequences of this attempt to erase and prohibit, however, is that no room is left to consider the semiotic, structural and critical capacities or workings of affective force, or the vitality and flux of these methods as they are put to work in different ways and contexts. Put simply, what of life produces them?

In this setting, we can see that the debate around affect theory is unquestionably about the ethics of exclusion, or what is deemed *properly* corporeal or vital. The assumption that questions of humanity, structure, culture and intention must be closed if questions of ecology, nature, things and potential are to be opened, presumes a rigid structure that fuels the existing critiques of affect theory's disciplinary and methodological closures. Critiques, such as Claire Hemmings's 'Invoking Affect: Cultural Theory and the Ontological Turn' (2005), explain that rather than extending a radical inclusivity, Massumi's theorisation of affect is actively involved in making judgments about *which* narratives and intellectual questions are worthy of attention – and this, very often in the name of refusing judgements. For Hemmings, these preferences direct attention away from important considerations about how affect can be social and structural and how the materiality of social facts is actively produced. Taking this cultural divide head on, Hemmings asks how Massumi would have other social scientists respond to the revelation that their current methods, indeed their desire to elucidate the mysteries of the socius, are entirely inadequate. Hemmings explains that,

> while many will concur with Massumi's scepticism of quantitative research in its inability to attend to the particular, we are left with a riddle-like description of affect as something scientists can detect the loss of (in the anomaly), [and] social scientists and cultural critics cannot interpret, but philosophers can imagine. (2005: 563)

With her incisive response, Hemmings aims to draw attention to the restrictions Massumi's conception of affect seemingly puts in place. 'How then can we engage affect in light of the critical projects we are engaged in', she asks, 'or are we to abandon the social sciences entirely?' (2005: 563).

It is in this vein of acknowledged engagement, and one that, with Bennett and Massumi, aims for 'openness', that I wish to bring the methodological stakes of critical shifts to the fore and ask, is it necessary to radically break from the methods and concerns of the recent past in order to leverage new ones? Or could we retain the critical questions of our forebears, however problematic, and read them differently? Clearly, critique is still being used in the very arguments that eschew critique, so what value can we ascribe to this method that denies method? As Bennett's argument highlights, questions of ideology and critical intervention are important to, and often motivate, discussions of posthuman ethics. And although occasionally self-negating, posthumanism demonstrates as much faith in human responsibility as the critical theories it opposes. As Karen Barad argues, 'causal interactions need not involve humans' (140), but these arguments' questions of scholarly ethics and methods are very concerned with the agency of humans, specifically the intellectual culture we are perpetuating. Quentin Meillassoux, for instance, claims that what has come to be known as speculative realism's project, a turn to the pre-human ancestrality of objects, is about getting outside of a human perspective: '*to get out of ourselves*' (2008: 27). But the project is clearly also about the kinds of philosophy scholars *should* be pursuing and writing.

To think ecologically, and to radically disperse agency, scholars need to rethink the boundaries of the human and what constitutes the intelligence and value of material life, but hopefully this need not entail a host of new exclusions, or new designations about what does not, or should not, *matter*. All intellectual interventions will privilege and discount particular perspectives to some extent, but need we win the value of our respective arguments by denigrating outright, even to the point of censorship and exclusion? Such an approach also risks negating how existing structures and methods, albeit differently conceived, already vitalise and leverage posthuman arguments. Retaining sociological questions of value and actualisation, for instance, the turn to ontology is immersed in questions of representational ethics, or how shifts in method reverberate ecologically. Grounded in critique, it summons questions of authorial position and method, namely, how method, as an ontology of orientation, has and will continue to matter, that is, to materially reconfigure life.

Questioning the ethics of anthropocentricism throughout, speculative realism longs for, but importantly is not itself, a 'pre-critical' philosophy – which Meillassoux defines as 'the non-philosopher's' capacity to be 'astonished' by, or credulous of, 'realism' (2008: 27). Retaining questions about critical value and professional ethics, Meillassoux retains a faith in the scholar's power to change the world by changing methods, to revise, though crucially not reject, human custodianship by refiguring critical authorship. In this way, questions of human responsibility and intention continue to anchor and drive many posthuman arguments about method and ecology. Both Bennett's and Massumi's projects, for instance, are invested in broader social, and socially contested, worries about society's self-perpetuating complicity in neo-liberal regimes of environmental looting and fear-mongering morality. They both aim to decentre the human and acknowledge and propagate value for the non-human agencies that are overlooked and sometimes denied by anthropocentric conceptions of the ecosphere.

Certain posthumanisms can appear to set up a division between epistemology and ontology, between realism and representation, or activism and critique; however, these arguments attest to a methodological shift in how scholars might think and write as the first step in activating and preserving ecology. What they seek to change, or deem to matter, are often the social facts, representations and structures that justify or produce certain unsustainable behaviours and economic priorities. Ways of positioning oneself in the world – whether anthropocentric or ecological – are seen as the cause, but importantly, also the means to transform environmental and civic degradation. The efficacy of social priority, ideologies and rhetoric involves errors that continue to energise the aims of posthuman arguments. Posthuman ethics, therefore, do not exclude humanist concerns. Indeed they are often expressions of, investments in, and pronouncements upon them. Surely, if we acknowledge and include this constitutive contradiction, as Bennett does when she explains that her elision of the human is driven by a concern for humanity, then the very temporality implied by the term 'post' becomes unsettled, and the terms of reference for all our debates a little more mired.

Notes

1. In *New Materialisms: Ontology, Agency, and Politics* (2010), Diana Coole and Samantha Frost also ask whether new materialist conceptions of reality can accommodate sociological concerns about social construction. They note that older works on the social construction of reality, such as those of Peter Berger and Thomas Luckmann (1966), or even Marx, can be seen to account for the materiality and realism of social ideologies and beliefs if read in a sympathetic way (2010: 26).

2. In the humanities, there are numerous and alternative method proposals that seek to make up for the ethical and explanatory failings of critical methods with novel forms of inquiry. In 'Reading with the Grain: A New World in Literary Criticism' (2010), for instance, Timothy Bewes proposes his own notion of 'reading with the grain' as an antidote to Walter Benjamin's suspicious 'reading against the grain'. Bewes underlines 'the need to outgrow our supposedly Benjaminian habits of reading against the grain – the phrase that functioned as a byword for theoretically informed criticism in the second half of the twentieth century' (2010: 4). In affect theory, for instance, Eve Kosofsky Sedgwick champions 'reparative reading' over 'paranoid reading' (1997), and Brian Massumi argues for a turn away from critique's judgement to affect's potential (1995). See also Zournazi (2002). Stephen Best and Sharon Marcus's 'Surface Reading: An Introduction' (2009), as described above, offers 'surface reading' as an answer to Louis Althusser's 'symptomatic', deep reading (Althusser and Balibar 1979). Other manifestos that pose preferable alternatives to critique include, Nigel Thrift's 'non-representational theory' (2007), Michael Warner's 'uncritical reading' (2004), Rachael Ablow's 'affective reading' (2010), John Law's 'mess as method' (2004), and 'fictocriticism' (Taussig 2010; Stewart 2007; Muecke 2010).

3. For a thorough discussion of Meillassoux's 'critique of critique' see Dolphijn and van der Tuin (2012: 167–72).

4. In addition to the critiques discussed below, David Cecchetto's 'Deconstructing Affect: Posthumanism and Mark Hansen's Media Theory' (2011), questions not so much the value of Hansen's interest, but why he must sideline the question of representation that his argument still clearly relies upon, and engages with, in important ways.

5. Massumi's differentiation of affect and emotion forms an important basis for several self-declared arguments about posthuman subjectivity. For instance, in their introduction to *Theory, Culture and Society*'s special issue on 'Naturecultures? Science, Affect and the Non-human' (2013), Joanna Latimer and Mara Miele outline that, in their volume,

> affect is being understood here not so much in its modern sense, as emotion or sentiment, but rather in terms of 'attachment' on the one hand and being 'moved' on the other. The sense of affect being invoked thus contrasts emotion and affect, the former being individuated and the latter being both embodied and relational. (2013: 8)

They cite Blackman and Cromby, who concur that in posthuman terms,

> affect is often taken to refer to a force or intensity that can belie the movement of the subject who is always in a process of becoming. Although affects might traverse individual subjects, for many scholars they undo the notion of a singular or sovereign subject. (Blackman and Cromby in Latimer and Miele 2013: 8)

For other posthuman utilisations of affect theory see Seaman (2007) and Protevi (2009).

References

Ablow, R. (ed.) (2010), *The Feeling of Reading: Affective Experience and Victorian Literature*, Ann Arbor: University of Michigan Press.

Althusser, L., and É. Balibar ([1970] 1979), *Reading Capital*, London: Verso.

Barad, K. (2007), *Meeting the Universe Halfway: Quantum Physics and the Entanglement of Matter and Meaning*, Durham, NC: Duke University Press.

Bennett, J. (2010), *Vibrant Matter: A Political Ecology of Things*, Durham, NC: Duke University Press.

Bennett, J., and W. Chaloupka (1993), *In the Nature of Things: Language, Politics, and the Environment*, Minneapolis: University of Minnesota Press.

Berger, P., and T. Luckmann (1966), *The Social Construction of Reality*, London: Penguin.

Berlant, L. (2011), *Cruel Optimism*, Durham, NC: Duke University Press.

Best, S., and S. Marcus (2009), 'Surface Reading: An introduction', *Representations,* Special Issue: 'The Way We Read Now', 108: 1, pp. 1–21.

Bewes, T. (2010), 'Reading with the Grain: A New World in Literary Criticism', *differences: A Journal of Feminist Cultural Studies*, 21: 3, pp. 1–33.

Cecchetto, David (2011), 'Deconstructing Affect: Posthumanism and Mark Hansen's media theory', *Theory, Culture & Society*, 28: 5, pp. 3–33.

Cole, A. (2013), 'The Call of Things: A Critique of Object-Oriented Ontologies', *The Minnesota Review*, 80, pp. 106–18.

Coole, D., and S. Frost (2010), *New Materialisms: Ontology, Agency, and Politics*, Durham, NC: Duke University Press.

Dolphijn, R., and I. van der Tuin (2012), *New Materialism: Interviews & Cartographies*, Open Humanities Press. An imprint of MPublishing, Ann Arbor: University of Michigan Library.

Felski, R. (2008), *Uses of Literature*, Malden and Oxford: Blackwell Publishing. Hemmings, C. (2005), 'Invoking Affect: Cultural Theory and the Ontological Turn', *Cultural Studies*, 19: 5, pp. 548–67.

Kirby, V. (2011), *Quantum Anthropologies: Life at Large*, Durham, NC: Duke University Press.

Latimer, J., and M. Miele (2013), 'Naturecultures? Science, Affect and the Non-Human', *Theory, Culture & Society*, 30: 7/8, pp. 5–31.

Latour, B. (2004), 'Why has Critique Run out of Steam? From Matters of Fact to Matters of Concern', *Critical Inquiry*, 30: 2, pp. 225–48.

Latour, B. (2010), 'An Attempt at a Compositionist Manifesto', available at <http://www.bruno-latour.fr/sites/default/files/120-NLH-finalpdf.pdf > (last accessed 25 March 2016).

Law, J. (2004), *After Method: Mess in Social Science Research*, New York: Routledge.

Leys, R. (2011), 'The Turn to Affect: A critique', *Critical Inquiry*, 37: 3, pp. 434–72.

Massumi, B. (1995), 'The Autonomy of Affect', *Cultural Critique*, 31: Part 11, pp. 83–109.

Massumi, B. (2002), 'The Autonomy of Affect', in *Parables for the Virtual: Movement, Affect, Sensation*, Durham, NC: Duke University Press, pp. 23–45.

Meillassoux, Q. (2008), *After Finitude: An essay on the necessity of contingency*, London and New York: Continuum.

Morton, T. (2013), *Hyperobjects: Philosophy and Ecology After the End of the World,* Minneapolis: University of Minnesota Press.

Muecke, S. (2010), 'Public Thinking, Public Feeling: Research Tools for Creative Writing', *TEXT*, 14:1, available at <http://www.textjournal.com.au/april10/muecke.htm> (last accessed 20 January 2011).

Nietzsche, F. W. ([1889] 1968), *Twilight of the Idols, Or, How to Philosophise with a Hammer*, trans. R. J. Hollingdale, London: Penguin.

Papoulias, C., and F. Callard (2010), 'Biology's Gift: Interrogating the Turn to Affect', *Body & Society*, 16:1, pp. 29–56.

Protevi, J. (2009), *Political Affect: Connecting the Social and the Somatic*, Minneapolis: University of Minnesota Press.

Seaman, M. J. (2007), 'Becoming More (than) Human: Affective Posthumanisms, Past and Future', *Journal of Narrative Theory*, 37: 2, pp. 246–75.

Sedgwick, E. K. (1997), 'Paranoid Reading and Reparative Reading; or, You're So Paranoid, You Probably Think This Introduction is About You', in *Novel Gazing: Queer Readings in Fiction*, Durham, NC: Duke University Press, pp. 10–39.

Smith, M. (2011), *Against Ecological Sovereignty: Ethics, Biopolitics, and Saving the Natural World*, Minneapolis, University of Minnesota Press.

Stewart, K. (2007), *Ordinary Affects*, Durham, NC: Duke University Press.

Taussig, M. (2010), 'The Corn-Wolf: Writing Apotropaic Texts', *Critical Inquiry*, 37: 1, pp. 26–33.

Thrift, N. (2007), *Non-representational Theory: Space, Politics, Affect*, London and New York: Routledge.

Warner, M. (2004), 'Uncritical Reading', in Jane Gallop (ed.), *Polemic: Critical or Uncritical*, New York: Routledge, pp. 13–38.

Zournazi, M. (2002), *Hope: New Philosophies for Change*, New York: Routledge.

CHAPTER 3

Sensory Substitution: The Plasticity of the Eye/I

Florence Chiew

When we think of perception most of us will call to mind everyday experiences of sight, smell, sound, touch and taste. Intuitively, we may also match the sensory perceptions we experience with their modal counterparts: we see with our eyes, hear with our ears, taste with our tongue, smell with our nose, touch with our skin. This classic definition of perception as an aggregate of different sensory modalities is also used in scientific approaches to the topic. In psychology textbooks, for instance, it is not uncommon to find stand-alone chapters devoted to explaining the functions and structures of each of the different senses (Chaudhuri 2011; Mathur 2009).

Implicit in this orthodox account is a causal and linear narrative: a discrete physical stimulus triggers a particular subjective response. Psychologist, George Mathur, explains the process like so: 'we may sense "sound" when air pressure waves *enter* the ear; and we may sense "light" when electromagnetic radiation *enters* the eye' (2009: 17, emphasis added). In a similar vein, perceptual psychologist, Avi Chaudhuri, describes how physical stimuli, as 'raw data', are transmitted via nerve impulses and sensory pathways to corresponding regions in the brain, where 'sensory inputs are biologically processed to ultimately produce the experience of perception' (2011: 36). While intuitive, these accounts of perception rest on a key assumption, namely, that the perceiver and the object of perception are discrete entities, separated by a biological or psychological interface through which sensory information passes. In other words, the process of perception relies on the object's externality from the perceiving subject or body.

In a similar vein, localisation is a foundational principle of modern neuroscience. Localisation theories posit that discrete regions in the brain are specialised for different functions (Kandel et al. 2013). Traditionally, neuroscientific explanations of sensory processing have been based on the 'labelled line' hypothesis in which 'a single neuron codes for a single pre-determined dimension' (Fotheringham and Young 1997: 48). According to psychologist Charles Gross, this hypothesis has also been termed the 'grandmother cell', indicating 'a neuron that would respond only to a specific, complex, and meaningful stimulus, that is, to a single percept or even a single concept' (2002: 512). In this approach, every neuron in the brain is believed to possess a unique 'hardwired signature', such that the firing of a single cell signals a distinct 'event' or concept as precise as 'light touch on my right elbow' (Ramachandran and Hirstein 1998: 1623). Accordingly, the goal of scientists is to find neural correlates of subjective experience so that all types of experience can be precisely explained in terms of the physical structure and processes of the brain (Kandel et al. 2013). Crucially, this view underpins a sense of determinism in conceptualising the nature of neurobiology and the functions that correspond to it. Put simply, specific neurons in the brain 'code' or represent individual objects in the world, such as faces, expressions, memories, places, relationships and so on.

Interestingly, however, more recent findings in the neuroscience of sensory substitution, or cross-modal plasticity, propose a different and unusual account of perception. Sensory substitution is the process by which information ordinarily acquired through the pathways of one modality is instead obtained through those that process another. Braille reading, for instance, is exemplary of the cross-modal interaction between visual and tactile information processing. Studies of neural activity in blind Braille learners show that the repeated stimulation of a particular body part, the finger tips, is accompanied by a growth in the cortical representation of the reading finger (Merabet and Pascual-Leone 2010; Pascual-Leone and Hamilton 2001; Hamilton and Pascual-Leone 1998). In proficient Braille readers, the enlargement of the 'finger tip' representation indicates the extent to which the sustained use of a body part modifies the neural circuitry corresponding to it. In short, such findings offer evidence of the malleability and adaptability of sensory function, in this case, how Braille readers learn to 'see' with touch.

In the same vein, prosthetic devices such as the tactile-visual sensory substitution (TVSS) system have been designed to compensate for the loss of vision by redirecting visual information into tactile stimuli (Bach-y-Rita et al. 2003; Bach-y-Rita and Kercel 2003; Bach-y-Rita

1972). Invented by neuroscientist Paul Bach-y-Rita, the basic model of a TVSS works by having a blind person wear computing devices that convert visual images taken by a mobile camera into vibrating tactile stimulators placed on different parts of the person's skin. Remarkably, with training and practice, TVSS users report experiencing a change in the modal quality and the originating source of the pulsating sensations. That is, they describe a shift in the location and individuation of perceptual experience, from an initial sensation of touch on the patch of skin receiving electrical stimulation, to the visual experience of images projected in front of them (Bach-y-Rita and Kercel 2003: 543). Compellingly, within a short period of time, the TVSS device seems to be integrated into the blind user's corporeal schema, challenging both the boundaries of the body and of biology, and the conventional notion of sensory modalities as discrete, pre-established entities.

Taken together, studies of sensory substitution would appear to call into question the traditionally atomic, linear and causal view of perception. Indeed, cross-modal plasticity offends two well-established scientific orthodoxies, namely, that a large proportion of the brain is devoted to processing visual information, and that biology is destiny or determinism.[1] Yet, curiously, the problem of determinism and the localisation of biological cause continues to plague interpretations of sensory substitution. As we will see, even though localisation theories are significantly complicated by findings of cross-modal plasticity, sensory substitution is still routinely understood in terms of discrete modalities that effect changes in each other (i.e., an 'injured' modality causes compensation by a separate 'intact' modality). The process of *how* this occurs is not something that is given much attention.

This chapter explores the implications of cross-modal plasticity for our understanding of perception and, importantly, it also questions the notion of deficiency as a lack of normal function. Using prominent case studies in the neuroscience literature, I show how findings of sensory substitution confound the distinction between 'biological' and 'environmental' determinants of development and individuation. Indeed, one of my central aims in this chapter is to flesh out the sociological insight that neurobiological processes are experience driven. To this end the phenomenologist Maurice Merleau-Ponty provides a pathfinding re-vision of the subject/object dichotomy, a dichotomy that continues to inform many of the current interpretations of the perceptual process. My argument is thus also a meditation on how empirical evidence of cross-modal plasticity suggests not only that sensory function is malleable, but that this malleability evokes a broader eco-logic of sensibility, one that allows us to think the plasticity of vision, the 'eye', as the plasticity of the subject of experience, the 'I'.

Braille and TVSS: What is 'Visual' Experience?

As vision is generally considered to be our dominant sense, neuroscientists working on sensory substitution are particularly fascinated by the role of the visual or occipital cortex in blind individuals. This line of inquiry is interesting as it captures a fundamental problem of origin and causality in theories of sensory substitution. As neuropsychologist Josef Rauschecker ponders,

> what is the kind of percept that a blind individual experiences when a 'visual' area becomes activated by an auditory or tactile stimulus? Do blind individuals 'see' their environment with their tactile senses . . . or does the visual area simply get transformed into an auditory or somatosensory representation by the new type of input? In other words, is the percept determined by the type of sensory input or by the (functionally preordained) brain region that receives it? (1995: 4)

Importantly, for Rauschecker, how this puzzle is addressed has deep implications for our understanding of the interface between perceptual experience and neurobiology, and in particular, whether the neurobiological apparatus underpinning perception is stable or protean. Put another way, at stake is a debate about where the biology of perception originates, and what it means to call something a 'visual' experience. Does the encounter of an object, a concept or a phenomenon depend on pre-given stimuli that the nervous system receives from the environment, i.e. a visual image stimulates (causes) a visual experience? Or, does determining an object's modality rely on the specificity of neural sites that process it? That is, does one experience sound, for example, only when a stimulus is processed in/by the auditory cortex? The riddle that provokes these queries is that even if the object is 'normally' visual, it seems possible that one's neurology could be rewired so that it processes this object as an auditory stimulus. In short, Rauschecker's question poses a debate between neurological determinism and contingency: visual experience is either determined by the 'functionally preordained' visual cortex or it is conditional on the brain's interpretation of a stimulus.[2]

Interestingly, then, although sensory substitution provides strong evidentiary support for the mingling of the senses, neuroscientists do not always agree on the *process* of cross-modal plasticity, that is, *how*

plasticity works. This difference in perspective is telling as it highlights the complexity of distinguishing the 'original' and 'substituting'
modality. The crux of contention rests on two contrastive approaches
to brain plasticity, that is, whether the recovery of a perceptual deficit is grounded in mechanisms of 'reorganisation' or 'unmasking'
(Finger and Almli 1985; Kadosh and Walsh 2006; Merabet et al. 2005;
Merabet and Pascual-Leone 2010; Zeki 1993). As cognitive neuroscientists, Roi Cohen Kadosh and Vincent Walsh explain, 'one possibility,
called the *reorganization hypothesis*, is that the reorganization of the
deprived brain leads to the establishment of new mediating pathways.
A second possibility, the *unmasking hypothesis*, is that damage induces
unmasking and strengthening of existing neuronal connections' (2006:
962, emphasis in original).

While the debate is seldom framed in this way, it is noteworthy
that the spirit of the dichotomy between determinism and contingency underlies these hypotheses. In an early review of neuroplasticity
research, scientists Stanley Finger and Robert Almli (1985) provide
a clarifying account of the assumptions underpinning the notions of
unmasking and reorganisation. On the unmasking hypothesis, they
explain, damage to sensory function means that 'while remaining
brain structures may be used to carry out a task, these structures are
not taking on new or "unusual" functions . . . the organism is simply
doing the best it can with that which is left' (1985: 178). On the other
hand, a reorganisation hypothesis proposes the 'sprouting' of new
neural connections such that 'intact axons sen[d] out new branches
or terminals to occupy synaptic sites vacated by other axons that are
degenerating or dying' (1985: 178). In brief, the notion of unmasking
assumes a view of the brain as stable and unchanging, whereas reorganisation suggests fortuitous, active changes in neural circuitry. Given
this comparison, it would appear that the former hypothesis retains a
deterministic flavour of neurobiological development, or at least, a
sense of its inevitability. Conversely, the latter hypothesis evokes the
play of contingency to the extent that 'sprouting' reflects newness and
creativity. But are these two hypotheses really that different?

In a series of experiments with Braille readers these hypotheses are
put to the test. Neuroscientists Alvaro Pascual-Leone and Roy Hamilton
(1998, 2001) find that in blind Braille readers, not only is the somatosensory cortex (the modality of touch) activated, as would be expected,
but the *visual* cortex also shows strong patterns of activation.[3] These
scientists suggest that 'in blind subjects the occipital cortex appears

capable of reorganizing to accept non-visual sensorimotor information, possibly for further processing' (1998: 170). In other words, the visual cortex of the blind actively participates in a tactile discrimination task such as Braille reading. Using a technique called repetitive transcranial magnetic stimulation (rTMS), Pascual-Leone and Hamilton are able to induce small and sustained decreases in activity in the part of the brain being stimulated. When rTMS is applied to the visual areas of blind subjects reading Braille, these subjects report interruptions in their reading ability. For example, they describe distortions in their perception of Braille symbols, saying that the Braille dots feel different, either 'flatter' or 'less sharp and less well-defined' (Pascual-Leone and Hamilton 1998: 170).

What can be extrapolated from these self-reports is that interfering with the visual cortex during Braille reading hampers the reading skills of these blind subjects. That is, the visual regions which are ordinarily assumed to be damaged in blind individuals continue to play a critical role in tactile tasks such as Braille reading. This specificity of the function of sight seems to be confirmed in control experiments. For example, when rTMS is applied to the visual cortex of sighted subjects working on tactile discrimination tasks (e.g., identifying embossed letters by touch), the subjects' performances on the tasks are not hindered. However, when rTMS is delivered to the somatosensory cortex, or the tactile processing centres of these participants, the participants' performances on the tactile tasks are interrupted. In these control experiments, tactile processing in sighted subjects reveals an activation of the perception of touch but *deactivation* of regions ordinarily devoted to primary and secondary occipital cortical areas (Pascual-Leone and Hamilton 1998: 170). Similarly, stimulating the visual areas of sighted subjects while they are in the middle of a tactile task does not affect their performance, *but* a similar stimulation disrupts their ability to work on a visual task (Pascual-Leone and Hamilton 1998: 170). Intriguingly, these findings seem to suggest that what determines the specificity of the functions of sight and tactility depends not on a fixed biological programme but on how they have been used over time – experience-driven biology. As Pascual-Leone and Hamilton (2001: 11) surmise, visual activation in the blind for tactile tasks may indicate a kind of 'tactile imagery' whose localisation in the visual cortex implies that 'expert networks of neurons in [tactile processing] have acquired, through competition, the ability to perform [visual] operation'. Accordingly,

Pascual-Leone and Hamilton propose that this ability of the senses to merge and differentiate is present in *all of us*. The individuation of the sensory modalities relies on the simultaneous experience of all modalities, such that long-term impairment or temporary loss of function can both impede and enable cross-modal plasticity.

Returning to the conflict between the unmasking and the reorganisation hypothesis, these findings are noteworthy as they illustrate a curious paradox whereby the functions of sight and tactility are both confounded *and* made specific. Fascinating, here, is the suggestion that the visual cortex is enacted differently in different subjects; visual processing in the nervous system is active in blind subjects reading Braille, but not active in sighted subjects learning to read Braille or working on other tactile discrimination tasks. Indeed, this paradox that confounds and specifies sensory functions is perfectly illustrated by case studies of people who have recovered from early blindness. According to Pascual-Leone and Hamilton, these blind patients report experiencing 'persistent difficulties in visual perception that may be related to these subjects' long term use of "visual" cortical areas for tactile information processing' (1998: 171). The 'once blind' describe 'gross misjudgements of distance and perspective, and difficulty in identifying objects by sight without the use of other sensory modalities' (Pascual-Leone and Hamilton 1998: 171). Here, it would appear that the apparently conflicting hypotheses of unmasking and reorganisation are *simultaneously* at work in the *same* individual. In fact, it is not even clear if they are separate, discrete processes.

The preceding case examples illustrate that the two hypotheses are in fact manifestations of a single process. Recall that unmasking is based on the idea that, post-injury, the neural system copes by strengthening existing connections and not by building new ones. In contrast, the reorganisation hypothesis rests on the claim that intact nerve fibres form new neural connections to take over dead or damaged pathways following an injury. Both hypotheses, however, have something in common.

They share the assumption that the workings of plasticity set in *after* the stability of the system has been disturbed. Yet, as we have seen in the examples, the process of individuation – locating an identifiable modality in its own right – relies on the simultaneous experience of 'all' modalities, since the specificity of a given sensory function depends not on biological fixity but on how, we might say, one experiences her biology differently, for instance, 'seeing with touch' as a confounded yet unique sense. In short, what is at stake is a problem of delineating the causal origin of sensation or sensibility itself.

To recall an earlier point, the phenomenon of neuroplasticity is fascinating because it challenges neuroscience's orthodoxy of localisation. Ironically, however, typical interpretations of cross-modal plasticity continue to assume that distinct sites belong to each of the senses, a thesis that in turn assumes that boundaries of the 'original' and the 'substituting' modality are intact. Put simply, the workings of plasticity are often only posed after the fact, when another sensory modality is said to have compensated for the damaged modality. On this assumption, plasticity is a second-order derivation from the *initially* stable neural organisation, motivated in the event of brain injury.

This explanation is the basis of Pascual-Leone and Hamilton's study. Although these scientists do not directly address the question of causality, their overall claim that cross-modal plasticity illustrates what they call the 'metamodal' brain would inevitably bear on rejecting a simple distinction between cause and effect, before and after. Yet, surprisingly, Pascual-Leone and Hamilton subscribe to a linear model of causality in their explanation of how the brain is multimodal. According to them, 'Braille reading in the blind is an example of true cross-modal sensory plasticity by which the de-afferented, *formerly* visual, cortex is recruited for highly demanding spatial-tactile tasks, making the acquisition of the tactile Braille-reading skill possible' (2001: 7, emphasis added).

For Pascual-Leone and Hamilton, this sense of recruitment is what makes the explanation of cross-modal plasticity compelling.

> The many studies that demonstrate processing of sensory information outside of the classically recognized cortical boundaries for that modality may not be examples of the brain being redundant or 'getting its wires crossed', but instead may represent the workings of an efficient metamodal brain, which uses inputs to those cortical regions . . . that seem best suited to execute their computations successfully. (Pascual-Leone and Hamilton 2001: 17)

At first glance, a metamodal rather than a strict localisation view of sensory substitution is promising. But it does not cohere with the explanation that proficiency in Braille is an example of how the *formerly* visual cortex is recruited for spatial-tactile tasks. In other words, when Braille reading is explained as the means by which the resources normally used to process vision are rechannelled and enlisted in touch, Pascual-Leone and Hamilton have already cast the workings of cross-modal plasticity in terms of the interaction *between* separate, bounded modalities, that is, a kind of seeing *with the help of* touch.

The problem with this understanding of plasticity is that it presumes autonomous modalities that precede their cooperation. *Before* damage to the brain has occurred, vision and touch are considered to be two self-contained modalities that serve pre-established functions. This reading is at odds with the empirical complexity of plasticity shown in Pascual-Leone and Hamilton's own experiments and case studies. In a truly metamodal brain, each sensory modality must always have been capable of receiving stimuli cross-modally. In other words, a metamodal brain would actually question the identity and location of what Pascual-Leone and Hamilton describe as the *formerly* visual cortex.

More pertinently, quarantining the process of sensory substitution as efficient computations in the brain does not account for its actual experience; not only seeing *with* touch, but how seeing *is* touch. To explore this point more closely, the following analysis draws on the case example of the celebrated prosthetic device, the tactile vision sensory substitution (TVSS) system. Like Braille, the success of TVSS is typically evoked as an example of the cross-modal communication between vision and touch. For use in blind navigation, Paul Bach-y-Rita's inspiration for TVSS emerged from his observations of how blind orientation always seemed to involve some kind of a 'transducer' for sensory information, for example, the fingertip of a Braille reader or the blind person's walking cane. Through the walking cane, 'experience is externalized to the point of contact between the object and the cane' (Bach-y-Rita and Kercel 2003: 542).[4] With this notion of a transducer in mind, Bach-y-Rita designed TVSS with the aim of redirecting visual information to stimulators in contact with the skin on various parts of the body, for instance, the back or the abdomen (Bach-y-Rita et al. 2003; Bach-y-Rita and Kercel 2003; Bach-y-Rita 1972).

More recent designs of TVSS feature a portable transducer, such as the tongue display unit that is connected to a video cable. Electro-tactile stimuli are sent to the tongue using electrode arrays positioned in the mouth. A camera, which is mounted on the head, captures images of the TVSS user's surroundings. The tongue unit display then converts these images or video data into sequences of pulse patterns that are delivered to the electrode arrays. As the electrodes activate touch sensors of the tongue, the TVSS user experiences sensation on the patch of skin receiving electrical or vibratory stimulation.

With learned proficiency in navigating TVSS one is able to make complex perceptual judgements, such as recognising faces or estimating distances and speed between objects. 'Equipped with the TVSS', researchers say, 'blind (or blindfolded) subjects are almost immediately able to detect simple targets and to orient themselves. They are also rapidly able to discriminate vertical and horizontal lines, and to indicate the direction of movement of mobile targets' (Lenay et al. 2003: 277). What is interesting about individuals who have adapted to the TVSS is that stimulation of their sense of touch gives rise not only to the experience of being touched but to the visual experience of the space in front of them; not just seeing *with* touch, but seeing *as* touch.

Something else is intriguing about this result. Insofar as the physical parameters of the modalities of touch and vision can be called into question, the specificity of functions is not blurred or indistinct. Here, again, we encounter the paradoxical confounding *and* distinction of the sense modalities. Indeed, experimental data on the workings of TVSS are striking precisely because they demonstrate that the specificity of a perceptual configuration remains utterly local. In other words, even though the objective of TVSS is to deliver visual information to touch sensors, the distinct experiences of vision and touch are not willy-nilly confused. For instance, Bach-y-Rita and Kercel observe that TVSS users 'learn to treat the information arriving at the skin in its proper context' (2003: 543). When subjects are tickled on the skin where the electrodes are applied, they report experiencing the tickle as a distinctly tactile sensation and do not mistake it for a visual one.

> At one moment the information arriving at the skin has been gathered by the TV camera, but at another it relates to the usual cutaneous information (pressure, tickle, wetness, etc.). The subject is not confused; when he/she scratches his/her back under the matrix nothing is 'seen'. (Bach-y-Rita and Kercel 2003: 543)

It is as if the perceptual apparatus 'recognises' the difference between vision and touch depending on the particular configuration of the perceptual experience. And when the experience calls for a cross-modal or inter-modal perceptual capability, both modalities can be straddled *at once*. The implication of this finding is incredible. If vision is simply missing or lacking in a blind person's perceptual apparatus, how would touch 'know' that (or when) it is not vision?

More crucially, findings of such profound 'intra-modal' plasticity not only raise peculiar questions about the interface between sight and tactility, but also between perceiver and perceived. If visualising is also externalising, an inter-subjective transposition seems to be in play. How is sight enabled by the experimenter's hand (that tickles the subject)? What grounds the spatial sense of self if one only lives *via* the environment? Indeed, what is the nature of this sociality if the other bodies and objects that apparently surround the subject also inhere within that subject's very personal and individual sense of space and being?

Merleau-Ponty and the Sensible Universe

In his final, unfinished project, *The Visible and the Invisible* (1968), Maurice Merleau-Ponty meditates on these difficult questions. Against the orthodoxy of the mind/body, subject/object distinction, Merleau-Ponty conjures a much more expansive understanding of the 'subject' of perceptual experience as 'the flesh of the world'. By insisting on the world as a general field of sensibility, and sensation as itself a form of apperception, a cognitive act of self-knowledge and realisation, Merleau-Ponty unsettles the routine separation between self and other, the body and the environment. He argues that any knowledge we have we can only acquire through living our bodies, for 'we are the world that thinks itself . . . the world is at the heart of our flesh' (1968: 136). Although counter-intuitive, to say the least, Merleau-Ponty's reconfiguration of perception as an ecological and a global phenomenon of life's self-encounter makes an invigorating contribution to our present discussion. As critical theorist and sociologist, Vicki Kirby, puts it, Merleau-Ponty's phenomenology of perception is 'so thoroughly comprehensive in its unqualified openness to the world that even closure is intrinsic to its makeup' (2011: 119). Given the pivotal significance of the notions of deficiency, loss and compensation for studies of sensory substitution, I want to focus on Merleau-Ponty's account of perception as an 'intertwining' of the body and the world – the body as the world – especially his radical reinterpretation of disability as an expression of life's tenacity and resilience.

In his essay 'The Intertwining – The Chiasm', Merleau-Ponty proposes a new conception of the body as a 'chiasm' or crossing-over. The word chiasm comes from the Greek term *khiasma*, 'a placing crosswise'. This notion captures the entanglement of subjective experience and objective existence insofar as for Merleau-Ponty the body is at once sentient and sensible. His remarkable insight lies in the way that he radicalises the intertwining of the body as subject and object. If the body touches and sees things, Merleau-Ponty writes,

> this is only because, being of their family, itself visible and tangible, it uses its own being as a means to participate in theirs . . . because the body belongs to the order of the things as the world is universal flesh. (1968: 137)

As we will see, this notion of the chiasmatic 'reversibility' of the flesh, that is, the flesh of the body *as* the flesh of the world, may help us meditate on the broader significance of cross-modal plasticity in an innovative way.

Indeed, in 'The Intertwining – The Chiasm', Merleau-Ponty's sustained attempts to *confuse* the experiences of vision and touch significantly reanimate our earlier discussion of Braille and TVSS. For the philosopher, sensory experiences such as vision and touch cannot be conceptualised as separate, discrete experiences, since in reality perception is holistic. However, and this is important, his account of the inseparability of sight and tactility does not rest on a simple understanding of combining or fusing otherwise discrete modalities. Holding together this intricate interface of inseparability and individuality, confounding and specificity, Merleau-Ponty writes,

> we must habituate ourselves to think that every visible is cut out in the tangible, every tactile being in some manner promised to visibility, and that there is encroachment, infringement, not only between the touched and the touching, but also between the tangible and the visible, which is encrusted in it, as, conversely, the tangible itself is not a nothingness of visibility, is not without visual existence. Since the same body sees and touches, visible and tangible belong to the same world. It is a marvel too little noticed that every movement of my eyes – even more, every displacement of my body – has its place in the same visible universe that I itemize and explore with them, as, conversely, every vision takes place somewhere in the tactile space. There is double and crossed situating of the visible in the tangible and of the tangible in the visible; the two maps are complete, and yet they do not merge into one. The two parts are total parts and yet are not superposable. (1968: 134)

In this lengthy yet wonderfully evocative passage, Merleau-Ponty deepens our appreciation of the ontological and empirical complexity of perception. For him, the roles of seeing and touching, or indeed, of any of the other senses, are 'reversible' because they are roles played by one body. However, this unity does not imply that there are no divisions or differences between the senses. Encouraging us to see the intertwining of the senses as a *worldly* phenomenon, a phenomenon that exemplifies the myriad cross-referencing that is life itself, Merleau-Ponty speaks to a broader eco-logic of sensibility that both individuates and collectivises. In other words, each sense, body, or perceiver is absolutely unique but its individuation, as such, is possible only in participation with and *as* the sensible universe.

Indeed, the meaning of sensory 'substitution' as a kind of 'superposing' is one with which Merleau-Ponty would likely disagree, since it neglects the complexity of time and space in suggesting that the experience of touch and vision can simply be overlapped, placed before, above or in the place occupied by the other. With Merleau-Ponty as inspiration, I propose that we take another approach to the phenomenon of cross-modal plasticity, and consider it as something of an *intra*-modal plasticity that is not a simple union of two or more discrete sensory modalities. In a very real sense, the 'information arriving at the skin' that has been collected by the camera, as Bach-y-Rita and Kercel (2003: 543) thought, has already *arrived* if it can anticipate where it ought to be. Rather than subscribe to the usual interpretation of plasticity as the process that occurs *after* the stability of the system has been disturbed (through injury or assault), it could be argued that the capacity for cross-modal plasticity must always have been alive and inherent in the perceiving subject/body.[5]

Significantly, this is an opportunity for us to rethink the logic of loss, deficiency and disability as that which is lacking in normal function and consequently needs to be replaced or replenished. Indeed, how is the 'normality' of vision secured if touch, which is apparently only a 'surrogate', as Bach-y-Rita (1983: 30) calls it, can *visualise*? The salient point that needs to be underlined is that the tactile-visual experience that characterises sensory substitution is not a meeting of temporally and spatially discrete modalities. Tactility is not an appendage to visual loss any more than the blind have lost the ability to see, or indeed, hone their visual acuity. By the same token, the identity of touch as a stand-alone modality that makes up for the absence of sight also undergoes a significant destabilisation when we re-examine the self-evident explanation of substitution as supplement or addition to the original. Both Braille and TVSS are provocative in their implications because they challenge the conventional dichotomy between sight and blindness, ability and deficit, and even the difference between human and machine (or reading apparatus in the case of Braille).

Alternatively put, if evidence of cross-modal plasticity significantly unsettles the integrity of any one sense as a bounded, separate modality that neatly corresponds to given kinds of sensory stimuli, what seems most compelling about sensory substitution is that it confronts the very Cartesianism (i.e., mind/body, psychological/physical, subject/world) that underwrites routine views of what perception is and how it works. This entanglement, or 'intercorporeity' as Merleau-Ponty (1968: 141) calls it, refuses the assumption that there are autonomous bodies or entities that make up the world. If perceptual experience is not a simple aggregation, connection, or separation of mind *and* body, subject *and* world, what needs reworking is the way this communicative interface is conceptualised. What is the *intra*-subjective form of contact at work here?

For Merleau-Ponty, a thing or a perception does not occupy a place 'in' the world, nor does the perceiver live 'in' the body, as if the body and the world are containers that house the perceiver and other objects (1968: 138). Rather, the parameters that supposedly circumscribe and differentiate the subject of experience from the object or world perceived cannot be defined outside of the constant acts of perceiving as a general field of sensibility. A passage in Merleau-Ponty's earlier and major work, *The Phenomenology of Perception*, helps me here.

> The patient therefore realizes his disability precisely in so far as he is ignorant of it, and ignorant of it precisely to the extent that he knows of it. This paradox is that of all being in the world: when I move towards a world I bury my perceptual and practical intentions in objects which ultimately appear prior to and external to those intentions, and which nevertheless exist for me only in so far as they arouse in me thoughts or volitions. ([1958] 2006: 95)

Merleau-Ponty's treatment of the relationship between subject and object captures the simultaneity of the confounding and specificity of individuation (of the senses, bodies and selves). In other words, his profound insight is that the production of the difference between perceiver and perceived, or we might also say between different sense modalities, does not occur prior to, or outside of, the moment of one's experience. If the world enables insofar as it is constituted by my body navigating my surroundings, I cannot have a removed perspective of it; I *am* it.

As discussed earlier, the workings of cross-modal plasticity significantly complicate the conventional sense of substitution as a replacement *of* one sense *by* another. In other words, the idea that substitution is a compensatory action that comes into existence secondarily, i.e., after or in the absence of a pre-existing sensory function, is itself problematised by the fraught origin of deficiency. Thus, if what enacts plasticity is a manifestation of neurology's inherently protean nature, 'substitution' cannot be a simple reorganisation of what was previously coherent and fixed. In short, reorganisation itself must be *originary*.

In this view, the findings of cross-modal plasticity in Braille reading and the TVSS demonstrate that touch is *already* visual rather than a supplement or corrective for vision. If the puzzle of *how* cross-modal plasticity is enacted cannot be readily resolved in terms of unmasking *or* reorganisation – because both explanations presume a model of intervention *following* deficiency – what is remarkable about cross-modal plasticity is its evocation of an originary synaesthesia in which the physical integrity of any *one* sensory modality is already broken open from the outset.[6]

A particular case study of phantom limb pain illustrates this sense of what is involved in intra-subjectivity. In their examination of a 26-year-old male soldier who had both his legs amputated following a serious injury in combat, neuroscientists Sharon Weeks and Jack Tsao discover the remarkably protean boundaries of the self and the body. They set up an experiment to see if the phantom limb pain that their patient experiences can be relieved by 'scratching' or 'massaging' the leg of another person (2010: 462). In particular, these scientists find that the volatility of corporeal plasticity takes on rather bizarre dimensions when tactile sensations are amenable to the 'projection' of one body onto another body, and even onto inanimate objects. Intriguingly, Weeks and Tsao observe that 'cramping or shooting pain in either phantom leg [in this patient] is alleviated by massaging the corresponding location on a friend's leg' (2010: 462). In addition, the relief that comes with this 'incorporation' of another person's leg into the patient's body schema lasts for a period of several hours (2010: 462).

Weeks and Tsao suggest that the pain relief their patient experiences may have to do with a sort of 'tactile empathy' that has been observed in studies using fMRI to track neural activity in subjects while they watched film clips of another person being probed on the leg with a stick (Keysers et al., cited in Weeks and Tsao 2010: 464). Weeks and Tsao believe that this finding is suggestive of a 'sensory mirror neuron system' in their patient in which 'observing the touch of his own hands on a foreign limb likely activates the sensory neurons in regions previously corresponding to his legs' (2010: 464). Further, Weeks and Tsao reason that this 'feeling of tactile empathy . . . supports the visual feedback [the patient] receives indicating that the legs he has assimilated into his body image are, in fact, being massaged or scratched' (2010: 464). This finding of what we might describe as an 'intra-social limb' radically calls into question the usual containment of the body as an atomic entity among others, separate from the environment around it.

Although Weeks and Tsao do not refer to Merleau-Ponty, it is worth noting that the notion of the body schema is one that the phenomenologist has written on extensively. In *The Phenomenology of Perception*, Merleau-Ponty argues that it is a misguided project to explain the experience of phantom limbs in *either* biological *or* psychological terms. Rather, he says, we need to consider the phenomenon through the more holistic perspective of 'being-in-the-world' ([1958] 2006: 94).

> What it is in us which refuses mutilation and disablement is an I committed to a certain physical and inter-human world, who continues to tend towards his world despite handicaps and amputations and who, to this extent, does not recognize them *de jure*. The refusal of the deficiency is only the obverse of our inherence in a world, the implicit negation of what runs counter to the natural momentum which throws us into our tasks, our cares, our situation, our familiar horizons. To have a phantom arm is to remain open to all the actions of which the arm alone is capable; it is to retain the practical field which one enjoyed before mutilation. ([1958] 2006: 94)

If perception is conceptualised holistically, as Merleau-Ponty suggests, losing the function of a limb or a sensory modality does not mean that the impaired person no longer has that arm or her sense of sight. The amputated arm survives for the amputee because the sociality and historicity of 'what it is' to have an arm, or the sense of sight, or whatever is deemed to be lost, endures because the flesh of the body *is* an 'intercorporeity' – the flesh of the world. For Merleau-Ponty, there was never an individual removed from the world because all individuation resides in the very ability of the universe to make sense of itself, to be present to itself, including its missteps and inadequacies. The point is not to undermine the heuristic devices that enable us to identify differences and to make distinctions, but to thoroughly complicate the conventional notion of deficiency as lack, as something broken or entirely absent.

The Plasticity of the Eye/I

By way of conclusion, if we read the phenomenon of sensory substitution alongside Merleau-Ponty's discussion of disability, it becomes clear that the site of deficiency (missing sense modality or limb) does not indicate a gap or space between the presence and then loss of a body part. Indeed, for the philosopher, the logic of substitution or compensation is not a productive way to appreciate the complexity of *individual* perception as a *field* because it is grounded in a restricted binary opposition between deficiency and recovery, or cast in quantifiable terms of more or less, addition or subtraction.

Interestingly, in its word root, deficiency does not mean lack. The etymology of this word comes from a combination of the Latin terms *de* and *facere*. As a Latin prefix, *de* means 'away from', 'down' or 'aside', and also has the function of undoing or reversing a verb's action. The term *facere* means 'to do' or 'to make' (Barnhart 2006). Taken together, *defacere* suggests some sense of an unmaking, evoking a rather different meaning than lack, which connotes without, or not having enough. Crucially, in the context of our discussion, undoing is not a system's failure or loss given that the very principle of plasticity demonstrates that life – biology *as* experience – makes and unmakes itself to generate different possibilities and fitness outcomes.

Thus, if we translate Merleau-Ponty's understanding of the flesh of the world into the terms of neuroscience, then it appears that cross-modal plasticity is an ecological involvement through which life enacts its own vicissitudes, 'repairs' and reinvention. As Merleau-Ponty says,

> while each monocular vision, each touching with one sole hand has its own visible, its tactile, each is bound to every other vision, to every other touch; it is bound in such a way as to make up with them the experience of one sole body before one sole world through a possibility for reversion, reconversion of its language into theirs, transfer, and reversal, according to which the little private world of each is not juxtaposed to the world of all the others, but surrounded by it, levied off from it, and all together are a Sentient in general before a Sensible in general. (1968: 142)

If the eye/I of experience is always/already something of an originary synaesthesia, then an eco-logic of sensibility in the spirit of Merleau-Ponty's thought does not so much refuse individuation; it makes it already a sociality, a community, a sensible universe from the start.

> It is not *I* who sees, not *he* who sees, because an anonymous visibility inhabits both of us, a vision in general, in virtue of that primordial property that belongs to the flesh, being here and now, of radiating everywhere and forever, being an individual, of being also a dimension and a universal. (Merleau Ponty 1968: 142, emphasis in original)

In sum, Merleau-Ponty's radical revision of perception as an intertwining of being and topology points to a fundamental paradox of location and causal origins. Regardless of whether we mean the subject, the biological body, or a sensory modality, individuation is not a simple act of becoming distinct or separate from the whole if we take seriously Merleau-Ponty's account of the sensible universe. Crucially, the simultaneity of the body (or a given sense modality) as at once subject and object reframes the very meaning of substitution as compensation or supplement by another entity. Indeed, Merleau-Ponty's pathfinding work offers what could be cast as something of a chiasmatic plasticity in which the current truism of neuroscience, 'experience driven biology', is significantly reinvigorated: the biological, the body, the perceiver *as* the world's experience of itself.

Notes

1. Up until the 1970s, the dominant account of neurological development maintained that there was a 'critical period' in the growth of a newborn or in the early stages of infancy, following which the capacity for regeneration of neural pathways was irrevocably lost (Ramachandran 1993; West-Eberhard 2003; Kelso 1995). It was thus believed that neurogenesis, the formation of new neurons and neural connections, could not have occurred in the adult brain as the mature brain was perceived to be resistant to change. As eminent neuroscientist, V. S. Ramachandran, puts it, 'far from being wired up according to rigid, prenatal genetic blueprints, the brain's wiring is highly malleable – and not just in infants and young children, but throughout every adult lifetime' (2011: 37).

2. Here, the ontology and autonomy of the brain as the distinct seat of perception is so self-evident it needs no explanation. Curiously however, even though scientists may agree that the sensory modalities are more fluid than discrete and non-overlapping, as traditionally conceived, the brain is nevertheless assumed to be the control centre and locus of all experience. We will return to this point later in the chapter.

3. Findings that show the contribution of the 'visual' cortex to perceptual processing in tactile discrimination have been supported by a number of different experiments. See Sadato et al. (1996), Buchel et al. (1998), Sathian and Zangaladze (2002), Kupers et al. (2011).

4. The example of the blind man's walking cane has been evoked in a number of different disciplinary and theoretical contexts seeking to complicate the conventional notion of the self as an atomic identity bounded by the skin. For instance, Gregory Bateson uses the analogy of the cane

to illustrate the implications of his ecological theory of individuation. Bateson asks,

> consider a blind man with a stick. Where does the blind man's self begin? At the tip of the stick? At the handle of the stick? Or at some point half-way up the stick? These questions are nonsense, because the stick is a pathway along which differences are transmitted under transformation, so that to draw a delimiting line *across* this pathway is to cut off a part of the systemic circuit which determines the blind man's locomotion. (2000: 318, emphasis in original)

This example has also been used by phenomenologist, Maurice Merleau-Ponty, to underscore the porosity of perception. See especially 'Eye and Mind' in *The Primacy of Perception* (1964).

5. Although writing in a different context, particle physicist and feminist scholar, Karen Barad, offers an invigorating take on this temporal complexity that may help demonstrate the broader relevance of my argument. In *Meeting the Universe Halfway* (2007), Barad discusses the implications of the famous 'two slit' experiment for our understanding of measurement and interference. Unpacking the work of physicist Niels Bohr, Barad argues that there is no sense in asking where an electron or entity is located *prior to* the measuring process. This is the basis of the indeterminacy principle in quantum physics which states that we cannot concomitantly know both the position and momentum of a particle because particles do not have fixed values of position and momentum (Barad 2007: 19). If a particular experimental arrangement is designed to respond to the particle-like character of the object of inquiry, then that is what is observed. One finds particle-like behaviour and not a diffraction or wave pattern. Correspondingly, if the experimental set-up is introduced to investigate the interference pattern of light or matter, the material specificity of that arrangement confirms it. For Barad, the gravity of the point being made is that value or evaluation does not pre-exist the apparatus; it is materialised in and as the specific process of measurement that is carried out, including the particular exclusions that are enacted. That is, the boundary between 'the object of observation' and the 'agencies of observation' is never fixed as such (2007: 114). Instead, the very possibility of making this subject/object 'cut' presents itself as the moment of measurement arises and where certain choices are made to the exclusion of others. Here, significantly, any exclusion is constitutive of the apparatus since it enables and provides the condition for establishing boundaries and measurement interactions. As Barad emphatically insists, 'we are not entitled to ascribe the value that we obtained for the position to some abstract notion of a measurement independent object' (2007: 113). For a further discussion of Barad's work, see Chiew (2014).

6. Indeed, Merleau-Ponty paves the way for me here when he suggests that,

> synaesthetic perception is the rule, and we are unaware of it only because scientific knowledge shifts the centre of gravity of experience, so that we have unlearned how to see, hear, and generally speaking, feel, in order to deduce, from our bodily organization and the world as the physicist conceived it, what we are to see, hear and feel. (2006: 266)

References

Bach-y-Rita, P. (1972), *Brain Mechanisms in Sensory Substitution*, New York and London: Academic Press.

Bach-y-Rita, P. (1983), 'Tactile Vision Substitution: Past and Future', *International Journal of Neuroscience*, 19: 1–4, pp. 29–36.

Bach-y-Rita, P., and S. W. Kercel (2003), 'Sensory Substitution and the Human-Machine Interface', *Trends in Cognitive Sciences*, 7: 12, December, pp. 541–6.

Bach-y-Rita, P., M. E. Tyler and K. A. Kaczmarek (2003), 'Seeing with the Brain', *International Journal of Human-Computer Interaction*, 15: 2, pp. 285–95.

Barad, K. (2007), *Meeting the Universe Halfway: quantum physics and the entanglement of matter and meaning*, Durham, NC: Duke University Press.

Barnhart, R. K. (ed.) (2006), *Chambers Dictionary of Etymology*, Edinburgh: Chambers Harrap Publishers Ltd.

Bateson, G. ([1972] 2000), *Steps to an Ecology of Mind: Collected Essays in Anthropology, Psychiatry, Evolution, and Epistemology*, Chicago: University of Chicago Press.

Buchel, C., C. Price, R. S. J. Frackowiak and K. Friston (1998), 'Different Activation Patterns in Visual Cortex of Late and Congenitally Blind Subjects', *Brain*, 121, pp. 409–19.

Chaudhuri, A. (2011), *Fundamentals of Sensory Perception*, Oxford and New York: Oxford University Press.

Chiew, F. (2014), 'Posthuman Ethics with Cary Wolfe and Karen Barad: Animal Compassion as Trans-species Entanglement', *Theory, Culture & Society*, 31: 4, pp. 51–69.

Finger, S., and C. R. Almli (1985), 'Brain Damage and Neuroplasticity: Mechanisms of Recovery or Development', *Brain Research Reviews*, 357: 3, pp. 177–86.

Fotheringham, D. K., and M. P. Young (1997), 'Neural Coding Schemes for Sensory Representation: Theoretical Proposals and Empirical Evidence', in M. Rugg (ed.), *Cognitive Neuroscience*, Cambridge, MA: MIT Press, pp. 47–76.

Gross, C. (2002), 'Genealogy of the "Grandmother Cell"', *The Neuroscientist*, 8: 5, pp. 512–18.

Kadosh, R. C., and V. Walsh (2006), 'Cognitive Neuroscience: Rewired or Crosswired Brains', *Current Biology*, 16: 22, pp. 962–3.

Kandel, E., J. H. Schwartz, T. M. Jessell, S. A. Siegelbarm and A. J. Hudspeth (2013), *Principles of Neural Science*, New York: McGraw-Hill Medical.

Kelso, J. A. S. (1995), *Dynamic Patterns: The Self-Organization of Brain and Behavior*, Cambridge, MA: MIT Press.

Kirby, V. (2011), *Quantum Anthropologies: Life at Large*, Durham, NC: Duke University Press.

Kupers, R., P. Pietrini, E. Ricciardi and M. Ptito (2011), 'The Nature of Consciousness in the Visually Deprived Brain', *Frontiers in Psychology*, 2: 19, pp. 1–14.

Lenay, C., O. Gapenne, S. Hanneton, C. Marque and C. Genouëlle (2003), 'Sensory Substitution: Limits and Perspectives', in *Touching for Knowing*, Y. Hatwell, A. Streri and E. Gentaz (eds), Amsterdam and Philadelphia: John Benjamins Publishing Company, pp. 275–92.

Mathur, G. (2009), *Foundations of Sensation and Perception*, Hove and New York: Psychology Press Taylor & Francis Group.

Merabet, L. B., J. F. Rizzo, A. Amedi, D. C. Somers and A. Pascual-Leone (2005), 'What Blindness Can Tell Us about Seeing Again: Merging Neuroplasticity and Neuroprostheses', *Nature Reviews Neuroscience*, 6: 1, pp. 71–7.

Merabet, L. B., and A. Pascual-Leone (2010), 'Neuronal Reorganization Following Sensory Loss: The Opportunity of Change', *Nature Reviews Neuroscience*, 11: pp. 44–52.

Merleau-Ponty, M. (1964), *The Primacy of Perception*, trans. J. M. Edie, Evanston: Northwestern University Press.

Merleau-Ponty, M. (1968), *The Visible and the Invisible*, trans. A. Lingis, Evanston: Northwestern University Press.

Merleau-Ponty, M. ([1958] 2006), *The Phenomenology of Perception*, trans. C. Smith, London and New York: Routledge Classics.

Pascual-Leone, A., and R. Hamilton (1998), 'Cortical plasticity associated with Braille learning', *Trends in Cognitive Sciences* 2: 5, pp. 168–74.

Pascual-Leone, A., and R. Hamilton (2001), 'The Metamodal Organization of the Brain', *Progress in Brain Research*, 134: pp. 1–19.

Ramachandran, V. S. (1993), 'Behavioral and Magnetoencephalographic Correlates of Plasticity in the Adult Human Brain', *Proc. Natl. Acad. Sci.*, 90: 22, pp. 10413–20.

Ramachandran, V. S., and W. Hirstein (1998), 'The Perception of Phantom Limbs: The D. O. Hebb Lecture', *Brain*, 121, pp. 1603–30.

Ramachandran, V. S. (2011), *The Tell-Tale Brain*, New York and London: W. W. Norton & Co.

Rauschecker, J. P. (1995), 'Compensatory Plasticity and Sensory Substitution in the Cerebral Cortex', *Trends in Neurosciences*, 18: 1, pp. 36–43.

Sadato, N., A. Pascual-Leone, J. Grafman, V. Ibanez, M. P. Deiber, G. Dolg and M. Hallett (1996), 'Activation of the Primary Visual Cortex by Braille Reading in Blind Subjects', *Nature*, 380: 6574, pp. 526–8.

Sathian, K., and A. Zangaladze (2002), 'Feeling With the Mind's Eye: Contribution of Visual Cortex to Tactile Perception', *Behavioural Brain Research*, 135: 1–2, pp. 127–32.

Weeks, S., and J. Tsao (2010), 'Incorporation of Another Person's Limb into Body Image Relieves Phantom Limb Pain: A Case Study', *Neurocase: The Neural Basis of Cognition*, 16: 6, pp. 461–5.

West-Eberhard, M. J. (2003), *Developmental Plasticity and Evolution*, Oxford: Oxford University Press.

Zeki, S. (1993), *A Vision of the Brain*, Cambridge: Blackwell Scientific Publications.

CHAPTER 4

Allergy as the Puzzle of Causality

Michelle Jamieson

In contemporary immunology and biomedicine it is generally stated that our understanding of allergy is limited because we have not yet definitively determined its causes. Like many other conditions, the identity of allergic disease is tied to the elucidation of a clear aetiology – the identification of faulty mechanisms or processes in the organism, or to the isolation of foreign, pathogenic entities. To date, attempts to conclusively determine the causes of this condition have come up short. Within immunology allergy refers to a class of disease bearing a strong genetic or biological basis, and caused by exposure to external, environmental substances (Janeway et al. 2005: 523). However the empirical data that supports this perspective is plagued with inconsistencies that cannot be explained by current knowledge and practice in immunology (Jarvis and Burney 1998: 607; Sublett 2005: 445). In the fields of psychology and psychosomatic medicine allergies are viewed as psychogenic, with various allergic conditions being diagnosed and treated using tools such as psychotherapy and hypnosis (Miller and Baruch 1956). Yet many practitioners and researchers in these areas acknowledge the existence of a biological, constitutional component that underlies the operation of psychological triggers and participates in allergic reactions (Dunbar 1938). Psychosomatic studies commonly report that allergic symptoms can be successfully alleviated with the use of psychotherapeutic tools, but that such tools cannot eliminate the biological predisposition itself (Hansen 1927; Diehl and Heinichen 1931). Here, the fact that allergic symptoms can be treated without altering the underlying predisposition complicates the identity and role of biology in allergic events.

The evidence from these disparate fields shows that the causes of allergy are both biological and psychological. This suggests that the aetiology of allergy cannot be resolved by deferring to an explanation that privileges one or another of its causes. Studies that recognise this dilemma, typically within psychology, psychosomatic medicine and psychoneuroimmunology, argue that a more comprehensive understanding of allergic disease is needed – one that accounts for the findings of psychological and biological investigations together (Banks Gregerson 2000). This perspective is exemplified in the turn toward multifactorial and biopsychosocial models of illness, which attribute the pathogenesis of allergy to a *confluence* of biological, psychological, social and other factors (Wilce 2003). As Mary Banks Gregerson explains, 'modern systemic approaches [within psychosomatic medicine] emphasize a multifactorial model of the complex interplay of biology, psychology, and, most currently, both the social and physical environments' (2000: 820). Allergic disease is thus increasingly viewed as the product of interactions between distinct factors.

Conceptually, these interdisciplinary approaches rest on the same notion of causality as the discipline-specific explanations they seek to unite – namely, a linear cause and effect relation between discrete, separated domains. However, these attempts at consolidating the insights of these diverse perspectives into one all-encompassing and comprehensive account actually reinstate the aetiological dilemma that allergies present. In attributing allergic disease to the actions of many different agents, multifactorial approaches raise the question of how these individual explanations (and the objects to which they refer) relate to, or interact with, one another. As a solution to the problem of a single original cause, this approach foregrounds the dilemma of *how* there are multiple, different, isolated factors that contribute to the production of disease. While the perceived benefit of multifactorial perspectives is that they *include* all possible variables and contingencies, it is precisely the nature of this inclusion – the reconciliation of these diverse perspectives into one – that is centrally at issue. How are we to make sense of these persuasive, though somewhat incommensurable, data sets together? How do biological causes actually relate to, and even inhabit, psychological causes?

Competing accounts of allergic disease problematise the idea that allergies are simply a biological condition, where biology is imagined to be separate from, and certainly prior to, those aspects of life deemed social, cultural, psychological and environmental. They challenge the view that biology alone – a fault located in the raw matter of an individual – is responsible for this pathology. As such, these conflicting bodies of evidence pose questions about the nature of biology itself: the diverse means by which allergies are both triggered and treated seem to contest a conventional view of biology as enclosed, given and natural. The fact that allergies can be triggered by phenomena other than allergenic substances, such as traumatic events and strong emotions (Jackson 2009; Miller and Baruch 1956; Dunbar et al. 1939) points to the impossibility of quarantining the psychological, social or environmental from the biological in any final sense. Moreover, it foregrounds that the very notion of aetiology – the belief in a discrete, immutable origin or cause – is problematic in itself.

This chapter argues that allergies complicate an orthodox understanding of biology as something divorced from psychology, sociality or the environment. Focusing on atopy, allergic diseases recognised as having a genetic component, it critically examines immunology's account of allergy's biological cause – immunoglobulin E (IgE), the antibody commonly identified as its primary causal agent. By concentrating on how IgE is animated *as* a biological cause, we will see that what constitutes IgE as 'causative' is a much wider context, one in which the biological is inseparable from one's environment, family, psychology or history. As the following discussion illustrates, attempts to attribute cause to a discrete entity such as IgE consistently run into the problem of how to locate immunological effects as properly, and only, biological.

This chapter explores empirical data and examples that problematise the attribution of biological cause in cases of allergy. With reference to issues such as gene-environment interaction and the role of inheritance in atopic asthma, we are confronted with evidence that the material body does not pre-exist its social and cultural contextualisation: phenomena often taken to be quintessentially biological actually evidence biology's social, psychical and historical complexity.

Biological Causes of Allergy

In 1921, German physicians Carl Prausnitz and Heinz Küstner conducted an experiment that successfully demonstrated the passive cutaneous[1] transfer of allergic sensitivity. The two investigators had been attempting to establish the presence of specific antibodies they believed responsible for allergic reactions in the serum of allergic individuals (Silverstein 1989: 226). Using themselves as guinea pigs, they sought to prove the existence of these entities by transferring serum from an allergic individual to a non-allergic individual. Serum was taken from Küstner, who was highly allergic to certain fish, and a small amount injected into Prausnitz's skin. A day later, the allergen (fish) was administered locally to Prausnitz. 'A typical wheal and erythema hypersensitivity reaction' (1989: 226) appeared at the site of infection, and persisted for over four weeks. With this experiment, Prausnitz and Küstner established the existence of particular antibodies that mediated the allergic response, and named this agent or substance 'reagin' (Prausnitz and Küstner 1921). In 1966, Japanese couple Teruka and Kimishige Ishizaka identified 'reagin' as immunoglobulin E (IgE), the specific antibody implicated in type I hypersensitivity – which is today commonly known as allergy (Silverstein 1989: 227).

Since the discovery of reagin, and later IgE, allergies have been characterised in terms of the presence and biological action of this antibody. At a basic level, allergy is defined as an antigen-antibody (IgE) reaction that produces a harmful inflammatory response in the host organism. Allergic reactions are widely viewed as overreactions to harmless substances that the immune system misrecognises as toxic – exaggerated defensive responses generated by an organism against its own tissues. According to mainstream immunology, these injurious reactions are caused by elevated levels of antigen-specific IgE in the organism's serum – IgE antibodies that bind with high affinity to specific allergens (for example, house dust mite) (Janeway et al. 2005: 519).[2] Allergic reactions are commonly referred to as IgE-mediated reactions, and allergic disease as IgE-mediated disease. This definition is summed up in the widely used textbook, *Immunobiology: The Immune System in Health and Disease*.

> Allergy is one of a class of immune system responses that are termed **hypersensitivity reactions**. These are harmful immune responses that produce tissue injury and can cause serious disease. Hypersensitivity reactions were classified into four types by Coombs and Gell ... Allergy is often equated with type I hypersensitivity (immediate-type hypersensitivity reactions mediated by IgE) (Janeway et al. 2005: 523, original emphasis)

IgE, and in particular, elevated levels of IgE, is broadly accepted as the principle biological and empirical marker of allergy. Moreover, high IgE is taken as concrete scientific evidence of a genetic predisposition to allergic disease. In clinical examinations, the exaggerated presence of this antibody confirms the status of an allergy as having a definitively genetic cause. Elevated IgE is determined using skin prick testing, a simple clinical diagnostic procedure that measures for antigen-specific IgE. Thus, IgE provides the evidence necessary to support a conventional biomedical explanation of allergy, that is, a taken for granted causal association between allergy and IgE. This is demonstrated in the definitions offered by standard-issue immunology textbooks: 'Much human allergy is caused by a limited number of inhaled small-protein allergens that reproducibly elicit IgE production in susceptible individuals' (Janeway et al. 2005: 519). Consequently, since the discovery of IgE, immunological investigations of allergy have been largely IgE-centric, usually involving demonstrations of how IgE participates in the aetiology of specific cases.

Troubling Evidence: Atopic and Non-Atopic Allergy

Elevated IgE levels are typical of individuals who suffer one or a combination of the three main allergic diseases: asthma, hay fever and eczema. In immunological parlance, the tendency to mount an exaggerated IgE response resulting in any of these conditions is called *atopy*, and the individuals who experience them are described as *atopic*. The term atopy refers to a group of allergic diseases recognised as having a tangible biological cause (IgE), and a strong genetic, familial foundation. James Sublett defines atopy as 'the genetic potential to manifest the trinity of classic allergic diseases – atopic dermatitis, allergic rhinitis (hay fever), and asthma' (2005: 445). Atopy is thus synonymous with both a genetic predisposition toward allergy and high IgE.

> As many as 40% of people in Western populations show an exaggerated tendency to mount IgE responses to a wide variety of common environmental allergens. This state is called **atopy**, has a strong familial basis, and is influenced by several genetic loci. **Atopic** individuals have higher total levels of IgE in the circulation and higher levels of eosinophils than their normal counterparts. They are more susceptible to allergic diseases such as hayfever and asthma. (2005: 523, emphasis in original)[3]

However, the view of IgE as the biological cause of allergy and evidence of atopy is as widely contested within the medical and scientific community as it is generally accepted. In immunology and other areas of health research, investigators have long noted significant inconsistencies in the correlation between elevated IgE levels and actual manifestations of atopy. Numerous studies indicate that high levels of antigen-specific IgE do not necessarily correspond with the presence of specific allergies – for instance, one can test positive for high IgE but never manifest an allergy, even upon encountering substances to which one has tested positive. And conversely, having normal levels of IgE is by no means a guarantee that an individual will be allergy-free – one can develop atopic allergies regardless of an absence of sensitivity. Deborah Jarvis and Peter Burney explain.

> Atopy is defined as the production of specific IgE in response to exposure to common environmental allergens, such as house dust mite, grass, and cat. Being atopic is strongly associated with allergic disease such as asthma, hay fever, and eczema, but not everyone with atopy develops clinical manifestations of allergy and not everyone with a clinical syndrome compatible with allergic disease can be shown to be atopic when tested for specific IgE to a wide range of environmental allergens. This is particularly so for asthma. (1998: 607)

Interestingly, instances of allergy both do and do not coincide with instances of elevated IgE. Indeed, there is a strikingly inconsistent relationship between IgE and allergy, or cause and effect, a fact that renders the status of IgE as biological evidence of allergy questionable. In what sense can IgE be understood to cause allergy if its presence only *sometimes* results in allergic reactions? What is a biological cause that does not always produce the same physical effect?

The ambiguous causal relation between IgE and allergy is elaborated in detail by Erika Isolauri et al. in their study of food allergy and irritable bowel syndrome.

> Detection of antigen specific IgE is invariably taken as an attribute of causality, a condition called 'IgE mediated disease' and, more specifically, of 'allergy'. However, empirical data are accumulating to suggest that transient increases in antigen specific IgE antibodies prevail in most healthy asymptomatic children during the first five years of life. Secondly, generation of these antibodies (sensitisation) on antigen exposure may not necessarily induce clinical disease (atopic disease). Thirdly, reducing the risk of atopic disease does not necessitate reduction of sensitisation and, finally, resolution or aggravation of clinical disease is not invariably associated with a corresponding alteration in antibody [IgE] concentration. (2004: 1391)

Isolauri et al. point to several incongruities that render the conventional equation of allergy with IgE questionable, if not scientifically untenable. In the studies they cite, the relationships between IgE, sensitisation and clinical disease cannot be explained by orthodox immunology. Instead, this body of evidence challenges the idea that the manifestation of atopy is governed by a fixed order of events (high IgE *then* allergy) or series of equations (high IgE = atopy, or low IgE = no allergy). These data show that no single or definitive causal narrative or set of rules reliably accounts for the relation between allergy and IgE. At stake in these inconsistencies is the integrity of IgE as a biological correlate of allergy, and thus also the identity of allergy as a genetically based condition.

Indeed, the ambiguity of the atopy-IgE connection throws this genetic foundation into question.[4]

The uncertain status of IgE as a genetic determinant of allergy is illustrated most starkly in cases of atopy that have *no* demonstrable biological basis. Sublett explains, 'all of the classic trio of diseases can present with identical clinical symptoms to their allergic counterparts, with no identifiable IgE-mediated response: atopic eczema/dermatitis syndrome (AEDS), nonallergic rhinitis, and intrinsic asthma' (2005: 445). In other words, a person can manifest an atopic illness in the absence of elevated IgE, and thus also in the absence of a genetic predisposition. This anomaly is confirmed in a case study by Hyman Miller and Dorothy Baruch (a physician and child psychologist team) that explores 'paradoxes in the physical pattern of allergy' (1956: 10). Examining the relationships between the results of skin prick tests, family histories of allergy and actual manifestations of allergy in a large experimental sample, they single out a category of allergy sufferers that experience some form of atopy but test negative for elevated IgE.

> There are individuals in whom the usual allergy tests, as well as eye tests, passive transfer tests, and inhalation tests are negative, apparently because there is no immunologic basis for their disease – that is, no reagins. They are not immunologically allergic, and yet their symptoms cannot be distinguished from those obviously resulting from immunologic roots. They develop the very same asthma, the identical hay fever, the same clinical manifestations of eczema. (1956: 12)

Remarkably, these data point to the existence of two types of atopy that are scientifically and genetically distinct, but *clinically indistinguishable*. While there are instances of atopy that are IgE-mediated, and thus conform to an orthodox immunological definition of atopy, there are simultaneously cases that have no demonstrated biological basis, but whose symptoms are identical to their IgE-mediated counterparts. This raises the question of whether we are dealing with the same group of conditions in both scenarios.

In recognition of this difference, contemporary immunology distinguishes between *atopic* and *non-atopic allergy*. Crucially, non-atopic allergy represents a statistically significant anomaly. In a study investigating the extent to which the incidence of asthma is attributable to atopy, Pearce et al. explain that 'standardised comparisons across populations or time periods show only a weak and inconsistent association between the prevalence of asthma and the prevalence of atopy' (1999: 271). Surveying a wide range of literature on this subject, they report, 'the available epidemiological evidence suggests that the population based proportion of asthma cases that are attributable to atopy is usually less than one half' (1999: 271). These statements show that non-atopic allergy is by no means an exception to the rule that atopy is predominately IgE-mediated: instances of atopic and non-atopic allergy are approximately *equal*.

The distinction between atopic and non-atopic allergy poses the problem of how these conditions can be clinically identical but constitutionally different. If these afflictions are evidenced by the same symptoms, in what sense can one, and not the other, be described as having a biological basis? Additionally, this division raises questions about the precise nature of allergy as a genetic, immunological condition. The fact that a set of symptoms, consistent with a specific genetic predisposition, arises frequently in individuals who do not possess this trait casts atopy's genetic basis into doubt. If atopy describes a genetic predisposition to allergy, what is a non-atopic (non-genetic) form of atopy? What is atopy if not – or when it's not – an IgE-mediated disease? The status of atopy as a clinical disease both with *and* without a genetic foundation compromises the evidentiary value of IgE as a biological marker of atopy, and renders the distinction between genetic and non-genetic increasingly hard to draw.[5]

At stake is the most basic understanding of biology. We normally think about biology as something whose fixed, organic nature separates it from the domains of psychological and social experience. The integrity of the biological is typically secured by its difference from these other aspects of life. But in the case of allergy, organic and non-organic, genetic and non-genetic, are entangled such that we cannot name one, and not the other, biological. Here, the complex involvement of the physical functions and processes of life with psychology and sociality emerges as biology's most distinctive feature.

Animating Atopy: Gene-Environment Interaction

These inconsistencies aside, even in the most straightforward cases of atopy the production of allergic symptoms is not reducible to the presence of IgE. High IgE (a genetic predisposition) is not alone responsible for allergy. Rather, a genetic predisposition must be animated by exposure to specific environmental antigens. That is, in order to become a biological cause, IgE has first to be triggered by contact with particular foreign, external substances. Sublett explains, 'the atopic state is a function of genetics waiting for environmental influences to manifest disease' (2005: 446). Similarly, Stephen Holgate states that 'gene-environmental interactions are critical to the pathogenesis of allergic disorders' (2004: 104). The necessity of this interaction is especially noted in cases of asthma (Janeway et al. 2005: 536; Martinez 1997: S117).

> In recent decades it has become routine to describe asthma as an atopic disease. A theoretical paradigm has evolved in which allergen exposure produces atopic sensitization and continued exposure leads to clinical asthma through the development of airways inflammation, bronchial hyperresponsiveness, and reversible airflow obstruction. (Pearce et al. 1999: 268)

These studies show that the cause of atopy is ecologically complex, and the riddles that appear are as relevant for how we understand the process of sensitisation as they are for what we mean by the presence of an innate predisposition. While elevated IgE signals the genetic potential to develop allergy, it is not a genetic determinant *unless* sensitisation occurs. The temporality of this process is difficult to comprehend as it involves a sort of temporal anticipation, where the 'original cause' *will be* determined *after* an event that has yet to occur. In crude terms, sensitisation causes elevated IgE to become a pre-existing biological cause. Counter-intuitively, sensitisation – an environmental encounter – determines whether a biological predisposition is, in fact, pre-existing. Yet even this account is challenged by evidence demonstrating that the specific sensitisation of genetically predisposed individuals doesn't always produce allergy. Several studies show that gene-environment interaction sometimes results in the opposite effect. For instance, Sublett notes that sensitisation can act to *suppress* or *prevent* allergic reactivity (2005: 445). Thus, despite exposure to antigen-specific IgE there is no guarantee that a harmful response will definitely occur.

Recognition of the role of environmental factors in awakening the allergic predisposition has led to the view that atopy is caused by a specific gene-environment interaction. It is widely accepted that the existence of a genetic predisposition, coupled with exposure to environmental antigens, leads to the development of atopy. Here, 'cause' is not located in the substance, IgE, but rather in an encounter between two things that are biologically inter-implicated: antigen-specific IgE and environmental allergens, or more basically, organism and environment.

Underpinning this view is the idea that the genetically predisposed organism and sensitising agent are fixed, separate entities whose physical interaction gives rise to allergic disease. The notion of gene-environment interaction presumes the prior existence of an organism that possesses certain genetic traits, and an external environment, populated by foreign life forms and substances. In other words, immunological accounts of the pathogenesis of atopy are based on the view that organism and environment are ontologically distinct, and that allergy is what happens when there is cross-contamination between them.

Yet, if we look closely at the conditions that enable sensitisation we find a situation that is not reducible to a simple conjunction of organism and environment. Rather, the very possibility of gene-environment interaction is already anticipated in the identities of the immunological components involved, namely, antigen and antigen-specific IgE. Antibody and antigen are each a corporealised response to the call or provocation of the other, a call which has yet to take place. The organism experiences an allergy once it has been triggered into action by exposure to something immunologically foreign and yet *already specified by that organism's own genetic potential*. In this context, the genetic predisposition, viewed as innate, does not straightforwardly precede the event of sensitisation: remarkably, the organism's production of antigen-specific IgE demonstrates that it has already been sensitised to this particular stimulus. Thus, the condition of atopic sensitisation is not the existence of two autonomous entities that are materially exterior to one another, but rather a complex interrelation of organism and antigen, genetics and environment, *in the first place*. Sensitisation shows that the organism-antigen relation is an ecological entanglement that is not initiated in any conventional sense: here, what makes immune responsiveness possible is the fact that neither component can precede the other.

This perspective has direct implications for our understanding of the aetiology of atopy. As the above discussion demonstrates, sensitisation is an immunological phenomenon that cannot be explained by using a framework of discrete interacting entities or consecutive moments. The ontological interrelation of genetics and environment means that cause cannot be located in any one body or event; it does not inhere in the substance of an antibody or in the genetic make-up of an individual, nor does it reside in a relationship in between these components. Atopy is genetically determined insofar as what constitutes it as a genetically based condition is a scene in which genetics and the environment have always been utterly inter-implicated.

These insights make it difficult to maintain a conventional idea of genetics as a set of pre-existing biological traits. The pathogenesis of atopy makes it impossible to properly demarcate genetics because its determinant quality arises in an already *anticipated* conversation with entities that are (apparently) non-genetic and alien to the organism.[6]

Consequently, the phenomenon of sensitisation forces us to critically consider what we mean when we describe something as genetic or biological. What concepts, substances or processes do we presume to define the biological against, and can we continue to do so?

Isolating Cause: Skin Prick Testing

The animation of atopy demonstrates that cause cannot be traced to a single biological entity (IgE or antigen) or event (sensitisation). Because organism and environment are an ecological intra-relationality, the origin of allergy cannot be located at a definitive point. Yet modern immunology favours a conventional understanding of what constitutes a cause. It conceptualises the immune response as a cause and effect relation between two discrete things, an antigen and an organism, or a stimulus and a response. The immune response is interpreted primarily in terms of a linear narrative of infection, in which the physical boundary of the organism is breached by the intrusion of a foreign element or substance. Organism and antigen are imagined as separate entities possessing fixed characteristics, which enter into relation in the event of a response.

However, this view of the immune response as an isolatable interaction between predetermined entities suggests the ontological interrelation of organism and antigen (or environment) is an *effect* of their meeting. As a model, it does not explain how these elements come to exist in a relation as different and opposed, and yet biologically correlative and implicated. That is, it cannot account for how a stimulus comes to be provocative for an organism that is already receptive to this very specific provocation. As such, this perspective actually obscures the question of *how* these unique biological pairings arise.

This model is epitomised in the skin prick test – one of the most common diagnostic methods of testing individuals for allergic disease. The procedure measures for levels of IgE and specific sensitivities by exposing the subject to a range of common environmental allergens typically associated with atopy (Walls 1997: 11–12). Although there is some variation in the way skin prick tests are conducted, the general procedure is as follows. First, the patient's inner forearm, which functions as the site of the test, is cleaned to remove any impurities and a large gridded stamp is imprinted on the skin (Walls 1997: 13). This rectangular grid, containing between ten and twenty squares, marks the site where a range of common allergens will be introduced under the patient's skin. 'Drops of glycerinated allergen extract are placed on the skin [in the centre of each square] and a prick is made through the drop with a . . . lancet' (1997: 13). In addition to these allergens (which may include house dust mite or different animal danders),[7] two control substances are included: normal saline is used as the negative control, which should yield no response, and histamine as the positive control, which should produce an inflamed response (1997: 13). The patient then waits for ten to fifteen minutes for a reaction to form. The result is a series of red welts on the skin – a wheal and flare response – whose appearance and physical size indicate a positive or negative diagnosis of allergy. Walls explains, 'a wheal equal to or greater than 3mm is taken to indicate a positive diagnosis, provided there is no reactivity to the negative glycerosaline control' (1997: 13).

The skin prick test provides a precise visual and temporal representation of a linear causal account of stimulus and response. The grid printed on the skin rationally and numerically organises the patient's responses to a variety of allergens. In demarcating individual welts in this localised 'field' of responses, the grid indicates that these are *separate immune events*. The physical organisation of neat rows and columns of little red bumps infers that each welt can be read in isolation, or rather, only in relation to the control substances.[8] This practice of quarantining individual responses, conceptually and biologically, suggests that each symptom can be accurately interpreted without reference to neighbouring substances or symptoms. Crucially, the structure of the test affirms that the patient's immune system deals with each substance specifically and autonomously of any other influence.

In conceptualising each welt as a stand-alone event composed of clearly discernable parts, the test treats the immune response as a phenomenon that can be delimited temporally, to the time frame of the test, and spatially, within the square of skin in which the welt appears. It locates the immune response firmly in a particular time and space. As a diagnostic tool, it does *not* accommodate the possibility that the boundaries of response might exceed the observable and measurable parameters of a single welt. For instance, some clinicians warn that if there is insufficient space between injection sites, 'large reactions can reflexively cause positive reactions in adjacent sites' (Walls 1997: 13). When injection sites are too close together, they literally infect one another, resulting in a general field of contagion from which individual responses cannot be objectively separated. Yet despite the clinical knowledge that a response may not be confined to the physical outline of a welt – that these responses are not necessarily immune to one another – the efficacy of the test rests on their capacity to be read as isolates.

Importantly, the test leaves no room for doubt about the identity of the allergen. Within the test, there is no sense that what causes or stimulates a specific swelling might be derivative of *more* than the inherent properties of a single allergen, or more interestingly, that the particular properties of this substance (its allergenicity) are emergent within a matrix of other factors. For instance, one could argue that the test abstracts grid, stamp, needle, clinic and clinician, as well as the other allergens present, from the materiality or agency of the stimulus, discounting them as external factors that do not affect the objectively controlled event of response. Here, cause is confidently located in (what is presumed to be) a fixed, immutable substance.

Governed by the logic of separability, the skin prick test compartmentalises stimulus from response, individual welts from one another, and individual allergens from one another. Most provocatively, it abstracts the event of the test itself from the wider context of the patient's reactivity. Viewed as an objective intervention, it is treated as an exceptional event that does not interfere with, or participate in, the patient's medical history of allergy. Yet every encounter between an organism and an antigen has the potential to trigger a process of sensitisation, *especially* where common environmental allergens are involved (for example, pollen or dust). As such, skin prick testing manufactures a set of circumstances that arguably increase the chances of sensitisation occurring. From this viewpoint, the diagnostic test cannot be sequestered from the broader clinical picture of the patient's reactivity; rather, it is one of many events that make up an individual's immunologic history.

The skin prick test neatly demonstrates the impossibility of the discrete bifurcations that it takes as its point of departure. Ironically, in the context of the test, nothing is strictly external to anything else – the very possibility of a response, and thus the efficacy of the test itself, are enabled by the contamination that (pre)conditions these divisions.

Allergic Biography: Inheritance and Atopic Asthma

Like gene-environment interaction and skin prick testing, the development of atopic asthma also points to the difficulty of isolating allergy's biological cause. The role of heredity in asthma presents a further complication to the task of aetiological explanation, as what is past and present, actually manifest and latent, become confused. To a larger extent than perhaps any other allergy, asthma highlights the relevance of history – or indeed the work of history – in the pathogenesis of allergic symptoms.

The association between allergy and IgE is so deeply sedimented in the scientific imagination that some immunologists have extended their investigations beyond antigen-specific IgE to IgE more generally. Pearce et al. argue that 'some type of IgE mediated process may be involved in almost all asthma cases, even when skin test reactivity to common allergens is not found' (1999: 270). This connection has been studied in detail by Benjamin Burrows, Fernando Martinez and others who demonstrated a correspondence between incidence of asthma and total serum IgE in subjects that tested positive *and* negative to common environmental allergens in skin prick tests (Martinez 1997: S119). They found that regardless of the presence of antigen-specific IgE, total serum IgE levels served as a reliable indicator of asthma.

In an effort to definitively demonstrate this correlation, Burrows et al. conducted further investigations, but this time centering their analysis on 'the intrafamily relations between total serum IgE and asthma' (Martinez 1997: S119). Burrows et al. examined 'the extent to which the strong familial aggregation of asthma could be explained by the known association between parental IgE levels and those of their children' (1997: S119). They sought to account for patterns of asthma inheritance in terms of the relationship between the total serum IgE levels of parents and their children. Martinez, one of the chief investigators, reports that the study made two important findings: firstly, it confirmed 'the expected strong parent-offspring correlation of . . . total serum IgE levels' (1997: S119), and secondly, it found that incidence of asthma in offspring was dramatically increased in cases where one or both parents also suffered asthma. Thus, Burrows et al.'s study singled out two variables associated with the inheritance of asthma – parental IgE and parental asthma.

Crucially, however, the study also showed that parental IgE levels and incidence of parental asthma were *not* simply interchangeable as variables. Remarkably, the authors 'found no statistically significant association between prevalence of asthma in children and serum IgE levels in their parents when the mother or the father did not have asthma' (Martinez 1997: S119). Martinez explains that,

> these results suggested that inheritance of a tendency to develop high total serum IgE levels is only one factor related to the inheritance of asthma susceptibility and that, by itself, it has limited ability to predict asthma inheritance . . . parental serum IgE seemed to increase the likelihood of developing asthma only when the parents themselves had asthma. (1997: S120)

In other words, the chances of inheriting asthma were found to be contingent upon one's parent(s) having a genetic predisposition toward allergy *and* the actualisation of this predisposition as asthma.

It is worth pausing here to consider the provocative implications of these findings. Burrows et al. observed that what was inherited by offspring depended not only upon the genetic traits of the parent(s), but on immunological events experienced by the parent(s) in his or her lifetime.[9] The child's inheritance was found to be directly related to circumstances and events in the parents' lives – factors presumably beyond the domain of biological characteristics. These findings suggest that offspring do not become asthmatic purely as a consequence of a given, genetic make-up. The significance of contingent, circumstantial factors in activating one's genetic inheritance challenges this conception. Here, the offspring inherits and materially manifests a genetic predisposition that has already been (or will be) awoken at a different point in time, in a different body (or bodies).

The role of parental asthma, rather than parental IgE, as a causal variable implicated in the inheritance of asthma disrupts the basic conventions of analysis, namely, the perceived given-ness of biology, and the assumption that bodies are fixed in time and space. For instance, it complicates any simple notion of this condition as genetically determined. The offspring's inheritance is not strictly genetic, in the orthodox sense of a set of pre-existent genetic traits transmitted, via birth, from one body to another. If what invests the parent's genetic make-up with its authorial capacity is a much wider field of factors that appear non-genetic, then the parent's biological legacy cannot be defined in terms of a fixed code in a bounded body. The inheritance of atopic asthma implies a far more enlarged sense of genetics, biology and the corporeal – one that challenges our ability to delimit the biological – materially, conceptually and historically.[10]

The complexity of genetic determination in atopic asthma also complicates a commonsense notion of inheritance. If one's genetic inheritance is decided by significant immunological events over the parents' lifetimes, then it is not clear that the inherited property strictly precedes its heir. If the determinant quality of a parent's genetics is realised in conversation with environmental factors, it follows that they might also be realised *after* the birth of the child. If this were the case, by what mode is this genetic potential transmitted or inherited? Like the contaminated scene of skin prick testing, the inheritance of asthma confounds a conventional idea of location – of discrete moments in time, or bodies in space.

The recurrence of parental asthma as a causal factor over many generations challenges a linear notion of causation, and thus also, the given-ness of the 'component' identities on which this model is based. The repetition of this variable suggests that the specific gene-environment interaction deemed responsible for the occurrence of asthma in one generation cannot be identified as an event that then determines its manifestation in the following generation. Instead, the recurrence of parental asthma means that any one instance of asthma must necessarily be caused by *all* other instances; parental asthma is only constituted as a cause of inherited asthma by the cases that comprise a whole atopic lineage. Thus, although any individual case of asthma is highly localised – it manifests in one body at one moment – it is simultaneously a unique possibility bodied forth by, and rooted in, a whole genetic, family history. The boundaries of any single case are compromised by the complex entanglement of its cause with/in many bodies, generations and moments.

Consequently, it is not clear that the asthmatic who reacts is straightforwardly the author of their attacks because what constitutes the individual's specific reactivity is a whole history. The asthmatic individual emerges as a biographical index that evidences the contamination of the genetic, familial and environmental. Viewed in this way, atopic asthma is symptomatic, not of an isolatable cause, but of the impossibility of circumscribing cause within a discrete domain, such as biology or genetics. This dilemma foregrounds the difficulty of locating sensitisation, temporally and spatially: it calls for a more entangled[11] sense of the relationship between past, present and future, and points to the need to complicate the idea of biology as a natural domain that comes before environment or family relations. More broadly, it highlights what is at stake in conceptualising any entity or phenomenon as ontologically enclosed (for example, organism, individual, ancestry, biology, environment).

This chapter has highlighted various difficulties involved in trying to isolate the biological basis of allergy. As we have seen, even the most seemingly straightforward cases challenge our ability to pinpoint effects or events that can be called definitively biological, and not simultaneously the work of other apparently non-biological factors. For instance, in gene-environment interaction, the determinant quality of genetics arises as an ecological event that speaks to the impossibility of quarantining the biological from the environmental. In the case of skin prick testing, what causes particular allergic swellings cannot be traced to the action of a single substance. Rather, cross contamination between test sites points to a broader scene of contagion that contests the simple location or aggregation of discrete causes and effects. And again, the role of heredity in atopic asthma complicates the task of identifying cause as every case expresses a whole atopic lineage.

Each of these examples illustrates that what we take to be biological, or what we routinely attribute to the action of biology, is actually an expression of the system of life as a whole. When it comes to matters of illness, it is common to separate biology out from other aspects of our lives. However, this approach leads to a diminished account of life's complexity, and by extension, a reductive understanding of biology. Conditions such as allergies call for a notion of biology that captures its ecological intricacies – its entanglement with psychological and other factors – rather than seeking to explain it away.

Notes

1. Of, pertaining to, or affecting the skin. (*OED*)
2. In non-allergic individuals, 'IgE is found in very low concentrations' in serum (Beers and Berkow 1999: 1015). Outside its role in producing pathological responses, IgE is believed to serve a protective function in the organism against multicellular parasites and other pathogens. Janeway et al. explain that IgE is part of a

   > defense system [that] is anatomically distributed mainly at the sites of entry of such parasites – under the skin, under the epithelial surfaces of the airways (the mucosal-associated lymphoid tissues), and in the submucosa of the gut (the gut-associated lymphoid tissues). (2005: 521)

   For more on the protective function of IgE, see Janeway et al. (2005).
3. Eosinophils are white blood cells that play a role in defending the host against the invasion of organisms such as multicellular parasites. Like IgE, eosinophils are found in tissues where these invasions typically occur – the gut, respiratory tract and urogenital tract. Because eosinophils are responsible for killing microorganisms and parasites, their action produces tissue damage and works to amplify the immune system's inflammatory response (Janeway et al. 2005: 531). Thus, higher levels of these cells in atopic individuals mean a more exaggerated inflammatory response.
4. Throughout this chapter, the terms 'genetic' and 'biological' are often used as synonyms. This is because in standard immunological accounts of allergy (immunology textbooks), confirmation of a genetic basis is often taken as an indication of a clear biological origin. The scope of this chapter and its disciplinary commitments preclude a more detailed examination of the genetics of allergy (which is an enormous field in itself). This chapter deals with the genetics of allergy in a broad sense.
5. The observation that some instances of atopy have a biological basis and others do not has strong resonances with the phenomenon of hysteria.

Although, historically, hysteria comes in many different forms, one of its defining features is its capacity to *mimic* organic conditions. Like allergy, the manifestation of hysterical illness problematises the distinction between organic (biological) and non-organic (psychological) illness. The fact that the hysterical body reproduces the symptoms of an organic condition suggests that anatomy and psychology are already involved in one another. Hysteria troubles the division between biology and psychology by destabilising the point of reference that secures our understanding of this difference. As Elizabeth Wilson explains, hysteria demonstrates that the capacity to mimic an organic condition is itself a possibility of biology: 'hysteria does not point to what is *beyond* the organic body . . . it directs us right back into the heart of organic matter; hysteria is one particular mode of biological writing' (2004: 78, emphasis in original). Similarly, the fact that atopic and non-atopic allergy share a common symptomatology poses the question of what constitutes the proper reference point for diagnosing allergic phenomena. For a detailed discussion of hysteria and its relationship to organic illness, see Wilson (1999; 2004).

6. A similar argument is made by Evelyn Fox Keller in *The Century of the Gene* (2000), where she complicates a conventional understanding of the gene as a stable biological trait that determines a specified outcome.

7. Walls explains, 'allergens are selected on the basis of the clinical history [of the patient] and are determined by their prevalence in the area from which the patient comes' (1997: 13).

8. The only other exceptions to this rule are cases in which the patient experiences a systemic allergic reaction, such as anaphylaxis. In these instances, individual responses to specific substances can no longer be physically located or pinned down on the body's surface. The complex, systemic, diffuse nature of the reaction (that is, hives all over the body and extreme difficulty breathing) compromises the neat compartmentalisation of responses required for an objective diagnosis of allergy in the skin prick test.

9. This finding speaks to the phenomenon of epigenetics – the inheritance of changes in gene expression caused by environmental factors (such as disease, diet, climate). As Noela Davis explains,

> epigenetics demonstrates that it is not genes in themselves that give form to an organism, but instead patterns of genetic expression that give the distinctive characteristics of a cell or tissue, and thus of the organism, through a dynamic crosstalk between genes, organism and environment. (2014: 68–9)

As Davis's article demonstrates, epigenetic research shows how factors normally considered outside the scope of biology come to be biological phenomena.

10. Mike Fortun's *Promising Genomics: Iceland and deCODE Genetics in a World of Speculation* (2008) discusses the increasingly expansive nature

of genetics and how contemporary genomic research is coming to terms with such an enlarged canvas. See Fortun (2008).

11. My use of the term 'entanglement' throughout this chapter is indebted to the work of feminist thinker and theoretical particle physicist, Karen Barad. In *Meeting the Universe Halfway: Quantum Physics and the Entanglement of Matter and Meaning* (2007), Barad uses the term to characterise the performative co-constitution of matter and discourse, nature and culture, subject and object, in scientific and other practices. Through the analysis of experiments and concepts in quantum physics, her work presents a critique of the metaphysics of individualism – the idea that the world is populated by things that have determinate qualities, properties and locations. See Barad (2007).

References

Banks Gregerson, M. (2000), 'The curious 2000-year case of asthma', *Psychosomatic Medicine*, 62: 6, pp. 816–27.

Barad, K. (2007), *Meeting the Universe Halfway: Quantum Physics and the Entanglement of Matter and Meaning*, Durham, NC: Duke University Press.

Beers, M. H., and R. Berkow (eds) (1999), *The Merck Manual of Diagnosis and Therapy*, 17th edn, Whitehouse Station: Merck Research Laboratories.

Davis, N. (2014), 'Politics materialized: Rethinking the materiality of feminist political action through epigenetics', *Women: A Cultural Review*, 25: 1, pp. 62–77.

Diehl, F., and W. Heinichen (1931), 'Psychische Beeinflussung allergischer Reaktionen', *Münchner Medicinische Wochenschrift*, 78, pp. 1008–9.

Dunbar, H. F. (1938), *Emotions and Bodily Changes: A Survey of Literature on Psychosomatic Interrelationships, 1910–1933*, 2nd edn, New York: Columbia University Press.

Dunbar, H. F., F. Alexander, D. Atchley, C. L. Hull, S. Cobb, H. S. Liddell, H. Davis and G. F. Powers (1939), 'Introductory statement', *Psychosomatic Medicine*, 1: 1, pp. 3–5.

Fortun, M. (2008), *Promising Genomics: Iceland and deCODE Genetics in a World of Speculation*, Berkeley: University of California Press.

Hansen, K. (1927), 'Analyse, indikation und grenze der psychotherapie bei bronchialasthma', *Deutsche Medicinische Wochenschrift*, 53: 35, pp. 1462–4.

Holgate, S. T. (2004), 'The epidemic of asthma and allergy', *Journal of the Royal Society of Medicine*, 97: 3, pp. 103–10.

Isolauri, E., S. Rautava and M. Kalliomäki (2004), 'Food allergy in irritable bowel syndrome: new facts and old fallacies', *Gut*, 53: 10, pp. 1391–3.

Jackson, M. (2009), *Asthma: The Biography*, Oxford: Oxford University Press.

Janeway, C. A., P. Travers, M. Walport and M. J. Shlomchik (2005), *Immunobiology: The Immune System in Health and Disease*, 6th edn, New York and London: Garland Science.

Jarvis, D., and P. Burney (1998), 'The epidemiology of allergic disease', *British Medical Journal*, 316: 7131, pp. 607–10.

Keller, E. F. (2000), *The Century of the Gene*, Cambridge, MA: Harvard University Press.

Martinez, F. D. (1997), 'Complexities of the genetics of asthma', *American Journal of Respiratory and Critical Care Medicine*, 156: 4, pp. S117–S122.

Miller, H., and D. W. Baruch (1956), *The Practice of Psychosomatic Medicine, as Illustrated in Allergy*, New York, Toronto and London: Blakiston Division, McGraw-Hill.

Pearce, N., J. Pekkanen and R. Beasley (1999), 'How much is asthma really attributable to atopy?', *Thorax*, 54: 3, pp. 268–72.

Prausnitz, C., and H. Küstner (1921), 'Studien über die Ükerempfindlickkeit', *Zentralblatt für Bakteriologie*, 86, pp. 160–8.

Silverstein, A. M. (1989), *A History of Immunology*, San Diego: Academic Press Inc.

Sublett, J. L. (2005), 'The environment and risk factors for atopy', *Current Allergy and Asthma Reports*, 5: 6, pp. 445–50.

Walls, R. S. (1997), *Allergies and Their Management*, Sydney: MacLennan and Petty.

Wilce, J. M. (ed.) (2003), *Social and Cultural Lives of Immune Systems*, London: Routledge.

Wilson, E. A. (1999), 'Introduction: somatic compliance – feminism, biology and science', *Australian Feminist Studies*, 14: 29, pp. 7–18.

Wilson, E. A. (2004), 'Gut feminism', *differences: A Journal of Feminist Cultural Studies*, 15: 3, pp. 66–94.

CHAPTER 5

Pregnant Men: Paternal Postnatal Depression and a Culture of Hormones

Rebecca Oxley

Introduction

The notion that postnatal depression (PND) may be experienced by fathers in a similar incidence to mothers (of around 10–13 per cent) is beginning to 'emerge from the wings' (Solantaus and Salo 2005), complicating ideas that PND may be understood as maternal hormonal fluctuations after the birth of a child. Even with the establishment of an overarching bio-psycho-social model of depression, however, it seems that fathers' PND has been elaborated in *juxtaposition* to that of mothers as primarily psycho-social in origin. Yet how can we ignore the biological evidence of what is happening within fathers' bodies over the puerperal period, especially considering that levels of cortisol, vasopressin, oxytocin, testosterone and oestrogen vary in fathers' bodies before, during and after the birth of a child? These hormones and their variations could be regarded as intrinsic to a mode of being that is, in a sense, *expectant*: just as men may embody PND, fathers, too, may be(come) pregnant. Yet how can we reach this understanding when it seems to defy the facts of biology? How can we situate this suggestion with regard to conventional dualisms that oppose sociality and biology, epistemology and ontology, mind and body, male and female? By investigating the sociality of hormones I will argue that the notion of a pregnant father and biologically postnatally depressed male is not made in defiance of biology; it is, rather, an active material engagement with it. Approaching contemporary anthropological, sociological and feminist debate on embodiment and hormonal constitution, my argument travels through and with fathers' bodies via key puerperal hormonal phenomena that pinpoint a few crucial ways in which the binary of nature and culture can be reconsidered and made more complex, more attentive to, and more *telling* of, somatic experience.

Endocrinological Actors

For centuries there has been an awareness that certain difficulties can accompany the pregnant and postnatal female body, and that this time is associated with risk to the health of both mother and child. What was to become classified as 'postnatal depression' in the 1950s after medical observation of a particular depressive pattern amongst new mothers (Everingham et al. 2006: 1745), seems to have been implied since Hippocrates' notions of disorders relating to the 'wandering womb' (Bleier cited in Nicolson 1998: 41; Ussher 2006: 91). This humour-based, gonadal understanding of female physiology and its link with puerperal melancholy would translate to later objectifications of PND perceived through the endocrinological body (Oudshoorn 2007). So too would the insistence of a biological basis for reproductive pathological mental illness: PND in women is, as it was, a disease.

By the middle of the last century PND was understood as a by-product of faulty chemical messaging between hormones and their influence on the brain. This has been described as a story of intrinsic feminine excess (Ussher 2006: 128), a leaky failure of female physiology to regulate and maintain reproductive hormones within range of a balanced norm. This is almost exactly how postnatal 'blues' have been described in an Australian health care context.

> Women with the 'baby blues' may feel tearful and overwhelmed, due to changes in hormone levels following childbirth. The 'baby blues' is common and to be expected following the birth of a baby. The 'baby blues' usually disappear within a few days without treatment, other than support. (Beyond Blue 2012, cited by the Australian Government 2012)

This statement details how feminine hormonal irregularity has been interpreted as normal, and yet the other branches of classified postnatal depression – PND and puerperal psychosis – while also common, are not typical and are considered pathological. The latter experiences interfere more strongly with the apparent natural bonds of mother and baby, and mothers' bodies may require assistance and treatment

to achieve the desired outcome. As such, PND and puerperal psychosis are more closely researched, and through continual questioning
the elaboration of symptoms has become more complex. They are, as
the National Medical Research Council of Australia (2000, emphasis
added) declares, 'not *just* the baby blues'.

To understand this complexity we might follow Edmund Husserl's
([1900/1901] 2001: 168) renowned proclamation, namely, to go 'back
to the things themselves'. What exactly are these hormonal things, secretions, chemicals, messengers, that appear to influence PND? Or more
precisely, at this stage of the analysis, how are they routinely conceived
in the literature?

The most crucial hormones that fluctuate after the birth of a child
are female gonadal steroidal (sex) hormones, the oestrogens of estradiol,
estriol and estrone, as well as progesterone. Levels of these hormones,
produced by the placenta, steadily rise throughout this period and acutely
drop after delivery with placenta removal (Hendrick et al. 1998: 93–5).
The femme fatale of these messengers is estradiol, useful in improving
the functioning of neurotransmitters through enhanced synthesis and
lowered serotonin (the 'happiness hormone') and dopamine breakdown
(the 'reward' neurotransmitter) (Hendrick et al. 1998: 93–4). A drop
in estradiol levels may thus contribute to PND with lowered serotonin
levels. This may be why there are reports of oestrogen being effective in
non-responsive cases of PND (Gregoire et al. 1996; Ahokas et al. 1999).

Progesterone, too, has been linked to PND, with the progester-
one-only contraceptive pill providing an effective treatment for some
depressed women (Richards 1990: 474). Progesterone's involvement in PND may also have something to do with the suppression
of menstruation, and when linked again with oestrogen that lowers
with menopause, may explain why sex hormones have been related
to depression throughout women's life cycles (Nicolson 1998: 30).
Research has also suggested that PND may cease or improve when
the menstrual cycle resumes (Dalton, cited in Nicolson 1998: 30),
furthering links that have been made between PND, premenstrual
tension and/or premenstrual dysphoric disorder (Miller 2002: 763).
Such associations with every aspect of a woman's life cycle bring
credence to Carol Gilligan's (1982: 6) claim that 'in the lifecycle, as
in the Garden of Eden, the woman has been the deviant'.

Oestrogen and progesterone are not the only hormones that may
play a role in experiencing PND. Prolactin, cortisol, as well as certain
thyroid (thyroxine and triiodothyonine) and pituitary (thyrotropin)

hormones may also be involved in the development of PND, given their puerperal variability. Excluding prolactin, crucial for breastfeeding, levels of each of these hormones should be back to normal between five days to three weeks after delivery. However this process of bodily regulation may take longer for some women, perhaps leading to depressive symptomatology. Yet, even those women whose processes are within standard norms can also be at risk of PND. As Brian Harris states, 'an alternative view is that hormonal profiles in [postnatally depressed] women are within normal limits, and that those normal peripartum changes trigger off other pathological mechanisms, at a neurotransmitter or receptor level, resulting in mood disorders' (1996: 27).

If both normal and abnormal hormonal processes may be causally involved with PND, then the evidence seems to suggest that women's bodies are intrinsically risky. Hormonal and other biological correlations, such as those found between PND and gestational diabetes, iron deficiencies and hypothyroidism, also have the effect of defining PND as an expected, if not normal, experience of the female body. What should concern us here is that such modes of analysis allude to women's bodies, particularly maternal bodies, as inherently pathological in terms of being naturally disease-prone and imbalanced. It is this line of thinking that makes certain abnormal behaviours in the puerperum somewhat 'understandable', if politically and socially awkward to accept (Ussher 2006: 91). Psychiatrist Margaret Spinelli explains this reasoning when she proposes that 'laws such as the *British Infanticide Act* acknowledge the biological vulnerability of parturition, including the potential for mental state changes related to plummeting hormone levels, the hypothalamic-pituitary-ovarian axis cascade and altered neurotransmitter function in the central nervous system' (2001: 812). Ornella Moscucci also elaborates this theme by suggesting that,

> the leniency with which women were treated in infanticide cases is one example of how this [biological] principle was applied in practice: at times of heightened sexual activity such as childbirth and the puerperium, women became physiologically and psychologically vulnerable and could not be regarded as criminologically responsible for their actions. (1993: 31)

In Australia, the New South Wales Infanticide Law (as per the Crimes Act 22A), similar to that in Britain, defines infanticide as the killing of a child less than twelve months old by the biological mother while suffering the effects of childbirth. Not surprisingly, there is little space for fathers to access the infanticide offence or defence as paternal PND is thought to result from psychological and/or social suffering rather than from biological reasons. Paternal PND is a probable result of their partner being depressed (an incidence of between 24 and 50 per cent (Zelkowitz and Milet 2001)), the changing of social roles, distressing early parenting experiences or feelings of exclusion in romantic relationships and/or with parenting. These same factors may also influence experiences of PND for women, and in an Australian health care context, care is taken that these factors are not viewed as less important than biological causes.

Nevertheless, and despite an appreciation that the aetiology of PND is complex, the dominant understandings of PND continue to privilege physiological data: the infanticide clause may be upheld as a consequence. Given this division of causality into either biological or social/cultural origin, it seems only logical that men may experience postnatal depression but not the baby blues. And it also follows that men may suffer from PND but not puerperal psychosis. However, can we simply assume that this sexual division of experience can provide an adequate account of the different manifestations of PND, or is it that assumptions about sexual difference precede these studies and organise the data accordingly? Is it possible that the answer to this riddle might be found by refusing to choose sides – either biological or socio-cultural – instead, elaborating how 'one side', here the hormonal/biological, already includes what is purportedly non-biological?

Nelly Oudshoorn (2007) and Celia Roberts (2007), while investigating cultures of contraception and HRT therapies, have both detailed how hormones considered to be 'male', namely testosterone, have been given secondary attention in reproductive issues when compared with those linked to the female body, such as oestrogen and prolactin. Anne Fausto-Sterling (2000: 177) dilates on this point, noting that even with scientific knowledge of testosterone and oestrogen being present in both males and females, pre-existing ideologies regarding sex characteristics pervade understandings of hormonal activity. In this sense, testosterone has been approached differently in medical thought and practice. While oestrogen has been elaborated as problematic, linked to reproductive pathologies and ageing, such as with the menopause for example, testosterone has been investigated and portrayed as virile, youthful and efficient (Fausto-Sterling 2000: 146–7). Contemplating these views, it is little wonder that very few scientific or medical studies attempt to measure or even consider the messaging of male hormones in instances of PND. The male body, unlike that of the female, is rarely represented in a way that foregrounds biology and vulnerability. The alignment of the feminine with an almost natural, or inherited helplessness, has a long history in metaphysics. As Vicki Kirby explains,

> although the Cartesian schema grants that man has a body, it is merely as an object that he grasps, penetrates, comprehends, and ultimately transcends. As man's companion and complement, woman *is* the body. She remains stuck in the primeval ooze of nature's sticky immanence, a victim of the vagaries of her emotions, a creature who can't think straight as a consequence. (1997: 59)

Yet the possibility of puerperal hormonal fluctuations in new fathers remains, and it is this phenomenon that is explored by Pilyoung Kim and James Swain (2007) in relation to paternal PND. In their review article they state that in the male, testosterone measures may decrease and oestrogen may increase during a partner's pregnancy and stay at respectively lower and higher levels several months after childbirth. These hormonal variations lead to improved attachment between father and child due to a decrease in 'masculine' qualities determined (or at least enhanced) by testosterone, such as aggression, as well as increased concentration in parenting, higher sympathetic response to infant crying and other 'maternal' qualities associated with oestrogen (2007: 42). Highlighting the complexities of apparent chemical messaging at this time, a decrease in testosterone, associated with male vitality (as normativity), may be linked to depression in men, but so too may a low level of oestrogen. The latter may result in a lack of father-infant bonding which is another key risk factor for experiencing PND. Hormonal balance, it seems, is crucial. Lower cortisol, prolactin and/or vasopressin levels (which increase after the birth of a child analogous to oxytocin levels in biological mothers) may also result in strained father-infant bonding and PND in men (2007: 42).

By investigating biological contributors to male PND, Kim and Swain implicitly question the notion that 'women, by virtue of their bodies and particularly as a consequence of their hormonal fluctuations, were "pathological specimens" of the human race' (in Moscucci 1993: 31). Yet they also explicitly reduce certain behavioural traits down to their essentialised, sexed, endocrinological properties. This allows them to draw, unproblematically, from a greater wealth of research, including those studies that concern non-human animal populations. Agreeing with conventional science, Kim and Swain understand oestrogen as the essence of femininity, equating it with communal bonding and child-rearing. Testosterone, in comparison and not surprisingly, becomes the essence of masculinity, denoting traits of individuality and aggression. By setting these two hormones in opposition, Kim and Swain still cling to notions of two easily identifiable biological sexes that each has determined attributes. This, in turn, leads to other, related dualisms that seem to naturally attach to, and describe, the bodies of males and females, such as public/private, state/family and production/reproduction in which males are understood and valued in terms of one realm and females the other (Williams and Bendelow 1998: 114). Not only may this have the effect of 'designat[ing] a woman's place within the family, the most basic biological and social unit' (Moscucci 1993: 4), but it also emphasises that,

> only culture, the mind and reason, social production, the state and society [may be] understood as having a dynamic and developmental character. The body and its passions, reproduction, the family and the individual are often conceived as timeless and unvarying aspects of nature. (Gatens cited in Williams and Bendelow 1998: 114)

The constraining logic of these dualisms, an invisible economy of hierarchical valuation, limits our understandings of the corporeal processes that animate puerperal bodies. So too does the pervading assumption of what actually constitutes the materially determined nature of sexed bodies. How then do we move away from such fixed notions about what bodies are and how they work? How can we understand hormonal activity or performativity in postnatally depressed women *and* men? Again, and now more pressingly, what, exactly, are hormones, given their privileged importance as explanatory objects in this field?

Hormone Cultures or a Culture Of Hormones?

In asking what it is that might constitute a hormone, one may well ponder what constitutes a body, or materiality more generally. Such questions have inspired the work of many leading scholars, and as such, a range of provocative enterprises have re-imagined and informed work on hormones and reproductive bodies. Fausto-Sterling (2000), seeking to clarify what secures the purported difference between sex and sexuality, details how the sexed brain, as with the (hormonally) sexed body, is as much a political object as it is a natural one. Oudshoorn (2007), in a similar vein, unpacks how the scientific endeavour actively brought such bodies into being. Indeed, it is now impossible to imagine the world today without hormones. Both scholars imply that science, as with feminism, has a political agenda that must take into consideration the context and timing of their specific motivations in the elucidation of 'hormones'. As such, Oudshoorn (2007: 150–1) notes that there are 'two faces' to what Roberts (2007) terms 'hormone cultures'; one that may be liberating, such as the freedoms offered by the contraceptive pill and the reduction of bodily suffering with HRT therapy, but also one that may be oppressive, as the need for bodily control may fuel the surveillance of 'women's problems'.

Annemarie Mol (2002: 102–3) provides a similar account of hormonal 'mixed blessings' (Oudshoorn 2007: 150). She describes the American feminist agenda that contests the view of 'biology as destiny', opposing access to oestrogen treatment in the menopause because it is unnatural and therefore unnecessary. Against this, groups in the United Kingdom, concerned by the neglect of women's problems, argue positively for this option. The different agendas that surround our approach to chemical secretions represent another type of leakiness. According to Elizabeth Grosz (1994: 21) their 'interimplications' require further investigation.

> The hole in nature that allows cultural seepage or production must provide something like a natural condition for cultural production; but in turn the cultural too must be seen in its limitations, as a kind of insufficiency that requires natural supplementation.

In other words, how these different agendas are contextually positioned highlights the notion that biology and culture (or politics for that matter) are not so easily separated: indeed, we may well find the political *within* the biological.

Celia Roberts (2007) follows this line of inquiry and illuminates how hormones may be understood as bodily messengers. In doing so she discounts the dualistic representation of hormones in scientific discourse which posits testosterone against oestrogen in determining sexed bodies. Roberts skilfully and intriguingly questions the 'disturbed and disturbing' nature of hormones, in terms of such conventional scientific approaches, by exploring what the phrase 'chemical messengers' means for sexually differentiated bodies. She asks 'if hormones are messengers of sex, what is the message? And to whom is the message sent? Is it from one part of the body to another or from the body to the world?' (2007: 21).

In contemplating this puzzle, Roberts first of all highlights the astounding complexity of the hormonal body and its interrelation with other bodily communication systems. Drawing upon the work of Bruno Latour (1988), Roberts then elucidates how hormones may be considered interactive in the production of somatic difference (such as sex and sexuality). She notes, with Donna Haraway (2003), that in such a way, hormones may be viewed as 'material-semiotic' actors that articulate with other active entities within bodies to prove that 'while hormones may excite or provoke sexual difference through their effects on bodies, they neither simply express nor produce sex' (Roberts 2007: 22). In other words, hormones may be viewed as natural and cultural collectives that are not biologically determined, and thus, in 'articulating endocrinology's body', Roberts looks to support 'a refigured view of hormones as messengers of sex, suggesting that hormones do not message an inherent or preexisting sex within bodies, but rather *are active agents in bio-social systems that constitute material-semiotic entities* known as "sex"' (22, emphasis added).

Robert's intention is to open up the many rigid assumptions in this field, approaching a historically informed 'hormonal messaging' materiality that leaves 'open space for variation or change' (2007: xv). This approach is widely gaining support in feminist and new materialist spheres for the novel way it understands hormones as actively provocative, given that 'etymologically hormone means to excite or provoke' (Roberts cited in Irni 2013: 43). Anna Sieben (2011), for instance, writing on heteronormative hormones, notes that her work,

> ties seamlessly in with Roberts' approach to sex hormones, sharing her desire to show the entanglement of the social and the biological in the production of sex hormones (pheromones respectively) without reducing one to the other and without rendering one active and the other passive. (2007: 264)

Yet, in my reading of Roberts's work, and consequently that of Sieben, a certain passivity and a lingering negativity seem to remain.

Roberts's work concedes that hormones do engage in the act of messaging, however, building on her argument, a further consideration here is whether they can also create or *be* the message. She describes how hormones participate, yet they do not appear to embody, communicate or converse. For instance, Roberts (2007: 105) makes use of Haraway's (2003: 20) notion of 'flesh and signifier, bodies and words: these are joined in naturecultures' such that 'there can be no reference to biology (to something like hormones) that is not a story, connected to other stories' (2007: 105). The import of the statement seems clear enough, but when we read more closely we find that whatever biology implies and includes it comes *before* its discursive reference and narrativisation. In this regard, while Roberts describes hormones as engaging actively in bio-social systems that constitute sex, there remains a haunting assumption that the materiality of hormones is somehow separate from the system with which they communicate. In this sense, hormones (biology) precede the interaction (social) which makes sense of them. While Roberts strives for an active view of hormones, this is not so different from the model of a *tabula rasa* in which 'inert matter merely receives and then bears an inscription without in any way rewriting its significance' (Kirby 1997: 77). Thus, Roberts's notion of what constitutes hormones is that they are determinable vehicles for culture, but cannot be actively cultural themselves. Considering this, can we expand the notion of hormones as messengers, to one of hormones *as* message, where *being the message* involves their own materiality with and through other actors?

Sari Irni, in her article 'Sex, Power and Ontology: Exploring the Performativity of Hormones' (2013), has offered a particular way to address the proposal of a hormone being a communicative embodiment through her posthuman performative approach. Utilising the work of feminist and physicist Karen Barad, she suggests that hormones be approached as material-discursive actors. Irni advises that sex hormones are active in bodies and societies, and are materially engaged as belief systems as well as chemical entities. For Irni, as with Barad, sex hormones can thus be considered as agentive phenomena, with their variability being key to their agency (as 'dynamicism *is* agency' (Barad 2003: 818, emphasis in original)). Concluding these insights, Irni details the importance of indeterminacy to the investigation of what comprises a hormone, and notes that 'the workings of so-called biological actants to a great extent remain to be explored' (2013: 54). Responding to this apparent gap in hormonal exploration, and building on the approach of Irni, the rest of this chapter is dedicated to understanding how hormones are materialised through their functionality. However, rather than elucidating hormones as active in bodies and societies, time will be spent pondering hormones as *already* bodies, and *already* social.

Thomas Csordas can help us here. A cultural phenomenologist, he conceived a mode of embodiment in terms of 'somatic modes of attention' or 'culturally elaborated ways of attending to and with the body with the embodied presence of others' (1993: 138). This embodiment is understood to be the 'existential ground of culture and self' (1994a: 269), a notion that allows us to 'question the differences between biology and culture, thereby transforming our understanding of both' (1994a: 288). Drawing from Maurice Merleau-Ponty's explorations of perception, Pierre Bourdieu's 'habitus' and Marcel Mauss's 'body techniques', Csordas offers us a way to view aspects of a lived body, such as hormones, as attentive, communicative and informative. As previously noted, hormones are certainly 'culturally elaborated'; they materialise (biological and social) space, temporality, and, possibly, narrative.

Csordas, by relating to Merleau-Ponty (1962), presents notions of a lived-through world in which knowledge is secondary to being. This is materialist in a sense, as it acknowledges that the world is the intersection of various perceptual experiences (Lock and Farquhar 2007: 109). Yet this view also seems to imply that biology precedes its agential capacity, and thus it is by complicating this facet of Csordas's argument, along with his undeniable and unapologetic focus on the human body, that we begin to see the prospects of what it might mean to elucidate a hormonal lived embodiment of PND in fathers. By approaching somatic modes of attention through investigating bodily *intra*-actions (Barad 2007), we may further entangle the 'dialectical partners' of text and experience, and of mental and physical health (Csordas 1994b: 12). Hopefully, we may be able to acknowledge a culture of hormones in (intra)action!

A Culture of Hormones in Practice?

As mentioned earlier, peculiar chemical fluctuations seem to take place in the male body throughout the puerperal months: testosterone levels drop and oestrogen levels increase. Somehow, these agential hormonal materialities vary, grow or adapt in enactment with the organs that secrete them, the neurotransmitters they communicate with, and the bodies they inhabit. Somehow, in communication with their world, these hormonal variations acknowledge what is happening on the 'outside', indeed, they seem to exceed the notion of 'communication with' to ontologise that very process as they prepare for fatherhood. They are attentive, and as culturally elaborated 'entities', their measures are seen to change. Through the flesh, the experience of becoming a father is altering flesh, altering biology, and a mode of 'being-in-the-world' (a 'self') for expectant fathers is changing.

Csordas (1993: 138) notes that 'attention' may be articulated at 'the existentially ambiguous point at which the act of constitution and the object that is constituted meet – the phenomenological "horizon" itself'. What we are seeing here is a different view of 'the how' of such attention that speaks to this very horizon. Hormones, attending to their materiality, forming of and as experience (given that their substance is linked to their enactments),[1] and as part of the bodily conversations of an impending father, are also attending with their bodies to the overall experience fathers are living through: their lived embodiment. Thus, by materialising as a somatic mode of attention, hormones not only engage with other biological entities, but also attend, in a wider sense, to *other's* bodies, towards other enwebbed materialities we identify and unify as human. Yet in the case of impending fathers this is not quite intersubjectivity, nor quite intercorporeality, as testosterone levels and oestrogen levels rise in *expectation* of an 'other'. Hormones, as with the father, are engaging and becoming *with* their future child, a child who, although yet to arrive, is strangely in evidence. In a way, we could risk suggesting that perhaps fathers, too, are pregnant.

Gail Weiss (1995: 5) writes that 'to describe embodiment as inter-corporeality is to emphasize that the experience of being embodied is never a private affair, but is always already mediated by our continual interactions with other human and nonhuman bodies'. Yet the previous example of hormonal transmutation has already shown the possibilities of an embodiment that is more than intercorporeality, if by this we mean two bodies interacting to produce a shared, but originally separate embodiment. While the notion of intercorporeality pushes the boundaries of what may constitute a body, assuming an extension of one body towards and with another body (Merleau-Ponty 1964: 168), searching the space *between* bodies, it does not fully concede the possibilities of one body being, already and always, inseparable *within* its materiality from another. Drawing from Karen Barad's (2007: 33) understanding of 'intra-actions' as signifying 'the mutual constitution of entangled agencies', there may be an 'intra-corporeality', a mutual-constitution of entangled biographical corporealities. Furthermore, these corporealities are agents of communication linking intelligibility, knowledge and performance. In this sense, although it has been calculated that 'men's hormones are generally related to the women's levels and not to the time before birth' (Storey et al. 2000: 90) – in other words, they can have little to do with the foetus – in understanding bodily intra-activity and how it is entangled with other(s) bodies, the baby is as much inside the father as it is the mother.

That 'men's hormones may be related to women's levels' (Storey et al. 2000: 90) is fascinating in itself. As Anne Storey and colleagues have discovered,

> men [may experience] significant pre-, peri-, or postnatal changes in [testoster-one, cortisol and prolactin], with patterns of change paralleling those found in women in this and other studies (Fleming and Corter, 1988; Fleming et al., 1997). Our results suggest that hormonal reactivity to social stimuli is also an important component of stage and individual differences in hormone-behavior dynamics, although these changes have not been the focus of as much research as the absolute hormone concentrations (but see Wingfield et al., 1990; Castro and Matt, 1997). *Hormone correlations between partners suggest that communica-tion within couples is related to the physiological changes the men experience.* (Storey et al. 2000: 90, emphasis added)

As alluded to earlier, other hormonal variations take place in the bodies of new fathers in unison with those of mothers who have recently
experienced childbirth. Vasopressin levels in fathers, tested through the
sampling of blood, seem to increase analogous to oxytocin levels in
mothers. In these hormonal examples a somatic mode of attention to
the movement of and within 'other's' bodies appears to be in evidence.
There is an intra-corporeal synchrony. But how can this be?

In attempting to explain, or at least, 'open up' a possibility for understanding this phenomenon, I find myself drawn to a similarly puzzling
example where biology seems to be conversing intra-corporeally and
changing bodily patterns. We have seen similar, mysterious, 'natural'
anomalies in the fundamentally contested phenomenon of menstrual synchrony. While a number of scientific studies (for example Ziomkiewicz
2006; Schank 2000) consider this experience imagined, others continue to
promote its reality. The most notable studies of the 'McClintock Effect'[2]
come from Aron Weller, Leonard Weller and colleagues, who have demonstrated 'by their own account' (Schank 2001: 3) that in fact a very
high degree of synchrony may be found among families, sisters, lesbian
couples, best friends and female co-workers (Weller et al. 1999a; Weller et
al. 1999b; Weller and Weller 1993). This synchrony may be explained by
exposure to pheromones (another chemical secretion released primarily
via the sweat glands) and sensory signals (such as odour) that are linked
to other female bodies. If such exposure does not occur, the phenomenon
may not arise.

What we can perceive from this is that the life-worlds of certain
agential beings (in this case females), according to their biographical
circumstances, have a certain 'somatic mode of attendance' to and with
menstruation. Menstruation is only cyclical as we make it cyclical. It is
variable, as the hormones that seemingly cause the experience are variable. Exposure to the intra-active corporealities of others is simultaneously happening internally and modifying embodiment. In this sense
we may also understand that vasopressin levels may rise, and may alter,
with oxytocin levels due to the experience they are embodying. This
has implications for fathers' PND, just as it would for maternal depression: it illustrates that intra-actions may express a different mode of
being-in-the-world, a means of becoming other. If attention to other
bodies (including that of the mother and child) is circumstantially different, vasopressin levels may be variable. Certainly fathers who have
had little contact with their child, or are not in a romantic relationship
with the mother of their child, seem to have a higher risk of PND and
lower levels of vasopressin.

Understanding hormones as inherently intra-active, as 'somatic modes of attention', also offers a possibility of teasing out Csordas's (1993: 146) call for a reinterpretation of couvade, in which,

> the core of the phenomenon is that an expectant father experiences bodily sensations attuned to those of his pregnant mate. Couvade has been understood in one of two ways in the literature. On the one hand, it is thought of as a rather odd custom in which the man 'simulates' or 'imitates' labor (Broude 1988; Dawson 1929; Munroe et al. 1973). On the other, it is regarded as a medical phenomenon, or 'syndrome' (Enoch and Trethowan 1991; Klein 1991, Schodt 1989). Thus, couvade is either exoticized as a primitive charade, or pathologized as a psychosomatic overidentification.

Csordas acknowledges with Laura Rival (1998: 628) and Albert Doja that,

> the different positions in the interpretation of couvade are kept as irreconcilable alternatives as long as we maintain the entrenched view that the social is grafted onto the biological, with the collollary proposition that biology is woman's destiny (De Beaviour 1949) or that female is to male as nature is to culture (Ortner 1974). (Doja 2005: 927)

Instead, if reconceived as a somatic mode of attention, couvade appears 'as a phenomenon of embodied intersubjectivity that is performatively elaborated in certain societies, while it is either neglected or feared as abnormal in others' (Csordas 1993: 146).

Just as couvade has been explained in dualist either/or terms, so too have hormones and the experience of PND. In reconfiguring couvade as a 'somatic mode of attention' we may see how perinatal hormonal fluctuations that act to and with the body in intra-active synchrony may also be a form of this experience. Depending on the biographies of agential materialities such as hormones within the body of a father, couvade may become and be enacted as pathological, as ritualised, or it might not be practiced at all. Indeed in 'Western' societies synchronised peri- and postpartum hormonal activity has been linked with the phenomenon of couvade syndrome, or the medicalised form of couvade, particularly in terms of pathologic hyperprolactinemia and irregular testosterone, oestrogen, prolactin and vasopressin levels. Fathers who experience more marked sensorial expressions of this intra-activity, such as growing breasts and/or an enlarged stomach, or feeling labour pains, may have higher levels of prolactin in their blood (Storey et al. 2000: 92). They may also have a higher level of paternal involvement in the pregnancy and rearing of their children. Additionally, it has been suggested that 'when men experience these couvade symptoms and changes in responses to babies, they may also be signalling their part-ners about their intention or ability to invest in the new baby' (Symons cited in Storey et al. 2000: 92). It seems fair to suggest that culturally elaborated intra-active communication abounds! Biology may converse through changing its form and substance in ways that can be under-stood by other material actors. Again, as Kirby describes it, 'nature reads, writes, articulates *itself* . . . [it] is, and always was, a self-record-ing' (2008: 230).

Paternal PND, as an abnormal experience, has also been related to couvade syndrome (Shapiro and Nass 1986). Yet if couvade may involve hormonal intra-activity, a somatic mode of attention to other bodies, then another possibility for the experience of PND in men may be highlighted: it may be related to the experience of maternal PND. Certainly, many fathers who experience PND in the state of NSW, Australia, are living with mothers who are also suffering. This in no way implies blame on behalf of the mother, where abnormal mater-nal hormonal fluctuations that may be involved in PND may cause or trigger a related condition in fathers. This again would posit the feminine as leaky or infectious. It also complies with a cause and effect model that understands biology as pre-existing the cultural and social forces that affect it from the outside. Instead of repeating these styles of explanation, with their uninterrogated political assumptions, the field of these changing materialisations may be more poignant, intimate and intricate. In the case of both mother and father experiencing PND, dependent on their biographical life circumstances, there may be an intra-corporeal mode of attendance giving rise to a mode of being that is more than just shared, more than the woman's stress being passed on in linear, causal fashion to the male partner. It may involve a scene of ontological entanglement. Culturally elaborated, they may both be suffering from PND.

Conclusion

> Speaking is a kind of sonorous touching; language is tissue in the flesh of the world. (Csordas 2008: 118)

Depression has been described as a 'mute illness', the 'silent killer' (Deb and Bhattacharjee 2009), and never has it been so quiet as in fathers suffering from PND, despite its emergence into Australian public health care and policy. Yet considering the distress that the experience may hold, this 'voicelessness' is not unexpected. As Arthur Frank (1995: 98) declares,

> the teller of chaos stories is, preeminently, the wounded storyteller, but those who are truly *living* the chaos cannot tell it in words. To turn the chaos into a verbal story is to have some reflective grasp of it. The chaos that can be told in story is already taking place at a distance and is being reflected on retrospectively. For a person to gain such a reflective grasp of [their] own life, distance is a prerequisite. In telling the events of one's life, events are mediated by the telling. But in the lived chaos, there is no mediation, only immediacy. The body is imprisoned in the frustrating needs of the moment. The person living the chaos story has no distance from [their] life and no reflective grasp on it. Lived chaos makes reflection, and consequently storytelling, impossible.

Yet as I have tried to make clear, the body is never mute. Through a description of the biosociality of hormones, it becomes possible to suggest that, indeed, the flesh is speaking to us as 'there is no outside of language' (Kirby 1997: 4). This use of language is one which lives in patterns within and through our bodies. It can involve the spoken word, or it can be in the way hormones are writing their own variability or how fathers embody their future child. As somatic modes of attention, hormones are intra-actively writing and telling their story, sharing the materiality of fathers' puerperal embodiment. In variable, culturally elaborated ways, hormones are conveying their (mutually constituted) tale of a possible lived embodiment of pregnancy, couvade and of PND. Complicating any simple division of nature and culture, hormones are irrevocably linked to what it *means* for fathers to experience these phenomena. In the sense of this argument, men may be(come) pregnant. Their experience may be one of 'developing offspring within the body', an experience that is 'full of meaning' and is 'of potentially great import' for understanding lived embodiment (Farlex 2014). Yet to be able to hear the stories of hormones and other bodily actors, we need to learn to listen in a different way, to become 'embodied sociologists' (Williams and Bendelow 1998) rather than those who study the sociology of embodiment as if it is an object, detached, distant, and somehow outside the very process of its own analysis. In doing so, we may find that by 'opening the question of corporeality through the nature/culture divide, we are confronted by the alien within – in the form of a very real possibility that the body of the world is articulate and uncannily thoughtful' (Kirby 1997: 5).

Notes

1. Roberts (2007: 58) notes that it is common physiological knowledge that 'what hormones are made of determines how they function in the body'. Polypeptide and glycoprotein hormones are water-soluble so they may travel throughout the body dissolved in blood plasma, while steroidal hormones are lipids that attach to plasma-carrier proteins that carry them through blood (Roberts 2007: 58). Acknowledging the agential properties of hormones, we may begin to see how the substance of hormones may be brought into being through their functional performativity. This difference in materiality affects the temporal activity of hormones or when they arrive at the target cell they communicate with (Roberts 2007: 58).
2. Menstrual synchrony has been named the 'McClintock effect' after the primary investigator who researched the phenomenon. Martha McClintock (1971) initially investigated menstrual synchrony and suppression in a female college dormitory.

References

Ahokas, A., J. Kaukoranta and M. Aito (1999), 'Effect of Oestradiol on Post-partum Depression', *Psychopharmacology*, 146: 1, pp. 108–10.

Australian Government (2012), 'Postnatal Depression', *Pregnancy, Birth and Baby*, <http://www.pregnancybirthbaby.org.au/postnatal-depression> (last accessed 10 September 2013).

Barad, K. (2003), 'Posthuman Perfomativity: Toward an Understanding of How Matter Comes to Matter', *Signs: Journal of Women in Culture and Society* 28: 3, pp. 801–31.

Barad, K. (2007), *Meeting the Universe Halfway: Quantum Physics and the Entanglement of Matter*, Durham, NC: Duke University Press.

Csordas, T. J. (1993), 'Somatic Modes of Attention', *Cultural Anthropology*, 8: 2, pp. 135–56.

Csordas, T. J. (1994a), 'Words from the Holy People: A Case Study in Cultural Phenomenology', in T. Csordas (ed.), *Embodiment and Experience: The Existential Ground of Culture and Self*, Cambridge: Cambridge University Press, pp. 269–88.

Csordas, T. J. (1994b), 'Introduction', in T. Csordas (ed.), *Embodiment and Experience: The Existential Ground of Culture and Self*, Cambridge: Cambridge University Press, pp. 1–24.

Csordas, T. J. (2008), 'Intersubjectivity and Intercorporeality', *Subjectivity*, 22: 1, pp. 110–21.

Deb, S., and A. Bhattacharjee (2009), *Mental Depression: The Silent Killer*, New Delhi: Concept Publishing.

Doja, A. (2005), 'Rethinking the Couvade [Social Thought and Commentary]', *Anthropological Quarterly*, 78: 4, pp. 917–50.

Everingham, C. R., G. Heading and L. Connor (2006), 'Couples' Experiences of Postnatal Depression: A Framing Analysis', *Social Science and Medicine*, 62: 7, pp. 1745–56.

Farlex (2014), 'Pregnant [Def.]', *The Free Dictionary*, <http://www.thefree dictionary.com/pregnant> (last accessed 3 January 2014).

Fausto-Sterling, A. (2000), *Sexing the Body: Gender Politics and the Construction of Sexuality*, New York: Basic Books.

Frank, A. W. (1995), *The Wounded Storyteller: Body, Illness and Ethics*, London and Chicago: University of Chicago Press.

Gilligan, C. (1982), *In Another Voice: Psychological Theory and Women's Development*, Cambridge, MA: Harvard University Press.

Gregoire, A. J. P., R. Kumar, B. Everitt and J. W. W. Studd (1996), 'Transdermal oestrogen for Treatment of Severe Postnatal Depression', *The Lancet*, 347: 9006, pp. 930–3.

Grosz, E. (1994), *Volatile Bodies: Toward a Corporeal Feminism*, Sydney: Allen & Unwin.

Haraway, D. (2003), *The Companion Species Manifesto: Dogs, People and Significant Otherness*, Chicago: Prickly Pear Press.

Harris, B. (1996), 'Hormonal Aspects of Postpartum Depression', *International Review of Psychiatry*, 8: 1, pp. 27–36.

Hendrick, V., L. L. Altshuler and R. Suri (1998), 'Hormonal Changes in the Postpartum and Implications for Postnatal Depression', *Psychosomatics*, 39: 2, pp. 93–101.

Husserl, E. ([1900/1901] 2001), *Logical Investigations*, D. Moran (ed.), 2nd edn, 2 vols, London: Routledge.

Irni, S. (2013), 'Sex, Power and Ontology: Exploring the Performativity of Hormones', *Nordic Journal of Feminist and Gender Research (NORA)*, 21: 1, pp. 41–56.

Kim, P., and J. E. Swain (2007), 'Sad Dads: Paternal Postpartum Depression', *Psychiatry*, 4: 2, pp. 36–47.

Kirby, V. (1997), *Telling Flesh: The Substance of the Corporeal*, London and New York: Routledge.

Kirby, V. (2008), 'Natural Convers(at)ions: Or, What If Culture Was Really Nature All Along?', in S. Alaimo and S. J. Heckman (eds), *Material Feminisms*, Bloomington: Indiana University Press, pp. 214–36.

Latour, B. (1988), *The Pasteurization of France*, trans. A. Sheridan and J. Law, Cambridge, MA: Harvard University Press.

Lock, M., and J. Farquhar (2007), 'Philosophical Studies or Learning how to Think Embodiment: Introduction', in M. Lock and J. Farquhar (eds), *Beyond the Body Proper: Reading the Anthropology of Material Life*, Durham, NC: Duke University Press, pp. 107–12.

McClintock, M. K. (1971), 'Menstrual Synchrony and Suppression', *Nature*, 229: 5282, pp. 244–5.

Merleau-Ponty, M. (1962), *Phenomenology of Perception*, trans. C. Smith, London: Routledge.

Merleau-Ponty, M. (1964), *Signs*, Evanston, IL: Northwestern University Press.

Miller, L. J. (2002), 'Postpartum Depression', *Journal of the American Medical Association*, 287: 6, pp. 762–5.

Mol, A. (2002), *The Body Multiple: Ontology in Medical Practice*, Durham, NC: Duke University Press.

Moscucci, O. (1993), *The Science of Woman: Gynaecology of Gender in England 1800–1929*, Cambridge: Cambridge University Press.

National Medical Research Council of Australia (2000), *Postnatal Depression: Not Just the Baby Blues*, Canberra: Commonwealth of Australia.

Nicolson, P. (1998), *Post-Natal Depression: Psychology, Science and the Transition to Motherhood*, London and New York: Routledge.

Oudshoorn, N. (2007), *Beyond the Natural Body: An Archaeology of Sex Hormones*, London and New York: Routledge.

Richards, J. P. (1990), 'Postnatal Depression: A Review of Recent Literature', *British Journal of General Practice*, 40: 340, pp. 472–6.

Rival, L. (1998), 'Androgynous Parents and Guest Children: The Huaorani Couvade. Curl Essay Prize', *Journal of the Royal Anthropological Institute*, 5: 4, pp. 619–42.

Roberts, C. (2007), *Messengers of Sex: Hormones, Biomedicine and Feminism*, Cambridge: Cambridge University Press.

Schank, J. C. (2000), 'Menstrual-Cycle Variability and Measurement: Further Case for Doubt', *Psychoneuroendocrinology*, 25: 8, pp. 837–47.

Schank, J. C. (2001), 'Menstrual-Cycle Synchrony: Problems and New Directions for Research', *Journal of Comparative Psychology*, 115: 1, pp. 3–15.

Shapiro, S., and J. Nass (1986), 'Postpartum Psychosis in the Male', *Psychopathology*, 19: 3, pp. 138–42.

Sieben, A. (2011), 'Heteronormative Pheromones? A Feminist Approach to Human Chemical Communication', *Feminist Theory*, 12: 3, pp. 263–80.

Solantaus, T., and S. Salo (2005), 'Paternal Postpartum Depression: Fathers Emerge from the Wings', *The Lancet*, 365: 9478, pp. 2158–9.

Spinelli, M. G. (2001), 'A Systematic Investigation of 16 Cases of Neonaticide', *American Journal of Psychiatry*, 158: 5, pp. 811–13.

Storey, A. E., K. J. Walsh, R. L. Quinton and K. E. Wynne-Edwards (2000), 'Hormonal Correlates of Paternal Responsiveness in New and Expectant Fathers', *Evolution and Human Behavior*, 21: 2, pp. 79–95.

Ussher, J. M. (2006), *Managing the Monstrous Feminine: Regulating the Reproductive Body*, London and New York: Routledge.

Weiss, G. (1999) *Body Images: Embodiment as Intercorporeality*, New York: Routledge.

Weller, L., and A. Weller (1993), 'Human Menstrual Synchrony: A Critical Assessment', *Neuroscience and Behavioral Reviews* 17: 427–39.

Weller, L., A. Weller, H. Koresh-Kamin and B. Shoshan (1999a), 'Menstrual Synchrony in a Sample of Working Women', *Psychoneuroendocrinology*, 24: 4, pp. 449–59.

Weller, L., A. Weller and S. Roizman (1999b), 'Human Menstrual Synchrony in Families and Among Close Friends: Examining the Importance of Mutual Exposure', *Journal of Comparative Psychology*, 113: 3, pp. 261–8.

Williams, S. J., and G. Bendelow (1998), *The Lived Body: Sociological Themes, Embodied Issues*, London and New York: Routledge.

Zelkowitz, P., and T. H. Milet (2001), 'The Course of Postpartum Psychiatric Disorders in Women and their Partners', *The Journal of Nervous and Mental Disease*, 189: 9, pp. 575–82.

Ziomkiewicz, A. (2006), 'Menstrual Synchrony: Fact or Artifact', *Human Nature*, 17: 4, pp. 419–32.

CHAPTER 6

Material Culture: Epigenetics and the Molecularisation of the Social

Noela Davis

Introduction

Recent sociological and feminist theorising about the body has recognised that past accounts had a tendency to bracket out biology in an often unconscious adherence to the received circumscriptions of the nature/culture dichotomy.[1] Now the focus has turned to an examination of the dynamism and productivity of bodies, to a consideration of what bodies can *do*. The body in these conceptualisations is not the passive substrate of past theory, something which is animated by the social, but, instead is seen *as* animation, agency and sociality. These accounts provide rich descriptions of the vibrant and lively capabilities of bodies, their capacities to affect and be affected, to effect changes to other bodies and to their environments. Such approaches are also a call to re-envisage our concepts of bodies, a warning to be wary of historical-progressivist accounts of our investigative endeavours and the attainment of knowledge. Making this point in a recent essay, Diana Coole (2010) reminds us that the philosopher Maurice Merleau-Ponty offered a cogent assessment of the problems that accompany a progressivist approach to research, one whose pitfalls still resonate with contemporary critiques. Her essay is a reminder for us not to forget the work of past theorists such as Merleau-Ponty, as former insights can remain pertinent to our current concerns.

Merleau-Ponty (2002) offers a critique of the assumptions and methodology of empiricism, contending that it effectively ignores and devalues the complexities of experience. Merleau-Ponty links empiricism to the sciences of chemistry, physics and mathematics (2002: 12, 26), but this methodology comprises a set of assumptions that can underlie any information-gathering venture, not just the sciences he identifies. The principles of empiricism align with our traditional, taken-for-granted world view and are, in summary: a linear conceptualisation of time; science as the progressive accumulation and mastery of knowledge; and the objects of science theorised as discrete entities with a temporal-spatial separation between them. It is a method that assumes that scientists are distanced from their objects of investigation and, similarly, that bodies are also separate objects, quite distinct in their function and capacity from the mind or culture which motivates them. Bodies, Merleau-Ponty claims, are reduced to mere processes of stimulus and response by such empiricist modes of inquiry (2002: 26). By concentrating only on the physico-chemical processes and make-up of objects, and not taking account of experience, feeling and context in its fullest sense, he argues that the empiricism of the above-named sciences removes the ambiguity and mystery from the world. This process of reduction and circumscription amounts, he claims, to a 'freezing of being', where living matter is rendered as just another object which similarly possesses fixed or given characteristics (2002: 60, 63).[2]

Merleau-Ponty insists that empiricism's atomistic approach cannot adequately account for the world, as our knowledge of it and of ourselves is not built up from the examination of discrete and determinable characteristics but is rooted in the intricate involvements of our embodied experience (2002: 27). Importantly, experience is not the addition of sensations or elements, nor is it the quantifiable 'thing' assumed by empiricism. It is instead a relationship between parts of the whole in which we are thoroughly implicated. Forces within this whole register in us in meaningful ways, but do not let us possess things or learn the (absolute) truth of the world, as empiricism would contend (2002: 39). Crucial to Merleau-Ponty's thesis is the insight that empiricist approaches do not address experience and its considerable contribution to subjectivity and knowledge. From an empiricist viewpoint, it is assumed that bodies and scientists do not alter the world they study; in other words, they are not considered active participants in the phenomena they investigate. Rather, it is presumed that bodies simply register impressions of an independent world-in-itself (2002: 8). Merleau-Ponty maintains that empiricism, contrary to the belief that it reveals independently existing truths, in an ironic twist actually falsifies the world (2002: 28). This is because the world is not given to us ready-made, nor is knowledge built up from the analysis of single elements, as empiricism presupposes.

Instead, Merleau-Ponty insists that knowledge comes from our sensory life experiences as we are immersed with/in the dynamic energies that circulate through the world: in short, we have an embodied relationship with our surroundings that gives meaning to our experience. For Merleau-Ponty, knowledge and meaning are relational, and are always produced in a specific context; consequently, as the context changes then so can our particular connection with it. Thus, truth is not progressively revealed, with each new truth adding to and extending the last as empiricism supposes, but is always immanent to the contingencies of the situation in which it is constituted (2002: 41).

As Diana Coole points out in acknowledgement of Merleau-Ponty's radical revisioning of the question of the objects of knowledge (2010: 96), his thesis shows how traditional approaches reify and separate processes and experiences which are in fact interconnected. His solution to the malaise of empiricism is to focus explorations on the lived, felt experience of being intimately entwined in the world. This is a theme notably adopted by affect theorists who level similar accusations against scientific enquiries. For instance, Bruno Latour (2004) insists that bodies should not be thought of as a container or possessor of properties, and when investigating how a body affects and becomes affected, he notes, 'one is not obliged to define an essence, a substance (what a body is by nature)' (2004: 205). Rather than trying to define what a body is, his advice is that we should instead direct our attention to what bodies actively do, what bodies are aware of (2004: 206). As Lisa Blackman and Couze Venn (2010) contend in their introduction to a special issue of *Body & Society* devoted to affect, bodies are processes, not entities. Echoing Latour here, we are again encouraged not to focus on what a body is, 'as if the body can be reified as a thing or an entity' (Blackman and Venn 2010: 9). Instead, Blackman and Venn direct us away from this seemingly static and 'given' sense of description towards the dynamic of corporeal activity (2010: 9). This movement towards action shifts the focus onto bodies as 'entangled processes . . . defined by their capacities to affect and be affected' (2010: 9). In taking this approach, such investigations give us insightful accounts of the vibrancy of bodies and their abilities to resonate with, and respond to, the forces that impact them. Such studies do a great deal to dispel any lingering assumptions that bodies are a mere static substrate underlying activity and affectivity.

Nonetheless, despite the vigorous and perceptive questioning of empiricist assumptions and circumscriptions found in such affective analyses, there still remains a curious reluctance to engage with bio-logical data. Enquiry into the physiological mechanisms of the body's dynamism is strangely foreclosed, with no apparent curiosity into *how* biology is able to develop vital, social capacities. The flows, intensities and forces that experience involves are certainly detailed, yet without investigating how these tensions are biologically, chemically, neuro-nally, hormonally and metabolically realised. As a consequence, the biology of the body remains an unexamined, unknown interior depth that is somehow outside the liveliness we experience.[3]

Elizabeth Wilson (2015) contends that this reluctance to engage with the biological is a common feature of much sociological and feminist theorising – a feature which Wilson labels 'antibiologism' (2015: 2–3). In investigating why social research seems to need to reject biology Wilson concludes that it is because we still see biology as inflexible and determinist, as apolitical and not relevant to social life. This attitude, in effect, re-consigns biology and culture to two separate and autonomous domains, each with their own logic and functioning. This lament for lost opportunities to engage in interdisci-plinary research does not come solely from the social sciences, either. Biologists are also concluding that their research could benefit from sociological insights and input, but note that only a 'handful' of social scientists are taking up the challenge (Nature Editorial 2012: 143). Wilson also reminds us that the social and natural sciences are not self-contained and closed off from each other but are interdependent. However, her call for greater use and interrogation of biological data comes with a caution not to be over-optimistic. She is not suggest-ing that the use of this research will somehow resolve all our social problems but, instead, argues that our understandings of ourselves, our bodies and the world will be poorer for not acknowledging inter-disciplinary entanglements and for not canvassing diverse sources of data (2015: 27).

The above arguments suggest that there are still two cultures, those of the physical and the social sciences, with the concomitant assumption that there are no crossovers or mutually relevant areas of enquiry. A question that arises is that of whether there can be a productive alliance between social and biological data. What ques-tions, puzzles and insights might be raised by a refusal to respect the (supposed) inviolability of disciplinary boundaries? In light of this, the question that will be addressed here is that of whether enquiry into the biology of bodies necessarily reifies them, freezes being and demystifies the wonder of our lived experiences with reductive descriptions. Instead of ignoring biological research, can we reread it in ways that challenge the implicit empiricist underpinnings found in many studies? Empirical research gives us much valuable knowledge about the world, and if approached within a different conceptualisation I contend that it can allow us insight into the entanglement of biology and the social.

To ponder these questions, this chapter will draw on epigenetic research into the intergenerational transmission of the health effects of social stigma, Vicki Kirby's theorisation of the world as an open system, and Karen Barad's detailed elaborations of how apparatuses materialise the world. Epigenetics is the study of the dynamic gene-body-environment conversations that enact the physiological mechanisms through which an organism's genome is expressed. That is, it is an investigation into how context shapes the genome, or how an organism's phenotype is materialised. The conversants are genes, bodies, biochemistry, diet, history, cultural practices, geography, economics, climate, even feminist theorising – to name but a few of the lived experiences that flow into the epigenetic exchange. In telling the story of these involved narratives, the exposition will necessarily take the form of a linear sequence and a temporal succession. But these appearances of linearity, temporality and cause and effect will be queered by the argument that the world is not an aggregation of atomic entities, separate events and chains of causality but rather a materialisation of differentiations within one system; and the contention is that epigenetics illustrates this entanglement.

In taking this approach, the argument will seek to challenge the suggestion that an investigation of physiological mechanisms necessarily constitutes a reification of matter. Contrary to studies that assume biology as a given starting point, the discussion here theorises physiology and bodies as already within the dynamic systematicity of the question under investigation. Enquiry into the workings of biological processes does not have to reduce bodies and matter to fixed entities without agency. Importantly, and ironically, to refuse exploration of the biological mechanisms through which matter expresses itself is, effectively, to limit the study of the materiality and capacities of bodies to the confines of a realm assumed isolable from biology. Such an investigation into the body's physicality does not have to halt its movement or demystify its capacities, but instead should give us even greater respect for the body's capabilities than can be obtained by only examining our lived encounters with the world, as if they could somehow be cut adrift from their physiological operations.

Practices that Matter

Both Barad (see 2007, 2010, 2012b) and Kirby (see 2011, 2012) offer theorisations of an entangled world where the constitutive cuts that form bodies and the world, discriminations that determine what matters and does not matter, do not come from an absolute outside but arise from within the phenomena under investigation. These conceptualisations do not start with the empiricist assumptions of separate, already existent, already identified entities, studies where difference is considered as 'separation from, or attachment to, another entity' (Kirby 2012: 203). Instead, the entangled world is materialised as differences within the world, materialised *as* particular entities. For Kirby, this system, this world, is Nature, and for her, there is emphatically no outside of Nature (2011: x). Culture and the social are not separate from or external to Nature, but instead express Nature's way of enacting itself differently. All the dynamism, intelligence, discursivity and agency we usually ascribe to culture are thus the 'internal torsions' of Nature/biology/matter in this account. There is no radical exterior or otherness but rather an entanglement wherein what appears to be other, separate or non-local is already systematicity at work (2011: x). As Barad provides a detailed elaboration of the mechanics of how this systematicity may operate, her work offers the potential for reconsidering the impasses that arise when biology and the social, in this case, are thought to reside in separate domains. The conundrum we are faced with if we assume an originary disjuncture between biology and culture is that of how two apparently incommensurate entities or realms can communicate, influence, understand, affect, and constitute, one another.[4] Barad sees bodies as differentiated materialisations of the world, and the cuts, or differences, between biology and the social are already internal – that is, the body is already its (purported) other.

Barad, like Kirby, stresses that she is not discussing interconnections between pre-existing things or events separated by space and time, but is concerned with the constitutive nature of the practices which enact the differences that matter in the world (2012b: 32). Bodies and matter are active practices of materialisation, rather than frozen or reified entities that possess independent and stable characteristics. The agent of this performative production is a material-discursive apparatus (Barad 2007: 146). Barad emphasises that an apparatus is not a pre-existing thing or a separate entity either, nor is it a mediator between objects and practices. On the contrary, apparatuses are processes of making determinate that arise from within the system's indeterminacy. As such, apparatuses contest the possibility of absolute separation and independent existence. It is a physical, intra-active practice; a process that produces, as it is produced by, ideas, knowledge, thinking, bodies, societies, environments, time, space – and other apparatuses (2007: 90–1, 148; 2012a: 12). As individual entities are not antecedent to the productive apparatus, this is not a logic of the aggregation of discrete entities. Instead, determinate entities and their interrelations and exclusions – and this includes the entanglement of one apparatus with/in another – are produced by the intra-active boundary-making practices that render the indeterminacy of the world meaningful (2007: 148; 2012b: 41).

Importantly for this analysis, in Barad's conceptualisation seemingly abstract aspects of the world – such as theories, concepts, social movements, and asymmetries such as racism and gender inequalities – are physical arrangements embodied in and through the apparatuses that produce, frame, and give them meaning (2007: 128–9). The social and conceptual are thus differentiations of matter that remain inseparable from it. The agential processes elaborated here, while presented as a series of events for heuristic reasons, must be understood as one doubly constitutive movement; that of the making separate that is the entanglement of 'spacetimemattering' (Barad 2012b: 32). This is one intra-active action that entangles as it divides, or what Barad terms a 'cutting together-apart' (2012b: 32, 46). Determinate history and potential future are produced as a sequence of cause and effect through an intra-action that temporalises. Enfolded within apparatuses are inheritance, memory and anticipation: the diffraction of a past that was never simply 'there' with an indebtedness to an always open future (2012a: 11). History is a hauntology where past and future are entangled, and where what is produced as past may anticipate the future (Barad 2010: 240). Kirby describes this paradox as a 'mysterious clairvoyance' where it is as if things or people are brought together before their actual meeting, where there is found a preparedness to receive a message that is yet to arrive, possibly yet to even be addressed. This is a message received before there is a specific addressee, yet it is delivered to the 'right' place, to a recipient that can read, understand and act on the missive. Kirby contends that this suggests that the certainty of the presumed identity of, or separation between, entities is compromised (2011: 9). This haunting by future possibility, as will be discussed, is a scene that is also played out in epigenetic findings.

Theorising Phenotype

I will examine the argument in Arun Saldanha's essay (2006) as he aims to offer an account of the dynamism of a phenotype's constitution, foregrounding bodies and physical events in his discussion of the ontology of race. However, despite his perspicacious grasp of the issues at play in the materialisation of phenotype and the attendant politics of race, it needs to be asked whether his work, ultimately, maintains a distance between nature and culture and, in so doing, provides an illustrative counterpoint to the entangled epigenetic theorisation of phenotype presented here.

Saldanha offers an incisive critique of works that take race to be a solely social construction, as well as those that suggest that race is merely a political category that could, and should, be dispensed with. Importantly, and this is refreshing, in the course of his critique he insists that we cannot adequately investigate race without 'serious engagement with its biological dimensions' (2006: 9). Bodies, he notes, cannot be considered to be solely produced by a circumscribed social or linguistic signification that excludes physiology. To do so, he insists, amounts to a disavowal of matter (2006: 12, 15). Saldanha argues that attempts to see race in purely cultural terms 'deontologise' it, as they imply that race could simply be a 'mental category' rather than a 'real' phenomenon. He contends that any theory that avoids an encounter with matter implicitly assumes that nature, biology, matter and the body are 'static and deterministic', and play no active part in politics and society (2006: 14–15).

In contrast, he seeks to offer an analysis of race in terms of phenotype as he sees the refusal to engage with the materiality of race as indicative of 'a wider anxiety in the social sciences about matter' (2006: 9), a concern that Wilson, as discussed earlier, also shares. Saldanha feels it is imperative to engage with the biological aspects of race for to do otherwise may leave the field open to reinstatements of biological-determinist justifications for racial hierarchies (2006: 10). Bodies, he emphasises, are not inert matter that possess a fixed characteristic called race, but are instead animated practices of racialisation produced through social and material encounters (2006: 18). In recognising this, Saldanha also argues that the politics of race must be acknowledged as a thoroughly embodied practice. He urges us to remember, as well, that race and racism are always geographically and historically specific instances. The asymmetries of race are not homogeneous or static but are always enacted in particular environments. So, he notes, any political or social policy considerations need to examine the distinctive characteristics of each occurrence of racism in its specific context (2006: 22).

Saldanha has given a thoughtful and constructive account of the issues with which a material account of race (or any other bodily materialisation of social asymmetry) has to contend. Nevertheless, his work still avoids delving too far into biological detail. He gives no account of the physiological processes involved in the expression of phenotype, nor of the incorporation of the physical responses a body makes to acts of racial discrimination. Perhaps some insights into this reluctance may be gleaned from Saldanha's critique of 'linguistic turn' theorists, in particular his discussion of Judith Butler's work. Butler, he contends, posits physical bodies as a constitutive outside to discourse, as an inert exteriority to language and signification (2006: 12). Saldanha wants to take a different path away from such conceptualisations in order to show us that active productivity is not limited to a circumscribed language, as Butler suggests. Rather than animation being bestowed on bodies by culture, Saldanha argues that bodies are 'productive in their own right, just like words' (2006: 12).

To illustrate his position, Saldanha examines a passage from Frantz Fanon where Fanon elucidates his response to a young boy's cry of 'look, a Negro . . . I'm frightened' (Saldanha 2006: 10). In acknowledging that Fanon's account describes the pain that is felt when one is subject to being stigmatised because of one's appearance, Saldanha explains that Fanon's phenotype is constituted by a multitude of social and physical factors, such as 'genetic endowments, environmental conditions, exercise, hormones, diet, disease, ageing' (2006: 12). However, even while theorising the implication of the social in the vitality of phenotypic constitution, Saldanha reveals a marked resistance to the suggestion that the boy's words could, in any way, affect phenotype for he emphatically states that Fanon's phenotype is 'not at all "performed" or "constituted" by the boy's exclamation' (2006: 12). Saldanha expands on his position by explaining that while language can charge or circumscribe a phenotype's possibilities, while it can affect what the stigmatised person is able to do or say in the particular circumstances, it does not alter the biological expression of a pheno-type (Saldanha 2006: 12).

Saldanha's insistence that language is not constitutive of phenotype gives rise to several questions. Does Saldanha, in critiquing Butler's clo-sure of language against physical bodies, nonetheless assume that the relationship between language and bodies is, as Butler contends, one of externality? In seeking to demonstrate the body's dynamism as a coun-ter to Butler's presumption that such liveliness is the sole preserve of discourse and culture, is Saldanha theorising a parallel domain of activ-ity where bodies and matter, while equally as productive and inventive as culture and language, are nevertheless removed from them? That is, is Saldanha critiquing only the theorisation of the body as inert, and taking it for granted that there is, indeed, a temporal-spatial gap between the realm of biology and matter and that of culture?[5] If so, in his apparent separation of such factors and their influences, Saldanha is still theorising a series of interconnections between discrete entities, rather than the systematic entanglement that Barad and Kirby present.

Saldanha makes this aggregative logic explicit when he speaks of the ontology of race. For him, the productive dynamism of space is a sticky 'viscosity'. Bodies, properties and events stick to each other, capturing more bodies here, or dissolving the collectivity back into its constituent parts there (2006: 18–19). That is, racial phenotype is theorised as an assemblage of properties, things and concepts and each seemingly maintains pre-existing and distinct boundaries and characteristics throughout. In doing this, together with his reluctance to consider that words can be materially constitutive of phenotype, Saldanha unfortunately reinforces the nature/culture divide in the name of contesting it – for as I will discuss, there is evidence that the experience of discriminatory remarks does indeed affect pheno-type. In other words, we could say that epigenetic research intimates that biology (in this case phenotype) *is* discursive, and is necessarily entangled with/in the social.

Epigenetics

While the etymology and earlier usage of the term 'epigenetics' sug-gest optional processes 'on top of' genetics, investigations of epigenetic mechanisms show them to be integral to an organism's development. Rather than being an additional, or supplementary level of genetic activity, epigenetic processes are essential to life and development as they are the mechanism by which cell differentiation takes place. All cells in an organism contain the same genetic complement, so there needs to be a method by which the differentiation of cells into the various organs and tissues – such as muscle, nerve, gut, skin, brain – can take place and thus produce the organism's phenotype (the patterning of genetic expression specific to this organism). Epigenetic processes regulate this differentiation by relaying biochemical and bio-electric messages – such as DNA methylation and histone acetylation[6] – that set how receptive a particular gene is to binding with the various proteins activated by transcription factors. These various mechanisms act to attenuate or amplify the degree of a gene's expression (Harper 2005: 344; Zhang and Meaney 2010: 442). An epigenetic viewpoint on the processes of development shows that it is not genes in themselves that give form to an organism. In other words, there is no pre-given, prescriptive code or genetic entity that determines what will materialise. Instead, the patterns of genetic expression that give the distinctive characteristics of a cell or tissue, and thus of the organism, materialise a phenotype in context through a dynamic crosstalk between one molecule and another, body organs, genes and environment, the organism and its surroundings.

While there are critical periods during early development when epigenetic processes have their greatest effect, research supports the contention that genetic expression is always open to environmental modification. These early exposures prime an organism's typical qualities and patterns of response to the environment, giving the organism its particular and individual characteristics, its resiliences and weaknesses, the personality that guides – but does not determine in advance – its future environmental interactions (see Kuzawa and Sweet 2009: 10; and Meaney 2010: 45, for an elaboration of this). Even though genetic expression is relatively stable, research demonstrates that the organism is at the same time always responsive to the specifics of its environmental context and its phenotype is always open to the possibility of further environmental modifications (Zhang and Meaney 2010: 447–8; see also Crepaldi and Riccio 2009). However, in noting the stability of bodies and their genetic expression it should not be presumed that this is a claim that bodies are inert and static. Somatic maintenance involves a constant gene-environment interrogation as the body strives to sustain itself in a perpetually changing context. In light of this evidence, phenotype can be seen as a continuing rematerialisation of an organism's epigenetic patterning in response to its surroundings.[7]

To assess the significance of epigenetic mechanisms for sociological research, we might ask at what point in development does environmental exposure begin? Is it at birth, prenatally . . . or even earlier? Evidence supports the hypothesis that this environmental conversation does not originate anew in each organism but that some elements can be passed on intergenerationally. Epigenetic modifications are not, as was previously thought, completely erased between generations and there is now a significant body of epigenetic research demonstrating the intergenerational transmission of environmental responses. While there is dispute over what, precisely, the mechanisms of some transmissions are, the important consideration is that there is agreement that the effects can impact over several generations (see, for example, Cropley et al. 2006; Gallou-Kabani and Junien 2005; Harper 2005; Hesman Saey 2013; Kuzawa and Sweet 2009; McGowan et al. 2009; Meaney 2010; Zhang and Meaney 2010).[8]

While we currently don't have a detailed understanding of how the earliest molecular developmental decisions are made, epigeneticists suggest that we are always already in conversation with the environment and with our inheritance. Lawrence Harper (2005) contends that 'to fully appreciate parental influence and the dynamic interplay between the individual and environment, the time frame for affecting the individual may be as early as gametogenesis' (2005: 352; see also Reik 2007: 430). Harper is not suggesting that epigenetic conversations only affect already formed individuals. The object of his theorising concerns the various possibilities that may or may not be realised in/as an individual, because there is a storehouse of environmental experience and propensities that work to confound received meanings of how an individual is normally defined. This organism is constituted as a gene-environment entanglement of potentiality, or to use Barad's terminology, it is haunted by its past and future possibilities. Before the particular individual can be said to exist, their genetic and environmental inheritances are already prepared to influence their developmental pathways, but always in context. The implications of these claims bear a similarity to the operations of Kirby's 'mysterious clairvoyance' (2011: 9). There is as yet no specific addressee for this epigenetic message but the history of a particular individual-yet-to-be is already 'apprised' of the possibilities for its future. This message is intended for the potential individual and has already met their potential future without yet meeting with them.

The implications of epigenetic theorising are that there is not first a biological body that is then worked on by a physical or social environment. Rather, we are always already environmental, and the relations of difference, between body and environment, biology and the social, are relations of externality *within* us, a 'difference [that] already inhabits the identity it would discriminate' (Kirby 1997: 55). Thus, the epigenetic conversation does not actually, as we would conventionally assume, take place between separately determinate entities but is always an entangled differentiation of systematicity. Indeed, the very status of the entity – here, the individual – is an enduringly tentative one whose apparent finitude can't even be clarified retrospectively, by the seemingly final cut of death.

Stigma

Stigmatisation has been linked to adverse physical health effects that can be traced across several generations. This research finding presents us with a puzzle, as stigma is a social labelling, a negative belief or a psychological denigration – in short, words. It is also an affective, lived experience where psychic pain is provoked in the stigmatised individual. The epigenetic evidence to be discussed strongly suggests that stigma is at the same time manifested in biology – and not just the biology of the person experiencing the stigma, but also, potentially, of their descendants.[9] This finding is in contradistinction to Saldanha's insistence that Fanon's phenotype was not constituted by his experience of discriminatory and stigmatising remarks (2006: 12).

Works by Bitte Modin (2003; 2008; 2009) and Rikke Lund (2006) and their respective colleagues have investigated the reproduction of social mortality patterns across generations. The subjects of Modin et al. were the children and grandchildren of people born out of wedlock in early twentieth-century Sweden and controls comprised descendants of people born within marriage in the same period. Their research found a correlation between the grandparents' illegitimacy and an increased risk of ischaemic heart disease in the subsequent two generations. Lund et al. studied the health effects of being born to an unmarried mother in 1953 in Denmark and they, too, found similarly increased disease risks in the offspring.

The research of Modin et al. showed a complex interplay of factors involved in these situations. Circumstances associated with being born out of wedlock at that time included poverty, inadequate nutrition, lack of social networks or support, lower social class, compromised mother-child relations, poor coping strategies and high psychosocial stress (2008: 823). But the salient point that Modin et al. and Lund et al. make is that they see social stigma, moral condemnation and exclusion from areas of social life as vital contributing factors to the increased incidence of intergenerational health problems in their experimental groups (Modin 2003: 493, 496; Modin et al. 2008: 823). Modin et al. maintain that there are differences between the experimental and control groups that cannot be explained by the shortage of material resources such as lack of food or inadequate housing that the subjects experienced. The crucial aspect of this research is their conclusion that stigma – seemingly a social, ideological and therefore abstract attribution – can manifest and be passed on physically. There is a transmission of values, attitudes and moral condemnation, which together have the ability to affect the physical health of the descendants of the stigmatised (Modin et al. 2008: 823–4). Lund et al. confirm that there is an intergenerational cumulative effect where each non-married generation added to the increased disease risk. They, too, note that the health problems they found could not be explained solely by the mental health problems or socio-economic status of the last generation under study, indicating that stigmatisation plays a part in the outcomes (2006: 499).

Although not longitudinal studies, other research into stigmatisation and discrimination (see, for instance, Hoffman and Spengler 2012; Kuzawa and Sweet 2009; Meyer 2003; Sweet 2010; Williams et al. 2010) similarly reports that the observed health outcomes of investigations into race, socio-economic status and sexual orientation could not be explained solely by measures of material resource availability or other concrete indicators. These studies, too, contend that the stigma associated with social marginalisation or lack of social status must be factored in to account for the development of disease.

Studies investigating family dynamics can help illuminate the mechanisms at play in these findings. Recent research investigating the health effects of stigma hypothesises stress reactivity as a mechanism for the development of illness. Researchers have proposed the notion of 'minority stress', which is stress the stigmatised or marginalised are subjected to, in addition to, and in excess of, the everyday stresses which we all negotiate (Meyer 2003: 675; Williams et al. 2010: 81).

Poor quality of family life, including factors such as abuse, neglect, poverty and other adverse social conditions such as stigmatisation or perceptions of a failure or inability to conform to society's norms, stress people. The stress hormones released – such as adrenaline, noradrenaline and adrenal glucocorticoids – produce several effects. One effect is to increase the availability of energy substrates that can promote, among other things, activation of inflammatory pathways, insulin resistance and hypertension. These can eventually manifest as diabetes and heart disease (Meaney 2001: 1163). At the same time, these increased stress hormone levels can also affect the methylation status of various genes, giving, for instance, reduced glucocorticoid receptor expression, leading to increased hypothalamic-pituitary-adrenal function. This can result in an increased release of hormones in response to stress, which indicates that the individual has developed heightened stress reactivity. In susceptible individuals this is often accompanied by hypervigilance, which is a constant state of being on guard to avert the possibility of stigmatisation or discrimination – and this itself is a state which increases stress and stress responses (McGowan et al. 2009: 342). These reactions have been shown to be associated with a sustained change in the expression of genes in regions that mediate responses to stress (Meaney 2001: 1170).

What, then, can play out are behavioural disturbances in the stressed individual, which may in turn elicit a further cycle of abuse or neglect from the parent, or further alienate the individual and entrench her further in a marginalised social position. And this can then provoke further increased stress responses that serve to reinforce the change in genomic expression and stress reactivity in the individual. What happens in this scenario does not simply take place at the level of behaviour or mental attitudes, for at the same time the parents' behaviour, or the social attitudes towards the stressed individual, are being made chemical, hormonal, metabolic. These attitudes and behaviours towards the individual are materialising, molecularised at the same time as the individual's responses to life are similarly becoming chemical, hormonal, molecular in ways that have been suggested to the body by its epigenetic past-future inheritance. The individual's very being is thus an active performativity.

Michael Meaney, another epigenetic researcher, describes the scenario of being born into a stressful environment as anticipatory development (2001: 1182), again reminding us of Barad's hauntology (2010: 240) and Kirby's clairvoyance (2011: 9). He sees that even before individuals have experienced the environment for themselves – even before they exist as an individual – they have in their inheritance messages from their environment already signalling their life conditions to them. They are born into stigma and the individual is already epigenetically prepared to respond to a high stress environment.[10] Enfolded in their history is a future possibility and this is already present at their birth as a past, present and future that is already in conversation.

Queering Epigenetics

This research and analysis suggests that the actions of epigenetic processes are twofold, and it is in this double practice that the notion that we are witnessing a linear, temporal-spatial progression is undone. Epigenetic mechanisms are, in Barad's terms, apparatuses – processes that resolve and materialise the indeterminacy of genes into determinate individuals with particular propensities, resiliences and characteristics. That is, if we apply Barad's argument, epigenetic mechanisms cut: they are boundary-making practices that differentiate the organism internally and, at the same time, differentiate it from its surrounding environment. Their cutting enactments also materialise the narrative of cause and effect. That is, there is not a linear trajectory of cause and effect, but specific configurations materialised as relations of cause and effect in the particular contingent phenomenon under investigation (Barad 2007: 149), in this case, the materialisation of an individual affected by stigmatisation.

But epigenetic processes simultaneously entangle. Biology and the environment – both physical and social – are inseparably materialised in the body, a molecular, chemical materialisation of environment as biology. The differences between them are internal to this body. In materialising the particular individual, past and future are also entangled. Anticipation and inheritance, and future possibility (of, for example, heart disease or good health) are enfolded and sedimented into the now of *this* individual in a diffractive entanglement of body and world.

As mentioned earlier, Barad explains this double action as 'cutting together-apart' (2012b: 46), which is her terminology to explain how the plenitude of the system is made meaningful. It is a phrase which reminds us that phenomena are not discrete entities but are the materialisations of an entanglement that has been framed in particular ways through apparatuses, apparatuses that have no one identifiable author, and which are made separate and identifiable through these very manifestations. Crucially, this is one intra-active movement that constitutes the phenomenon through this movement, and is not a succession of actions. Barad offers a further way of expressing the productivity of this systematicity. It is, she says, a 'differentiated indivisibility' (2010: 253) which again serves to reiterate that phenomena are entanglements. In this we see delineation but no absolute separation, which has echoes of Kirby's account whereby what we take to be discrete entities are actually the 'internal torsions' of a systematicity that cuts and differentiates itself from itself (2011: x). Otherness and heterogeneity are thus already within this system as its own constitutive conditions. History and memory, future possibilities and present circumstances are all written into the materialisations of bodies (Barad 2007: 383). All parts of bodies – flesh, molecules, hormones, both physical and mental capacities, affective sensations, and so on – are reconfigured as the memory of their particular enfoldings. Physical bodies and biology are not static vessels, which are then inscribed by the social or by history, but are the dynamic, discursive, performative rematerialisations of all their constitutive conditions. The social is materialised as, and in, this body, (re)configured in its molecular and hormonal history, a biology always already social.

Conclusion

Epigenetics shows that at the body's molecular level, the social and biological are intimately woven with/in each other and their particular environmental histories.

Environment, biology, economics, history, politics, morality, and so on, are constitutive of bodies and are entwined in a mesh of mutual reconstitution and reconfiguration of the world because they are, at the same time, corporeally enacted. Stigmatisation, or any form of discrimination or verbal abuse, is at one and the same time a discursive experience, an affective lived sensation, an embodied hostility, and a molecular biochemical process – as bodies discourse, ideate and perpetrate this violence on other bodies. It is this entanglement that gives them the capacity to produce such 'consequences', that gives bodies the depth of feeling that is experienced. Analysing empirical research into these processes does not reify or 'freeze' the body or reduce it to an essentialised, static object devoid of mystery. The relations of stimulus-response or cause and effect are not a linear trajectory in the progress from the past through to the present and into the future, but are actively and performatively produced as an enfolding of past-present-future in one constitutive movement. Importantly, this is no simple recuperation of prescriptive determinacy.

It is through these seemingly paradoxical condensations that we are alerted to potential social and political ramifications of epigenetic enfoldings, effects that can shed light on difficult social issues. If we consider how to intervene into a social problem in order to bring about affirmative change, epigenetic research presents us with a challenge. As Saldanha notes, politics must be sensitive to a multitude of contingent manifestations of race and racism. These are always historically specific occurrences, each requiring its own particular attempts at a solution, telling against any generic or universal prescriptions (Saldanha 2006: 22). This, too, supports Wilson's (2015: 28) insistence that biology is political and politicised and internal to our social concerns. Because of the intergenerational hauntings by both past and future that epigenetics suggests, we are not merely interposing our remedies into a linear trajectory. We are not simply contending with the situation today if the past is still active within it as a potential future. Sustained action is required as interventions must reconfigure the embodied future potentials that are being made possible by the past, anticipations that may have been projected across several generations.

Epigenetics also suggests that words and language matter – in all senses of this term. Biology is not quarantined from injury by words; insults cannot necessarily be brushed aside but can physically wound, again and again, across generations. This epigenetic knit confounds the notion that we can, a priori, specify the boundaries of biology and the social, psyche and soma, discourse and body, past and present, the human and the non-human or human and environment. As discussed, there are many studies investigating the productivity of bodies and matter that ask perceptive questions about our experiences of embodied being. Yet in critiquing the assumptions and circumscriptions of 'empiricism' in order to emphasise the active participation of bodies in life, they appear, nonetheless, to inadvertently introduce their own foreclosures. There is Saldanha's insistence that language doesn't materialise phenotype, and affect theory's apparent proscription of investigating physiological mechanisms. The epigenetic research sampled here suggests that we should be wary of any attempts to impose circumscriptions on bodily enactments, whatever their variety. These studies instead indicate that the biological and the social are implicated within one another and distinctions we find between them are not absolute but are always materialisations that make separations in and through what is mutual in their constitutive processes. The argument here is not simply that bodies are just as productive as culture and discourse, yet still separate from them; rather, it is that bodies are *already*, through and through, everything that we conventionally imply when we speak of cultural and discursive performativity.

Notes

1. For recent research detailing this argument see Alaimo and Hekman (2008), Coole and Frost (2010) and Wilson (2015).

2. Merleau-Ponty's criticism is still of relevance. Many researchers in the physical sciences still study physiological processes in isolation as the object of enquiry. As Merleau-Ponty noted, the body is treated as chains of physico-chemical stimulus and response between discrete processes or objects, as, for example, Abramowitz and Bartolomei (2012), Cortessis et al. (2012), and Waterland and Jirtle (2003) illustrate. However, we need to ask what the root of the problem is, for we cannot deny that research in this tradition, even as we decry the methodology as purportedly erroneous, informs us of the world. The issue, I contend, is not this practice in itself, but rather, the non-recognition that phenomena are always an embodied, active, contextual entanglement, such that discrete entities of study are materialisations of how the world separates itself into seemingly independent parts.

3. For example, an affective analysis of bodies that specifically claims to be developing a 'materialist model' – yet does not engage with biology – is that of Julian Henriques (2010: 58). In examining the transmission of affective energy through dance vibrations in the Jamaican dance hall scene he wants to give a 'vibrational' rather than a social account of sound wave dynamics through a medium, in this case, the corporeality of dancers' bodies (2010: 58). Henriques offers an engaging and vivid account of the connectedness that comes from the crowd's visceral experience of the sound. The scene energises dancers, enables the music to raise them out of themselves and inspires them to dance all night (2010: 68). But despite discussing the physics of wave propagation and sound, he does not give any consideration to what effects these sound frequencies might physically have on the body (as an aside, epigenetic research suggests that physical forces such as electric fields, shear stresses, mechano-transduction and pressure – forces which encompass sound pressure waves from music – can affect gene expression (Davies 2013a: 38–9; 2013b). Nor does he investigate what biochemical or metabolic states might accompany the rapturous state of the dancers: for instance, what physical state enables participants to dance until morning on a dance night? Although providing a highly charged account of the affective forces that impel and connect the dancers, Henriques overlooks biological responsiveness when he describes the states of intense interconnectedness found in the dance scene.

4. Some perceptive research in epigenetics discerns that the social manifests in biology but struggles to come to terms with the mechanisms behind this as researchers still hold a version of the empiricist assumption of separation between discrete, self-contained fields. There is still an underlying belief that the social and the biological are separate, qualitatively

and quantitatively different domains, which sit beside each other and can somehow interact. While on the one hand researchers are asking for interdisciplinary engagement from the social sciences they nonetheless assume that there is a body which is *then* worked on by the social or the environment. This is revealed in statements such as, 'disentangling the genetic and environmental contributions to cardiovascular risk is difficult, and interactions between the two factors over time can complicate the understanding' (Vik et al. 2013: 569); Satoshi Toyokawa and his colleagues include a graph delineating the relative contributions of genetics and the environment to disease (Toyokawa et al. 2012: 68); and the query of how the social environment 'gets into the mind' (Toyokawa et al. 2012: 68) or 'under the skin' (Galea et al. 2011: 400) are exemplary of this pervasive division. The logic behind these positions is that we can maintain (and calculate) the separation between biology and its environment, rather than the position that will be elaborated here, namely, that the biological is *already* social; that is, the social is always already 'under' the skin and we cannot ultimately disentangle biology from culture.

5. While Saldanha appears to state that Butler ultimately posits bodies as 'an inert exteriority to language' (Saldanha 2006: 12) her position is more complex. For Butler, biological bodies can actively resist culture's attempts to script and narrate them, so this seemingly does not preclude an active biology. However, such activity is limited to a reactivity – for Butler, these bodies do not initiate their own actions.

6. DNA methylation and histone acetylation are two of the many epigenetic mechanisms so far identified, and the ones about which scientists have the most information. The highly compressed structure of DNA makes it relatively inaccessible to the transcription machinery that inhibits or facilitates a gene's state of expression. Acetylation allows other transcription factors greater access to DNA as it lessens the electrical bonds between molecules. DNA methylation is a chemical bond between DNA and methyl groups that can either attenuate or amplify the degree of a gene's expression. The specific effect methylation has depends on many factors, including the location on the genome, and the actions of other transcription factors operating in the vicinity of the gene (Blewitt 2013).

7. See, for example, Alasaari et al. (2012), Rönn and Ling (2013) and Unternachrer ct al. (2012) for studies supporting the hypothesis that there can be immediate and ongoing epigenetic adjustments in response to environmental changes.

8. On this point see also Hannah Landecker (2011). She offers a comprehensive review of epigenetic evidence for the enfolding of history and the social within the body through food and nutrition.

9. Epigenetic processes and outcomes are not limited to the negative and dysfunctional. However, by studying the dysfunctional we can gain

insights into the usually invisible normal: what we consider normal is, just like the dysfunctional, materialised through epigenetic apparatuses of genes-in-context. All possible expressions of individual propensity are already environmental.

10. Meaney emphasises that stress reactivity is neither good nor bad in itself but must be viewed in context. Heightened stress responsivity, he notes, can actually help an individual born into challenging life circumstances to survive to adulthood. It is an individual and particular cost-benefit analysis as to whether this outweighs the propensity for later disease and the mortality risks associated with this life situation (2010: 65–6). In other words, the results are not already determined for they remain open to other forces, which nevertheless include this inheritance.

References

Abramowitz, L. K., and M. S. Bartolomei (2012), 'Genomic imprinting: recognition and marking of imprinted loci', *Current Opinion in Genetics & Development*, 22: 2, pp. 72–8.

Alaimo, S., and S. J. Hekman (2008), 'Introduction: Emerging Models of Materiality in Feminist Theory', in S. Alaimo and S. J. Hekman (eds), *Material Feminisms*, Bloomington: Indiana University Press, pp. 1–19.

Alasaari, J. S., M. Lagus, H. M. Ollila, A. Toivola, M. Kivimäki, J. Vahtera, E. Kronholm, M. Härmä, S. Puttonen and T. Paunio (2012), 'Environmental Stress Affects DNA Methylation of a CpG Rich Promoter Region of Serotonin Transporter Gene in a Nurse Cohort', *PLoS ONE*, 7: 9, e45813. doi:10.1371/journal.pone.0045813

Barad, K. (2007), *Meeting the Universe Halfway: quantum physics and the entanglement of matter and meaning*, Durham, NC: Duke University Press.

Barad, K. (2010), 'Quantum Entanglements and Hauntological Relations of Inheritance: Dis/continuities, SpaceTime Enfoldings, and Justice-to-Come', *Derrida Today*, 3: 2, pp. 240–68.

Barad, K. (2012a), 'Intra-active Entanglements', *Kvinder, Køn & Forskning/ Women, Gender & Research*, 1–2, pp. 10–23.

Barad, K. (2012b), 'Nature's Queer Performativity', *Kvinder, Køn & Forskning/ Women, Gender & Research*, 1–2, pp. 25–53.

Blackman, L., and C. Venn (2010), 'Affect', *Body & Society*, 16: 1, pp. 7–28.

Blewitt, M. (2013), 'Epigenetic control of gene expression', available at <https://www.coursera.org/course/epigenetics> (last accessed 2 July 2013).

Coole, D. (2010), 'The Inertia of Matter and the Generativity of Flesh', in D. Coole and S. Frost (eds), *New Materialisms: Ontogeny, Agency, and Politics*, Durham, NC: Duke University Press, pp. 92–115.

Coole, D., and S. Frost (2010), 'Introducing the New Materialisms', in D. Coole and S. Frost (eds), *New Materialisms: Ontology, Agency, and Politics*, Durham, NC: Duke University Press, pp. 1–43.

Cortessis, V. K., D. C. Thomas, A. J. Levine, C. V. Breton, T. M. Mack, K. D. Siegmund, R. W. Haile and P. W. Laird (2012), 'Environmental epigenetics: prospects for studying epigenetic mediation of exposure-response relationships', *Human Genetics*, 131: 10, pp. 1565–89.

Crepaldi, L., and A. Riccio (2009), 'Chromatin learns to behave', *Epigenetics*, 4: 1, pp. 23–6.

Cropley, J. E., C. M. Suter, K. B. Beckman and D. I. K. Martin (2006), 'Germ-line epigenetic modification of the murine A^{vy} allele by nutritional supplementation', *Proceedings of the National Academy of Sciences*, 103: 46, pp. 17308–12.

Davies, P. (2013a), 'Exposing cancer's deep evolutionary roots', *Physics World*, 26: 7, pp. 37–40.

Davies, P. (2013b), 'Physicist versus cancer', available at <www.abc.net.au/radionational/programs/breakfast/physicist-versus-cancer/4872614> (last accessed 8 August 2013).

Galea, S., M. Uddin and K. C. Koenen (2011), 'The urban environment and mental disorders: epigenetic links', *Epigenetics*, 6: 4, pp. 400–4.

Gallou-Kabani, C., and C. Junien (2005), 'Nutritional Epigenomics of Metabolic Syndrome: New Perspective Against the Epidemic', *Diabetes*, 54 (July), pp. 1899–906.

Harper, L. V. (2005), 'Epigenetic Inheritance and the Intergenerational Transfer of Experience', *Psychological Bulletin*, 131: 3, pp. 340–60.

Henriques, J. (2010), 'The Vibrations of Affect and their Propagation on a Night Out on Kingston's Dancehall Scene', *Body & Society*, 16: 1, pp. 57–89.

Hesman Saey, T. (2013), 'From Great Grandma to You: Epigenetic changes reach down through the generations', *Science News*, 183: 7, p. 18.

Hoffmann, A., and D. Spengler (2012), 'The lasting legacy of social stress on the epigenome of the hypothalamic-pituitary-adrenal axis', *Epigenomics*, 4: 4, pp. 431–44.

Kirby, V. (1997), *Telling Flesh: the Substance of the Corporeal*, New York: Routledge.

Kirby, V. (2011), *Quantum Anthropologies: Life at Large*, Durham, NC: Duke University Press.

Kirby, V. (2012), 'Initial Conditions', *differences: A Journal of Feminist Cultural Studies*, 23: 3, pp. 197–205.

Kuzawa, C. W., and E. Sweet (2009), 'Epigenetics and the Embodiment of Race: Developmental Origins of US Racial Disparities in Cardiovascular Health', *American Journal of Human Biology*, 21: 1, pp. 2–15.

Landecker, H. (2011), 'Food as exposure: Nutritional epigenetics and the new metabolism', *BioSocieties*, 6: 2, pp. 167–94.

Latour, B. (2004), 'How to Talk About the Body? The Normative Dimension of Science Studies', *Body & Society*, 10: 2–3, pp. 205–29.

Lund, R., U. Christensen, B. E. Holstein, P. Due and M. Osier (2006), 'Influence of marital history over two and three generations on early death. A longitudinal study of Danish men born in 1953', *Journal of Epidemiology and Community Health*, 60: 6, pp. 496–501.

McGowan, P. O., A. Sasaki, A. C. D'Alessio, S. Dymov, B. Labonté, M. Szyf, G. Turecki and M. J. Meaney (2009), 'Epigenetic regulation of the glucocorticoid receptor in human brain associates with childhood abuse', *Nature Neuroscience*, 12: 3, pp. 342–8.

Meaney, M. J. (2001), 'Maternal Care, Gene Expression, and the Transmission of Individual Differences in Stress Reactivity Across Generations,' *Annual Review of Neuroscience*, 24, pp. 161–1161.

Meaney, M. J. (2010), 'Epigenetics and the Biological Definition of Gene x Environment Interactions', *Child Development*, 81: 1, pp. 41–79.

Merleau-Ponty, M. ([1962] 2002), *Phenomenology of Perception*, trans. C. Smith, London: Routledge Classics.

Meyer, I. H. (2003), 'Prejudice, Social Stress, and Mental Health in Lesbian, Gay, and Bisexual Populations: Conceptual Issues and Research Evidence', *Pyschological Bulletin*, 129: 5, pp. 674–97.

Modin, B. (2003), 'Born out of wedlock and never married – it breaks a man's heart', *Social Science & Medicine*, 57: 3, pp. 487–501.

Modin, B., D. Vågerö, J. Hallqvist and I. Koupil (2008), 'The contribution of parental and grandparental childhood social disadvantage to circulatory disease diagnosis in young Swedish men', *Social Science & Medicine*, 66: 4, pp. 822–34.

Modin, B., I. Koupil and D. Vågerö (2009), 'The impact of early twentieth century illegitimacy across three generations. Longevity and intergenerational health correlates', *Social Science & Medicine*, 68: 9, pp. 1633–40.

Nature Editorial (2012), 'Life Stresses', *Nature*, 490: 7419, p. 143.

Reik, W. (2007), 'Stability and flexibility of epigenetic gene regulation in mammalian development', *Nature*, 447: 24 May, pp. 425–32.

Rönn, T., and C. Ling (2013), 'Effect of exercise on DNA methylation and metabolism in human adipose tissue and skeletal muscle', *Epigenomics*, 5: 6, pp. 603–5.

Saldanha, A. (2006), 'Reontologising race: the machinic geography of phenotype', *Environment and Planning D: Society and Space*, 24: 1, pp. 9–24.

Sweet, E. (2010), '"If your shoes are raggedy you get talked about": Symbolic and material dimensions of adolescent social status and health', *Social Science & Medicine*, 70: 12, pp. 2029–35.

Toyokawa, S., M. Uddin, K. C. Koenen and S. Galea (2012), 'How does the social environment "get into the mind"? Epigenetics at the intersection of social and psychiatric epidemiology', *Social Science & Medicine*, 74: 1, pp. 67–74.

Unternaehrer, E., P. Luers, J. Mill, E. Dempster, A. H. Meyer, S. Staehli, R. Lieb, D. H. Hellhammer and G. Meinlschmidt (2012), 'Dynamic changes in DNA methylation of stress-associated genes (*OXTR, BDNF*) after acute psychosocial stress', *Translational Psychiatry*, 2: August, e150 doi:10.1038/tp.2012.77.

Vik, K. L., P. Romundstad and T. I. L. Nilson (2013), 'Tracking of cardiovascular risk factors across generations: family linkage within the population-based HUNT study, Norway', *Journal of Epidemiology and Community Health*, 67: 7, pp. 564–70.

Waterland, R. A. and R. L. Jirtle (2003), 'Transposable elements: targets for early nutritional effects on epigenetic gene regulation', *Molecular and Cellular Biology*, 23: 15, pp. 5293–300.

Williams, D. R., S. A. Mohammed, J. Leavell and C. Collins (2010), 'Race, socioeconomic status, and health: Complexities, ongoing challenges, and research opportunities', *Annals of the New York Academy of Sciences*, 1186, pp. 69–101.

Wilson, E. A. (2015), *Gut Feminism*, Durham, NC: Duke University Press.

Zhang, Tie-Yuan and M. J. Meaney (2010), 'Epigenetics and the Environmental Regulation of the Genome and Its Function', *Annual Review of Psychology*, 61, pp. 439–66.

CHAPTER 7

Racialised Visual Encounters

Xin Liu

The question of race is often approached as an epistemological problem, predicated on readings and representations of visible differences, such as 'hair type, nose shape and skin colour' (Alcoff 2002: 14). On this account, race is understood discursively, as 'an ideology, a narrative' (Saldanha 2006: 9). Importantly, in this line of inquiry, the seemingly neutral act of seeing is subjected to scrutiny. The practices of visual representation – 'the King of the senses' (Braidotti 2011: 107) – are considered to be crucial to the genesis of the modern human subject. For example, in her analysis of 'the process of speciation', Megan H. Glick argues that visual representation as a form of 'ocular anthropomorphism' entails 'the dualistic movement between processes of racialisation and speciation' (2012: 99). Similarly, drawing on a Foucauldian conceptualisation of the 'Classical episteme', Linda Martin Alcoff notes that Western fetishistic classifying practices which delineate and differentiate natural terrains and types, such as map-making and table-drawing, emerged simultaneously with the 'metaphysical and moral hierarchies between racialised categories of human beings' (2002: 13).

In reconfiguring what is taken as self-evidently visual in racialised and anthropocentric perceptual practices, the above accounts provide strong critiques against an 'ocular consciousness' (Glick 2012: 99), characteristic of the sovereign and disembodied human subject, coded as white and masculine. Moreover, the immediacy of phenotypes is now considered 'a produced obviousness' (Alcoff 2002: 14). In other words, the direction of essentialism's logic of causality is reversed, so that the visible racial differences are understood as the result of, rather than the cause and justification for, various forms of racism.

And yet we should not be surprised that, despite such interrogations, the visual registry continues to function as a powerful determinant, mediating everyday racialised encounters. As Alcoff writes,

> the processes by which racial identities are produced work through the shapes and shades of human morphology, and subordinate other markers such as dress, customs and practices. And the visual registry thus produced has been correlated with rational capacity, epistemic reliability, moral condition and, of course, aesthetic status. (2002: 16)

Given the primacy of the visual in racialised social relations, Alcoff argues for the importance of taking into account the practices of the visual, without falling back into any naturalising appeal to phenotypic race in terms of original essence. For Alcoff, one of the ways to achieve a contextual and located understanding of racial designation is to situate the analysis in a phenomenological description of the visual mediation that informs 'the way we read ourselves and the way others read us' (2002: 16).

In attending to the terms through which racialised visual practices operate, it may be argued that racialised and feminised others could appropriate the gaze in situated encounters, and produce an 'oppositional gaze, of looking back or claiming the visual field, rather than looking down or being the object of visual inspection' (Griffin and Braidotti 2002: 223). Yet, in this model of encounter, the self-presence of an ocular consciousness, the very stuff of how it works or what it is, is left unquestioned, which unwittingly returns to the logic of presence/absence that has enabled the white racist gaze in the first place. Even when the process of subjectification is acknowledged, it remains contested as to whether and how to approach the materiality of phenotypes (Saldanha 2006). And further to this, it is unclear exactly how the field of the visible can be transformed, given the deep-rooted racial prejudices that often take the form of stereotypes. Is it at all possible to read otherwise?

The Materialisation of Racialised Bodies

In light of these concerns, Judith Butler's engagement with the question of race in 'Endangered/Endangering: Schematic Racism and White Paranoia' proves important, for it offers a performative account of seeing that real-ises racialised bodies. In this piece, Butler offers a critical commentary on the Rodney King case, where the video evidence was thought by many at the time to be self-evidently an attack by police on King, and not the other way around. Central to Butler's analysis is the workings of a 'white racist episteme', as a 'historically self-renewing practice of reading' (Butler 1993a: 22) which structures the visual field. It functions as the *precedent* and *antecedent* of regulatory norms that order the messy field of the visual into a coherent and intelligible narrative. As Butler writes, 'the white paranoiac forms a sequence of narrative intelligibility that consolidates the racist figure of the black man' (1993a: 16), whose 'body is circumscribed as dangerous, prior to any gesture, any raising of the hand' (18).

Butler depicts a scene in which the white racist episteme materialises or real-ises racialised bodies. In examining the *how* of the interpretation processes that render the beaten body as the source of violence, Butler argues that seeing is not a direct or neutral perception. Rather, it is a political construal of the visible, symptomatic of a racialised visual episteme, which is 'hegemonic and forceful' (Butler 1993a: 17). This means that what is seen is itself a racial formation, integral to a racialised visual economy that discriminates, 'orchestrates and interprets (Butler 1993a: 20). Positing the body as a sign, Butler's account radically calls into question the referential stability of phenotypical differences as the immutable ground and the incontestable truth of hierarchical racial positioning. Importantly, this provocative argument does not simply reverse, but radically confounds the terms of linear causality that inform most racist narrative. As Butler makes explicit, 'This signification produces as an *effect* of its own procedure the very body that it nevertheless and simultaneously claims to discover as that which *precedes* it own action' (1993b: 30; emphasis in original).

The (re)production of what counts as valuable and intelligible is, for Butler, kernel to the political economy that (re)produces hierarchical differences that justify forms of violence, exclusion and denigration. At stake here is the condition of limit-ing, or the 'logic of morphing' (Kirby 2006: 84). According to Butler, the bodily contour is a permanently shifting and negotiated interface of interior and exterior, self and other. Drawing on several theoretical frameworks, Butler's conceptualisation of contour/threshold is understood in terms of 'interpolation [*sic*] (Althusser), enunciation (Benveniste), body imago (Lacan), and inscription (Foucault)' (Kirby 1997: 126). Given that Butler's reading of race here draws on Franz Fanon's notion of a 'historico-racial schema' (Fanon cited in Butler 1993a: 20), which challenges the Lacanian model of the mirror stage (for it shows that a racialised and racialising dynamic is already present in the formation of a bodily image (Ahmed 2000: 59–60)), I want to focus on Butler's reading of bodily contour in terms of bodily imago.

In Lacan's thesis of the imago, individuation and identification take place through the unstable dynamic of projection and misrecognition of imaginary bodily contours. This specular image is an idealised totality that confers a visual integrity and coherence, which is in fact a compensatory mask of the irretrievable loss of original unity. Significantly, the inevitable ambiguity of bodily ego/imago – as 'a visual fiction', 'a site of *méconnaissance*' (Butler 1993b: 138) – has profound implications for the earlier discussion of ocular consciousness in racialised encounters. First of all, given that the ego as imago is the relation of identification, which can never be finally achieved, the phantasy of a self-present subject – capable of exercising an objectifying gaze that is itself coherent – is radically qualified. Secondly, since the morphological scheme that inaugurates the ego also provides grids of intelligibility – 'the threshold of the visible world' (Kirby 2006: 58) – the racist phantasy that renders racialised others radically different and separate will prove futile. As Vicki Kirby observes,

> how we perceive the difference between people, objects and their inter-relationships (the shape and definition of otherness) will be extruded through a corporeal imaginary which has constitutive force: the subject *is* this process, where the differentiation of world and ego emerge in the same reflex/reflection. (2006: 58)

Not only is the question of 'who sees and reads' in racialised encounters radically confounded, but the materiality of racialised bodies is also cast in a new light. Following Franz Fanon, Butler argues that 'the black male body is constituted through fear, and through a naming and a seeing' (1993a: 18). This reading is exemplary of Butler's conceptualisation of corporeality and materialisation. For Butler, there is no outside of signification, for 'every effort to refer to materiality takes place through a signifying process which, in its phenomenality, is always already material' (1993b: 68). It is important to note that the term 'material' here does not connote the 'in-itself of matter' (Kirby 2006: 69). Kirby's reading of this detail is especially informative. As she writes,

> the argument that the body's substance is a sign rather than a fixed solidity or prescriptive referent is furthered in the happy coincidence between the words 'matter' and 'materialize'. While these words evoke a *notion* of physical substance, these signs are also synonyms for 'meaning' and the larger semantic process of meaning-making . . . (2006: 69; emphasis in original)

Butler posits the phenomenality of the visual (and the aural) as the materiality of the signifier, which 'will signify only to the extent that it is impure, contaminated by the ideality of differentiating relations, the tacit structuring of a linguistic context that is illimitable in principle' (1993b: 68). Given Butler's vigorous attention to initial conditions, in this account, the nature of phenomenality is assumed, and problematically rendered as 'the substantive, material anchor of signification' (Kirby 1997: 110). For if 'what appears only signifies by virtue of those non-phenomenal relations, i.e., relations of differentiation' (Butler 1993b: 68), it seems that the process – the *how* of appearing visibly and aurally – is severed from what is understood as non-phenomenal.

Undoubtedly, Butler's examination of the maintenance work that enables the anticipating and inscriptive efficacy of white paranoiac visual perception is an important intervention, for it is precisely the denial and erasure of its operation that reproduces 'a white racist imaginary that postures *as if* it were the unmarked frame of the visible field, laying claim to the authority of "direct perception"' (1993a: 19; emphasis in original). Nevertheless, its implication is undercut by virtue of the incommensurable gap that Butler installs between signifier and signified, as well as between sign and referent. For Butler, the irretrievable loss of the referent or a prior moment, determines the sign's purported failure, and functions as the momentum that propels its recitation. Given this, Butler argues that it is precisely within the historicity of the sign – the necessity of its reiteration – that the potential for transformation, that is, for reading otherwise – is located. For if seeing is a political construal, a cultural formation, then its inherent instability (because of the slippage of meaning) necessarily involves the process of re-signification. It follows then that it is only through reiterated readings that 'the workings of racial constraints on what it means to "see"' (Butler 1993a: 16) may be called into question.

However, if the racialised visual episteme is equated with an oppressive notion of power that always already delimits perception as cultural imprint, then it remains unclear how to read differently within the 'racially saturated field of visibility' (Butler 1993a: 15). As Butler herself acknowledges,

> it is not, then, a question of negotiating between what is 'seen', on the one hand, and a 'reading' which is imposed upon the visual evidence, on the other. In a sense, the problem is even worse: to the extent that there is a racist organization and disposition of the visible, it will work to circumscribe what qualifies as visual evidence, such that it is in some cases impossible to establish the 'truth' of racist brutality through recourse to visual evidence. (1993a: 17)

Eye-to-Eye and Skin-to-Skin Encounters

In feminist theory, Sara Ahmed's work is regarded as contributing significantly to the discussion of affect and racialisation. Nevertheless, there is a similarity in Ahmed's and Butler's frameworks in respect of their structural commitments to, and political investigations of, difference understood as a gap, or break, which calls for further analysis. For example, Ahmed locates the analysis of race in encounters, understood as involving various forms of gaps between: histories of encounters and the present moment of contact, the visual economy and the affective economy or the modality of eye-to-eye and skin-to-skin, 'unconscious emotions' (2004: 44) and conscious recognition. Taking cues from Butler's formulation of performativity, Ahmed understands these gaps as the inevitable consequence of the cut from histories of encounters and the repression of ideas 'to which the feeling may have been first (but provisionally) connected' (2004: 44). Because of an 'imperfect translation of the past' (Ahmed 2004: 184), these gaps inevitably implicate potentially transformative moments of hesitation 'between the domain of the particular – the face to face of this encounter – and the general – the framing of the encounter by broader relationships of power and antagonism' (Ahmed 2000: 8).

Finding in Butler's consideration of bodily boundary the important attention to historicity, Ahmed supplements the economy of the visual with the affective. Whereas the former involves 'techniques for differentiating' (Ahmed 2000: 3) through racialised visual coding, the latter is a process in which emotions and feelings, as impressions felt on the skin, 'circulate between signifiers in relationships of difference and displacement' (Ahmed 2004: 44). For Ahmed, an encounter implies both eye-to-eye and skin-to-skin modalities that converge on the surface of the body. Conjoining the affective with the visual, Ahmed argues that an intervention into any one perceptual modality will always involve other, related concerns.

First, the configuration of skin as 'a border that feels' (Ahmed 2000: 45; emphasis in original) affords an account of racialisation that is attentive to the lived experiences of racialised others. Second, the metonymic sliding of affects critiques 'the tyranny of the visible' (Alcoff 2002: 19), which marks the hyper-visibility of racialised others that renders unassailable the invisibility of whiteness. As Ahmed dilates,

> the skin is not simply invested with meaning as a visual signifier of difference (the skin as coloured, the skin as wrinkled, and so on). It is not simply implicated in the (scopophilic) logic of fetishism where the visual object, the object which *can* be seen, becomes the scene of the play of differences. (2000: 44; emphasis in original)

The proposition that the surface of skin as a bodily boundary 'is felt only in the event of being "impressed upon" in the encounters we have with others' (Ahmed 2004: 25), significantly qualifies the racist phantasy of segregation and homogeneity. On this account, affective contamination is always already implicated in the boundary formation of a supposedly pure and undifferentiated whiteness. For example, commenting on the economy of xenophobia, Ahmed argues that it 'involves not just reading the stranger's body as dirt and filth, but the re-forming of the contours of the body-at-home, through the very affective gestures that enable the withdrawal from co-habitation with strangers in a given social space' (2000: 54).

Last but not least, drawing on critical insights from psychoanalytic accounts of unconscious emotions and Marxian notions of value, Ahmed posits that repression – the '"absent presence" of historicity' (2004: 45) – motors the affective, all the while contributing to the stickiness of signs that accumulate affective value as they circulate. The question, 'what sticks?', centres on Ahmed's interrogation of the repetition and reproduction of stereotypes and racial prejudices. As she writes, '"What sticks?" . . . is a reposing of other, perhaps more familiar, questions: Why is social transformation so difficult to achieve? Why are relations of power so intractable and enduring, even in the face of collective forms of resistance?' (Ahmed 2004: 11–12).

Especially this last point needs to be read in relation to Ahmed's general political project. Ahmed's primary concern is to account for the specificity of hierarchical differences, that is, which differences come to matter, a question that moves beyond the essentialist reification of racial differences that feeds racism. She is also critical of the postmodernist indifference to the specificity of difference, here, that of racialised others, as well as the privileging of mobility in narratives that celebrate nomadism, indeterminacy and the free-floating play of difference. As Ahmed notes, 'that chain of endless deferral, that seemingly open fluidity, is halted at certain points, partially fixed in the process of becoming intelligible' (1998: 129). With this in mind, it becomes clear that Ahmed's anti-essentialist account of race requires an economy of signification that operates without positive terms, and one which is manifested in the visual and the affective. In order to keep the question of origin moving, Ahmed endeavours to hold in tension the processes of circulation and blockage that resonate with the 'determined, but not fully determined' (2000: 6) nature of racialised and racialising encounters.

This approach is significant to Ahmed's analysis of 'relations of othering' that 'contest[s] the model of race as a bodily attribute' (2004: 16). A good example of this is Ahmed's reading of the 'effect and affect' (2004: 59) of economies of hate. Let's first recall Butler's reading of the Rodney King case. Butler's analysis of the racialised visual episteme makes explicit the ways in which the inverted projections of white paranoia render the black man's body hateful and fearsome. Similarly, Ahmed acknowledges the racialising effect of the visual, whereby phenotypical differences function as 'the visual prompt that triggers identity thinking' (2000: 129). And yet, Ahmed worries that a mere focus on the visual registry may run the risk of reinstalling the assumption that hate resides in particular bodies of/as signs because of the 'fetishisation of skin colour' (2000: 130), which is 'seen to hold the truth of the subject's identity' (131). When, for example, Ahmed reads John Griffin's *Black Like Me*, 'an autobiographical account of a white man who receives medical help to alter the colour of his skin so that he can "discover" the truth of being black' (2000: 130), she writes,

> his transformation into a stranger, where he passes as black in the mirror, produces the naked face of the black man, a face that immediately gets coded as fierce and glaring, as monstrous and bestial. In passing as black in his own mirror image, the vision of the black face is hence over-determined by the 'knowledges' available of blackness central to the violence of colonialism. (131)

For Ahmed, bodies of/as signs of hate tend to stick 'because they become attached *through* particular affects' (2004: 60; emphasis in original), which are 'visceral and bodily' (58). In light of this, Ahmed asserts that at stake is the question of how emotions are actually produced in racialised encounters, for thinking through this aspect of the puzzle assists in making visible the 'contingent rather than necessary' (2000: 54) association between objects and emotions, as the term 'sticky' indicates. Related to this, Ahmed offers a performative account of hate that operates 'by providing "evidence" of the very antagonism it affects' (2004: 52). As she explicates, 'in *seeing* the other as "being" hateful, the subject is filled up with hate, which becomes a sign of the "truth" of the *reading*' (Ahmed 2004: 52, emphasis added). In laying bare the contingency and historicity of the subject and object of emotions, Ahmed hopes to open up possibilities for seeing and knowing differently.

Nevertheless, as Ahmed's description of the performativity of hate makes clear, her account of affect remains primarily visual. To put this differently, the histories of visual perception, limited by social regimes of significance, structure and condition the realm of the affective within the horizon of cultural intelligibility. In a similar vein to Butler's theorisation of visual perception, the affective economy in Ahmed's account focuses upon the problem of limiting conditions. Again, we are made to wonder about the actual possibility of generating alternative readings that might enable political contestation, for it seems that an oppositional and prohibitive conception of power, one that also informs how signification works, foregrounds Butler's and Ahmed's interpretation of limit-ing conditions in the first instance. This is evident, for example, in Ahmed's understanding of sociality as an antagonistic differentiation, opposed to inclusion and the with-ness of corporeal generosity. Butler's and Ahmed's interventions rest on the shared notion that prohibition induces a reconfiguration of approach. Inasmuch as perception always moves, it will never faithfully represent a referent that escapes culture, and this implies that a certain failure of fit, a mis-measure, is inevitable. However, it is precisely this movement that heralds the possibility of change. Nevertheless, Butler and Ahmed understand this 'within-ness' as a failure to see what is really there, what could be there if we weren't encumbered with prejudice. The problem with this position is that if affective visual perception is always negative and oppressive in the first and last instance, then it is unclear exactly what will enable and substantiate the leap to its potential undecidable and subversive outcome, or, in terms of what Butler hopes for, how 'a contest within the visual field, a crisis in the certainty of what is visible' (1993a: 16) might be achieved.

Moving Beyond the Visual

Writing in the context of the racialisation process of the turbaned Sikh, Jasbir Puar acknowledges the importance of Butler's and Ahmed's interventions, but remains unconvinced of the political efficacy in the performative reiteration of seeing. If the visual field is so thoroughly saturated by the historic-racial schema and constrained within the realm of the cultural and the discursive, then, according to Puar, it seems that the only way out of this epistemological, ocular economy is by moving beyond and outside its confinement. As she writes,

> Butler and Ahmed rely on acts of reading to contest epistemological truths; that is, the logic of visibility is challenged through the logic of visibility by pointing out the instability of visual evidence, rather than moving aside the visual, however momentarily, as the primary epistemological terrain of racial knowledge. Similarly, the logic of signification is contested through pointing out the instability of signs. (Puar 2007: 189)

Part of Puar's concern is that the pre-emptive and anticipating force of the visual entails a paranoid logic that will endlessly confirm and reconstitute its own racialised reading. Instead, Puar opts for the perceptual realm of the tactile (and/or the haptic). Following Brian Massumi, Puar approaches affect and bodily matters not as an effect of cultural inscription, but as 'the body's "visceral sensibility"' which 'precedes sense perception' (2007: 189) and 'reasserts ontological rather than epistemological knowing' (194). For Puar, the implication of the disparities between conceptions of bodily participation is considerable. Instead of rendering the body as a sign, Puar argues that the antedating nature of bodily visceral sensibility provides a site of intervention *before* and *beyond* the 'discursive baggage' (2007: 184) and 'representational weight' (191) of racial prejudice.

Rather than focusing on the limiting conditions, Puar attends to the conditions of emergence. Whereas limit-ing conditions, or the logic of morphing, concern the operation of regulatory norms that always already structure and constitute what counts as intelligible, the condition of emergence sheds light on the ontogenetic priority that is itself a field of affective intensity. In light of this, discursive structures, or cultural grids of intelligibility, are understood as forms of relative stasis that derive and emerge from a state of flux, that is, *affect before representation*. Instead, Puar understands affect in its 'ontogenetic dimension', 'as prior to representation – prior to race, class, gender, sex, nation, even as these categories might be the most pertinent mapping of or reference back to affect itself' (215). Whereas visuality freezes bodies in cultural frames of sorts, the ontogenetic difference takes the expression of 'movements, intensities, emotions, energies, affectivities, and textures as they inhabit events, spatiality, and corporealities' (215). In accordance with this reading of affect, Puar endorses Saldanha's theorisation of phenotypical encounters, attentive to 'the matter of phenotype and how phenotype matters' (190). Given the visual connotations of phenotypes, the proposition that the tactility of phenotypical encounters is somehow before and beyond visual perception is indeed curious and confusing. For how are phenotypical differences perceived as such?

In contrast to Ahmed's reading of encounters wherein the regulatory and hegemonic mechanism of racialisation imposes itself upon bodies 'through the force of historically blighted signifiers that metonymically link and bleed into each other' (Puar 2007: 190), in Puar and Saldanha's formulation, phenotypical difference in itself is regarded as operating through the autonomous affect that is 'unmediated, in all of its *connective glory*' (Saldanha 2006: 22, emphasis added). This unmediated and autonomous phenotypical encounter is understood as,

> the encounter of smell, sweat, flushes of heat, dilation of pupils, the impulses
> bodies pick up from each other, the contagion of which *we know little*, the sense
> of being touched without having been physically touched, of having seen without having physically seen. (Puar 2007: 190, emphasis added)

In sum, by rendering encounters in corporeal terms Puar aims to 'comprehend power beyond disciplinary regulatory models' (215). Of particular importance to Puar's 'affective politics' (215) is the common ground she shares with Butler and Ahmed, namely, the taken-for-granted understanding of what constitutes an ocular economy – visuality as seeing through the eyes (which Puar interprets as the physical fact of seeing) – as an overdetermined, epistemological and cultural construction where power's intention is to restrict and to prohibit. Ironically, given Puar's vehement challenge to the fixation of difference in poststructuralist epistemology, her investment in the affective must nevertheless depend upon and therefore reinstall this reading, interpretation, and representation of the visual as fixed and somehow incorporeal when compared to tactility.

Returning to the question of sensorial, translative involvement posed earlier, we will recall that Puar holds that bodily affective contagion cannot be known to us, because '"something recognizable" [is already] a quality (or property)' (Massumi cited in Puar 2007: 281). However, given this, the question remains as to how the 'subtraction' (Massumi 2002: 58) and registration of 'excitation' and '*intensity*' (2002: 61) from the purported fixity of the symbolic order might actually proceed. This puzzle is clearly exemplified in Puar's elaboration of bodily visceral sensibility:

> 'It anticipates the translation of the sight or sound or touch perception into
> something recognizable associated with an identifiable object'. So the lungs
> spasm even before the senses cognate the presence of a shadow in a 'dark street
> at night in a dangerous part of town'. The 'dangerous part of town' and the
> shadows are *then* the identifiable objects for which epistemic force is confirmed
> only *after*, or more accurately, as affective response *has taken place*. (2007: 189,
> emphasis added)

In the above description, there is a clear sense of a mind/body split, in the form of a temporal and spatial linearity. The very meat of the body, the lungs in this case, generate affective and active response *before* intellection, understood as culturally constrained epistemological knowing. Yet, Puar is quick to assert that affect as ontogenetic difference is not a matter of '"pre" . . . through temporality' (2007: 214), nor is it in a relation of 'relay between stasis and flux' (215). It is 'a temporality and a spatialization that has yet to be imagined' (214).

If, as Puar claims, affect occupies an ontologically different order 'yet to be imagined' – quite different from an epistemological one which presumably is imaginable, then we are left with something of a riddle. Simply put, given this radical abyss, this in-between the ontogenetic and epistemological, it is unclear how one can perceive these bodily responses at all. What is it that falls between these two orders of experience? After all, how can the ontogenetic affect exist 'outside' our ability to be affected by it? Recall that in Ahmed's formulation of racialised encounters, individuation and differences are said to arise from encounters. As she notes,

> identity itself is constituted in the 'more than one' of the encounter: the designation of an 'I' or 'we' requires an encounter with others. These others cannot simply be relegated to an outside: given that the subject comes into existence as an entity only through encounters with others, then the subject's existence cannot be separated from the others who are encountered. As such, the encounter itself is ontologically prior to the question of ontology (the question of the being who encounters). (Ahmed 2000: 7)

Distinct from the immediacies of affective corporeal sociality in Puar's and Saldanha's propositions of phenotypical encounters, Ahmed posits encounters as performative, which 'cannot, then, be detached or isolated from such broader relations of antagonism' (2000: 9). In other words, the absent present historicity, as the limit of intelligibility, foregrounds the very designation of '"the encounter" as such' (Ahmed 2000: 9). Interestingly, Ahmed concedes that an encounter 'involve(s) surprise', because it 'is not a meeting between already constituted subjects who know each other: rather the encounter is premised on the absence of a knowledge that would allow one to control the encounter, or to predict its outcome' (2000: 8). This description of encounter seems to be echoing that of Puar's, at least in terms of the surprising, multi-layered and enlivening possibilities that may be generated. Are these two notions of encounter radically different? Or can we entertain the possibility that the enclosure and limitation of performative encounter confined within the social/the cultural is implicated with/in the corporeal sociality in phenotypical encounters?

If we can agree in the main with Ahmed's postulation of encounter as the foundational framing that accompanies any ontological question, and if we add this to Puar's reading of ontogenetic differences, could we perhaps interpret these seemingly different encounters – their enclosure within two distinct and segregated orders – as a bifurcation which is affected by, through and as, a generalised self-encounter which the organism has with itself?

In sum, what seems to be presented here are two expressions of the same racialisation process. Butler and Ahmed locate the transformative potential in the instability of signs and various gaps. Puar, following Saldanha and Massumi, stresses the necessity to account for bodily experiences before and beyond the visual register. It is unclear, however, how the tactile and the haptic can be neatly severed from the visual (before, beyond, outside of), because as Puar herself concedes, phenotype is experienced 'through the haptic where the visual induces the sensation of touch' (2007: 190). But what is most intriguing here is that in segregating 'ontological becoming' *and* 'epistemological knowing' (Puar 2007: 196), as well as the bodily sensation in itself *from* the visual – because mediated by the racialised economy of signification – two modes of racialisation, isolated temporally and spatially, are said to be at work.

However, in an attempt to both explain and counter prejudice, is it possible to close off the realm of the sensible as if it exists as an absolute exteriority? If so, what would be the locatable difference, the in-between that mediates and communicates with these two modalities of racialisation? To put this differently, if bodily, visceral sensibility precedes culturally mediated perception, as Puar understands it, and by extension, if the neurobiological precedes the socio-political as nature precedes culture, then the question remains as to where and how the transition from the former to the latter can proceed.

It is to this extent that the conceptualisation of racialised encounters seems unnecessarily circumscribed in both frameworks. And yet a generalisation of encounter that affirms the historicity and specificity of visuality and tactility, *with* Butler and Ahmed, could be read in a way that will acknowledge Puar's concern about corporeal sociality, not as an absolute exteriority, but as always already knitted into an economy of signification. For if encounter is what affords ontological interrogation of the question 'what is', as Ahmed notes, as well as the production of any difference, any identity, then the construction of the insurmountable barrier that severs corporeal substance as an absolute exteriority (outside and beneath) from the materialisation (cultural construal) of skin is radically qualified. Vicki Kirby offers a compelling contribution to this issue that can assist us here.

> By remaining on the body's surface its internal meat needn't be mentioned: it is simply excluded from corporeal reinscription, its process and registration. Thus, although signification is an operation whose very experience and possibility is registered and forged through the entirety of the body's biological and perceptual apparatuses – our neurological maps, cognitive representations, sensate recordings, expressions and translations, and so on – Butler's thesis must refuse any suggestion that biological substance might be semiological in nature . . . What is it that actually creates and receives inscriptions if it is not the body's interior complexity? And if that interiority reads and writes those inscriptions (because it must be in the nature of biology to do this), then need we assume that flesh itself is outside, or before, textuality/language? (2006: 83)

What could be a more illuminating argument that continues to address political concerns might be to conceive encounter as 'the relational dynamic of sociality itself' (Kirby 2006: 114) in order to open up the very identity of power, language, corporeality and visuality as the generative nature of the Sensible that encounters and produces itself in all its expressions. If reading and writing as seeing is approached as corporeography (Kirby 1997: 83) or curiosity in corporeal terms, then visuality is a tactility that is 'utterly referential' (Kirby 2011: 124). Instead of conceding to the interpretation of visuality as seeing with eyes, vision is recast as 'a sort of wild associational and synaesthetic conversion, a supersaturation within and across all perceptual modalities, such that we hear visually, taste aurally, and so on' (Kirby 2011: 128). Thus, in this 'radical interiority of the Sensible' (Kirby 2011: 124), 'the flesh of the world' (Kirby 2011: 118), as subjectivity in general, interrogates and acquires knowledge of itself through self-encountering. 'Perception is instead likened to an ontological organ of *con*ception. It is a desiring organ that seizes upon its own alienness, and in the wonder of the encounter, is reconceived' (Kirby 2011: 120; emphasis in original).

How a Tongue Encounters its own Corporeal History

It seems fitting at this juncture to illustrate how this implicated reading of racial encounters might operate in context. Let me use as an example my practice of the Finnish rolling r, which has been one of the major difficulties in my experience of learning the Finnish language as a Chinese immigrant in Finland.

> Abril: 'Place this pen, breadthwise, in your mouth. Bite it. Now push your tongue against it. Do you feel the tip of your tongue?'
> I nod.
> Abril: 'Good. Now try to move it up and down, say, rrr.'
> 'lll'.
> Abril: 'No, no, come on, chinita, say rrr.'
> 'lll'.
> Abril: 'No, you have to practise', my Mexican friend laughed.

I am recounting this story because of encountering my own tongue in a strangely self-conscious way during my laborious practice of the rolling r. Frustrated by the stubbornness of my tongue, I tried the pen. This was said to be a trick to practise the rolling r when my Mexican friends were kids. With the tip of my tongue I pushed against the body of the pen: it was difficult to tell apart the fleshy soft surface of the tongue and the cold, hard plastic body of the pen. But this entangled feeling did enable a bodily awareness of and forceful attention onto the tip of the tongue.

The key to achieving the rolling r, or in its phonetic terminology, the alveolar trill, lies in the activation of the tongue tip in the form of 'a series of very rapid tap-like closures' (Michael and Maidment 2005: 59). This movement channels the airstream along the centre of the tongue. The Finnish voiced alveolar trill requires both the vibration of the tongue tip and the vocal chord. In fact, the pronunciation of the alveolar trill can be difficult for Finns as well. Many Finnish children have to train with a speech therapist at a very young age in order to achieve the trill pronunciation. And this is certainly interesting given that Finns often remark on the toughness of the Finnish rolling r as opposed to the softness of its Swedish counterpart – characteristic of the Finnish language in particular and the identity of Finnishness in general.

Given the considerable difficulties, it is understandable how anxious I feel every time I need to pronounce a Finnish word involving the alveolar trill. Moreover, the 'mispronunciation' of the Finnish rolling r as the consonant l, is often acknowledged as characteristic of Chinese or Asian accents. It is undoubtedly with good intentions that my Finnish teachers would often address this issue with Chinese and other Asian students at the beginning of Finnish for Foreigners courses. Stating up

front that Chinese speakers have a problem with the rolling r is meant
to smooth Chinese students' anxiety and confusion with its difficult
pronunciation. 'But it might come with practice' was an encouragement that immediately followed in most instances.

The following example is telling of such a stereotype. In the second
session of a class on Finnish for Foreigners at Turun Iltalukio, a local
evening school in the city of Turku, Finland, I conducted participant
observation, studying the process of Finnish language learning among
adult migrants. Because it was a beginner's level Finnish language
course, students were given instructions on how to practise pronuncia-
tions of the Finnish alphabet. I sat at the back of the classroom, assuming that this position would provide a better view of the whole class
and the events that would transpire. When the teacher approached me,
I was concentrating on taking notes about the practice of pronunciation – the noise of playing with tone and pitch that bodied forth from
all corners of the room. When my Finnish teacher asked if I could try to
pronounce the rolling r, a one-on-one instruction, I felt the sudden attention focused upon me. Other students nearby turned towards me and
stopped their practice. For some reason, I became nervous, feeling their
sharp gaze, their silent scrutiny and anticipation. I was fully aware that
my success rate in articulating the rolling r was (and in fact still is) very
low. The chance of getting it right in conversational situations is random, especially when I feel anxious. Nervously, my tongue tip pushed
and rubbed against the alveolar ridge. A stream of air from my lungs
was blocked by my tongue tip so that it vibrated, leading to a quick
tapping movement. 'Rrr' I voiced, a success that took me completely by
surprise. The teacher was similarly shocked and commented, 'Chinese
cannot pronounce that, which can be sometimes very problematic for
others to understand.'

What happens if this scene is approached in terms of Butler's racialised visual field? Recalling Butler's description here, the racialised body
is always circumscribed and read in certain ways, prior to any actual
gesture of the body. In other words, racialised visual regulatory norms
are 'the narrative precedent and antecedent to the frames that are
shown' (Butler 1993a: 16), which orders and rearranges the visual field
and its pluralities into a coherent fiction. In light of Butler's account
of seeing as reading and writing in the general sense, this scene can be
interpreted as a performative encounter/enactment. That is, the way in
which I was seen already performatively anticipated and materialised
how I might be heard. However, using Ahmed's account of the affective
porosity of skin, we can further argue that while the racialised visual

field sets limits to intelligibility – how I might be read and why I would probably fail – the feeling, for example, of such nervous apprehension in being read by others made me aware of the bodily boundaries and differences that set me apart from others. Yet, with Puar and Saldanha as our guide here, we also want to account for the haptic encounter, for example, the tension felt on my tongue tip – its activation, its rubbing, pressing, licking, tapping – and the blockage formed by the interaction of the tongue tip and the air stream. But how do I come to feel and register these tensions? How are they limit-ed and made intelligible? How do they emerge?

My articulation of the rolling r bodies forth the audible and palpable movement of the vibration of airstreams and articulators, a strange self-encounter that occurs *within me*. What confused and shocked the teacher and other students that gave rise to a conflicting reading of my race cannot be reduced to the ocular epistemological economy that equates seeing with perception with eyes. Rather, this visual perception of my Chineseness is already a saturated field of perception that involves a complex and intricate transvaluation and translation of the tone, pitch of my utterance and the vibration of my tongue.

In order to digest this scene from a different perspective I want to turn to Florence Chiew's work on sensory substitution. Here, we are offered another approach that again questions the rather automatic assumption that sensory modalities are somehow independent of each other. Working with research in neuroplasticity, her account of its wiring is one of interimplicated connectivity, which Chiew goes on to elaborate as an ecology of mind, or ecological tangle. As Chiew argues, 'the individual experience of perception is not separable from the general ecology of phenomena' (2012: 48). Calling into question the locatability of the origin of perception, the where and what it is that confounds the difference between perception and sociality, Chiew draws on a familiar example in phenomenological research and discusses 'the points of contact between the blind man, the cane, the object/ground'.

> The blind person's perceptual experience is oddly 'externalized' from the hand to the point of interaction between the cane and the object/ground, suggesting that the cane has been incorporated into his body schema, and one might say indeed that the cane is the hand, or that the cane *is* the eye – and even that the ground is the eye! (2012: 51; emphasis in original)

The tongue becomes tense when faced with the rolling r challenge. Can the tongue see the approaching of the teacher and the judgemental gaze of other students? Can the tongue hear the teacher's pronunciation of the rolling r? Can the tongue predict and anticipate my potential failed attempts, my accented foreign pronunciation? Do the modalities of perception re-call each other?

Chiew's work on neuroplasticity and sensory substitution cogently shows that the emergence of any modality, any 'locus' of perception, in fact any entity, involves the whole system of translation and differentiation. Rather than an absolute break or separation of *entirely* foreign entities, we could say that the origin of encounters remains strangely open, local and dispersed, a constant that continually reads and rewrites *itself*. In light of this account, the tongue sees and hears through tonguing and being tongued in practicing the rolling r. I see this scene as a stuttering moment of race not only because it is a crisis of perception that *is* the performative reiteration in which power as visibility as sensibility as sociality is astonished and confused, but one which also confirms the alienness within itself – between its own anticipation of perceiving the condensation, translation and 'convers(at)ion' (Kirby 2011: 68) of Chinese accented speech production and its actual substantiation. In doing so perception as sociality re-reads and re-writes itself, even appearing as 'not Chinese' sometimes and thereby changing for everyone what the living signifier of Chinese identity actually is. Tonguing tongued encounters *are* expressions of the scene of writing of origin, a scene which includes the intricately involved condition of limit-ing with/in emergence, integral to the performative reiterations in which race's 'arrival' will always founder and stutter.

References

Ahmed, S. (1998), *Differences that Matter: Feminist Theory and Postmodernism*, Cambridge: Cambridge University Press.

Ahmed, S. (2000), *Strange Encounters: Embodied Others in Post-Coloniality*, London: Routledge.

Ahmed, S. (2004), *The Cultural Politics of Emotion*, Edinburgh: Edinburgh University Press.

Alcoff, L. M. (2002), 'Philosophy and Racial Identity', in P. Osborne and S. Sandford (eds), *Philosophies of Race and Ethnicity*, London: Continuum, pp. 13–28.

Braidotti, R. (2011), *Nomadic Theory: The Portable Rosi Braidotti*, New York: Columbia University Press.

Butler, J. (1993a), 'Endangered/Endangering: Schematic Racism and White Paranoia', in R. Gooding-Williams (ed.), *Reading Rodney King, Reading Urban Uprising*, New York: Routledge, pp. 15–22.

Butler, J. (1993b), *Bodies That Matter: On the Discursive Limits of 'Sex'*, New York: Routledge.

Chiew, F. (2012), 'Neuroplasticity as An Ecology of Mind', *Journal of Consciousness Studies*, 19: 11–12, pp. 32–54.

Glick, M. H. (2012), 'Ocular Anthropomorphisms: Eugenics and Primatology at the Threshold of the "Almost Human"', *Social Text 112*, 30: 3, pp. 97–121.

Griffin, G., and R. Braidotti (2002), 'Whiteness and European Situatedness' in G. Griffin and R. Braidotti (eds), *Thinking Differently: A Reader in European Women's Studies*, London: Zed Books, pp. 221–36.

Kirby, V. (1997), *Telling Flesh: The Substance of the Corporeal*, New York: Routledge.

Kirby, V. (2006), *Judith Butler: Live Theory*, London and New York: Continuum.

Kirby, V. (2011), *Quantum Anthropologies: Life at Large*, Durham, NC: Duke University Press.

Massumi, B. (2002), *Parables for the Virtual: Movement, Affect, Sensation*, Durham, NC: Duke University Press.

Michael, A., and J. Maidment (2005), *Introducing Phonetic Science*, Cambridge: Cambridge University Press.

Puar, J. (2007), *Terrorist Assemblages: Homonationalism in Queer Times*, Durham, NC: Duke University Press.

Saldanha, A. (2006), 'Reontologising Race: The Machinic Geography of Phenotype', *Environment and Planning D: Society and Space*, 24: 1, pp. 9–24.

CHAPTER 8

Microbiology as Sociology: The Strange Sociality of Slime

Jacqueline Dalziell

The attribution of consciousness has always been the bedrock of how we understand and compare species being. Evolution's prized end product, it is the most prominent marker of the profound difference that identifies human achievement. Consciousness markers such as cognition, language and memory are considered to be either specific to the human, or most complex and superior in their human manifestations. That is, human consciousness is understood *as* consciousness, or, consciousness perfected. It seems fair to say that little has changed on this front since Descartes's famous dictum, 'Cogito ergo sum'. The human is still unquestionably considered *the* rational animal.

However, more recently there have been broad, interdisciplinary moves to refine our understanding of the nature of consciousness. Although productive, discourses such as animal studies and posthumanism have a tendency to rely on the logic of supplementarity for their interventionary impetus, adding or subtracting certain abilities in order to make things right. Within this framing of the problematic, the attribution of agency, for example, might be distributed to other creatures.[1]

However such redemptive gestures, which aim to transfer to the animal what were previously considered human capacities, inadvertently recuperate the very logic of anthropocentrism they claim to contest. Although the denial of cognitive capacities to animals is a political determination that is certainly questionable, it may prove that the confirmation of animal cognition is equally problematic. To grant intelligence to animals, even in an attenuated or calibrated form, continues to use a very anthropocentric understanding of intelligence as a comparative yardstick: it subsumes animal difference into a particular normative template. More to the point, it leaves the dilemma of what, exactly, we mean by intelligence very much intact – something to be affirmed or denied rather than questioned. Further, these theoretical sleights of hand make it difficult to pose a more fundamental question, namely, why the determination to locate and aggressively defend such criteria persists.

My attempt to dilate upon the subject of consciousness from a different vantage point, using slime moulds as a heuristic, provokes this foray into the natural sciences.[2] Underpinning my interest in rethinking the human/animal divide is its corollary, the two cultures problem, whose founding supposition contends that the study of culture can be neatly isolated from the scientific study of the natural world. In thinking about such divisions we enter something of a tautological impasse, wherein what we mean by consciousness informs how we conceptualise cognition and what it means to be human: put simply, each term explains and defines the other. Compellingly, pondering consciousness with slime moulds evokes an uncanny resonance with these very complicities, as it embodies a peculiar contestation of the traditional partitioning of matter from mind, nature from culture. To this end, this chapter poses certain questions: Is there humanity in the cell? Is there sociality? Is there consciousness? Indeed, could it be that within the *microbiological* we might find humanity's self-inquiry, a form of self-reflection yet one whose refracted involvements do not return us to anthropocentrism in any straightforward way?

Physarum polycephalum is an acellular slime mould. Typically observed in its plasmodial form, it resembles a small patch of bright yellow fungi. *Physarum* can embody a diversity of different microscopic and macroscopic forms, ranging from several millimeters in diameter to table size: it usually lives in damp leaf litter, slowly swarming through its environment to engulf bacteria and fungi. Visible to the naked eye, its quivering, twitching protoplasm courses almost fast enough to see it grow, and it is one of the easiest eukaryotic microbes to grow in culture.

In recent years, *Physarum* has attracted interest from the biological sciences, due in part to its unexpected level of cognitive literacy. Utilised by economists, biologists, physicists, mathematicians and cognitive scientists, *Physarum* has been chosen as a working model of decentralised modes of organisation. Its ability to consistently calculate and take the shortest path to any destination, and with what scientists are learning is a surprising level of sophistication for a brain-less organism without a nervous system, has proven astonishing. Research has discovered that slime moulds 'learn', 'memorise' events and routes, 'make decisions', 'form preferences', selectively forage for food, and solve with unexpected accuracy a range of complex challenges that scientists have set them. So far *Physarum* has accurately anticipated the itinerary of the Silk Road, outwitted human engineers in transport network organisation, solved puzzles which supercomputers cannot, replaced machines to control microchips, and driven robots (Adamatzky 2010; Adamatzky 2012; Tero et al. 2010; Waugh 2011; Tsuda et al. 2006). It consistently performs beyond expectations in a battery of psychological and cognitive tests, and in many of the experiments thus far, outperforms humans.[3]

Importantly, most of the experiments are forms of intelligence testing. A range of studies has been conducted to deduce whether *Physarum* holds some of the capacities and hallmarks of what is classically thought of as intelligence (memory, rationality, forethought), and how they measure up to a scientific determination of consciousness. *Physarum* has maintained the interest of scientists because, as it turns out, it measures up rather well. Experimentation on slime moulds has increased rapidly in a short period of time, and the findings of what *Physarum* is capable of, and subsequent tests on top of these findings, is still ongoing. This work has featured in the prestigious journals *Nature*, *Science* and *Proceedings of the National Academy of Science of the United States of America*, and has made international media on several occasions. Some of the more pioneering experiments have been conducted by a team of researchers at The Social Insects Laboratory at the School of Biological Sciences at Sydney University, Australia, with whom I have been in conversation. It is these experiments that will provide the framing for our discussion here.

Physarum was initially thought to be a kind of fungus, but was later discovered to be a protist. According to biologist Chris Reid of The Social Insects Laboratory, this taxonomic group embraces 'everything we don't really understand' (cited in Jabr 2012). In terms of both taxonomisation and species being it is, for scientists, unsettlingly indeterminate. Slime moulds get classified as protists because protists are unicellular, however *Physarum* is both unicellular and multicellular simultaneously. Often referred to as the 'many headed slime', its interior is a sac of cytoplasm containing a multitude of individually nucleated cells. If you cut a plasmodium in half you get a 'copy' of the original, although they will not mirror each other's behaviour, instead acting as two separate organisms. If you place them back together they fuse and exist as one creature. *Physarum*'s actions manifest locally – individual cells oscillate, responding to the oscillators of their neighbouring cells, as well as to environmental cues – and on a larger scale, in the movements and actions of the *Physarum* when 'acting' as one giant organism with seemingly no designated controller. The drive of the 'wills' of millions of different oscillators is what motors the organism and makes it appear as one creature. However, as there is no *one* agent to 'decide' *Physarum*'s movements, it is unclear whether *Physarum* should be treated as one giant system, one organism, a system of replicates, a series of clones of one original, authentic *Physarum*, or a collection of individual organisms simply residing within close proximity. In this way, one could argue that there has only ever been *one* slime mould: spatially plural, yet ontologically singular.

The scientific atomism of taxonomic classification (cutting things up into smaller and smaller pieces to then reconstruct the characteristics of the system from its parts) seems inadequate in this case, as there is no part one could isolate and study as if it were a smaller, simpler supplement of a larger whole; no part that isn't similarly a reflection, an expression, of its expansive genealogy. Even scientific descriptions of *Physarum*'s life cycle differ considerably, as there is no actual 'beginning' to the 'cycle'. Both its morphology as well as the location of a discernable moment where its life lapses into its death does not follow any kind of causal chain or temporal order. Those working with *Physarum* certainly acknowledge these dilemmas. Tanya Latty, of the Social Insects Laboratory, reflected,

> I try to actually avoid deciding whether it's an individual or a group. I mean, for our experiments, we consider each time we cut it each of those things is an individual, it's a replicate. But I mean you could argue that that's not really the case, because when you put them all back together again and they're perfectly happy to coexist . . . but then there's individual fragments, you can cut them at the same time and the same size but they'll behave differently from each other. They don't all do exactly the same thing . . . It gets really confusing . . . We actually go back and fourth over whether we call it a group or an individual, because it's really unclear what you call something like that . . . it's not a community in that you don't have actual individuals . . . I try to avoid talking about them and defining them. (Latty 2012, pers. comm., 14 September)

Ontologically speaking, determining how and where to place *Physarum* is a problem of causality as much as it is of spatio-temporal positioning.

Given this irresolvable puzzle of identity, there is no uniform way in which the organism is referred to in the literature. It is often called a 'network', a 'system', or an 'aggregation' (Tero et al. 2010: 440, 441; Scmickl and Crailsheim 2007: 2), although all these terms seem to miss the paradox in its biographical detail, or perhaps attempt to ignore it.

In essence, what we are contending with is an organism for which the concept of 'species' does not hold, an organism which has no evident point of birth, whose being cannot be circumscribed as either individual or collective, and whose internal traffic cannot be satisfactorily explained by resorting to a notion of assemblage, interaction or admixture. It seems reasonable to ask, then, given that scientists have defined *Physarum* as a 'self-organised' system: what is being organised, and where is this agential 'self' located? As we could read 'individual' as 'identity', we might query if there is a kind of sociality at work here.

Interestingly, these same questions which the researchers are struggling with in this *scientific* context, have a history in sociological thought – indeed, they were some of the very same questions that motivated Émile Durkheim, the discipline's founding father, to muse over the exact nature of the object of sociology. Throughout his *oeuvre*, Durkheim traced questions that were reminiscent of similar riddles: the problematic of authorship and agency, and causality and determinism, in order to demarcate what should properly define sociological inquiry. His work posed several questions that remain central to methods of sociological analysis. For example, what are the differences that secure the uniqueness of an individual, albeit one indebted to, and born of, the social fabric? Or, to recall his own words, 'How can we belong entirely to ourselves, and entirely to others at one and the same time?' (1973: 152).

Durkheim's project was to carve sociology out from the social and (expressly) the natural sciences in order to secure its inquiry as an exact science, with a distinct object, autonomous from other disciplines. In his field-defining *Rules of Sociological Method*, he outlined sociology as the study of social facts; 'ways of thinking and acting', he declared, that 'constitute the proper domain of sociology' (1996: 4). Social facts are 'external to the individual', and are 'endowed with coercive power, by virtue of which they impose themselves upon him' (1996: 2). Due to their collective origin, social facts exist prior to, and outlive, individual consciousness, even if they animate individuals and are enacted through them. For Durkheim, social facts do the work of explaining the seemingly unpredictable or tumultuous decisions and occurrences that materialise in any given society as the result of a structured, pre-scripted, pattern of sociality, a pattern knitted together by social facts. And yet, inhering within the social fact, that kernel of what was to be sociology's objective and clear sense of evidence, we find the very equivocation of individual/collective agency at play.

Rehearsed throughout the entirety of his cannon, Durkheim's meticulous empirical research led him to view what he termed 'the social organism' as haunted by the same predicament of individual versus collective intention. Understanding society *as* system, he argues, 'something else in us besides ourselves stimulates us to act' (1973: 153). Durkheim locates the causal thrust of individual, and social, behaviour in 'a totality of energies that determine us from outside to act', collective currents and forces that bend and animate an individual so that she is 'only an intermediary' through which the social realises its aims ([1897] 2006: 343; 1933: 404). The force of sociality, he argues, 'is *in* the whole as it is *by* the whole', and is in this sense beyond individuals: 'each individual contains a part, but the whole is found in no *one*' (1953: 26, emphasis added). For Durkheim this motoring force compelling society, that which propels and obligates individuals to act, *is* the social. The constraints and contracts, or social facts that pull on an individual to act, are 'to be found in each part because it exists in the whole, rather than in the whole because it exists in the parts' (1996: 9). Put otherwise, even if manifested in individuals, the origin of this power is definitively collective.

As I read Durkheim, he is interrogating the fundamental essence of sociality, aiming to magnify all of its fascinating enigmas, to mould a theory on the problem of the individual, or that which binds us. Accordingly, and perhaps not surprisingly, his conclusions raise vital questions and contradictions. For instance, how sustainable is the notion of an externality that imposes itself *upon* an individual in Durkheim's line of argument? If the individual is an individuated expression of sociality, then how can a social force possibly be 'imposed' from an external vantage point? Isn't any external point, or even notion of exteriority, an expression of the very socius that generated it? Put otherwise, if an individual emerges through and as a living manifestation of the histories and socialities that birthed her, then where is the caesura that discovers a single and original source of agency within this morass?

However, as if acknowledging the recondite nature of his subject matter while not quite knowing how to think it, this very meditation on sociality 'runs headlong into a problem of general philosophy which goes far beyond it: why are there individuals?' (1983: 20). From time to time, Durkheim will complicate his own position (that society is *the* agential force behind individual and collective will), and some of his musings attest to certain hesitations in his thinking. In a footnote, Durkheim states,

> let us add, to avoid any misunderstanding, that we do not believe that there is a precise point where the individual ends and the social begins. The association is not established at once and does not at once produce its effects; it needs time to do so and there are consequently moments at which the reality is imprecise. ([1897] 2006: 347)

If, as Durkheim argues, there is no 'precise point' demarcating the individual from the social, how is it that he can theoretically sustain their differentiation (347)? Correlatively, if there is no 'precise point' how can there be 'moments' where it is 'imprecise' at the same time as 'moments' where it is not (347)? As his formulation postulates that this 'association' is not 'established' originally but requires time as a prerequisite to become established, we might question *how* this imprecision coalesces into a bifurcation. Given the complex workings of the social organism, one could argue that it is no longer clear where the boundaries surrounding the individual lie, as any such boundaries, understood as borders that separate, are also the bindings to and through the collective. Related to this, Durkheim asks, 'if society is composed solely of individuals, how can there be something outside them?' (347). This question astutely raises the problem of what could possibly be 'outside', given that the 'conscious collective' or 'social' that Durkheim locates agency in/as are the very individuals that bend them to 'its' will.

To rethink Durkheim from a contemporary posthumanist perspective, we could argue that what Durkheim in fact elucidates about the challenge of causality is that any individual, or part, is already both constituted by, and an iteration of, its expanded socius, or whole (Chiew 2012; Lehman 1993). The 'whole' is both refracted through and enacted in/as its 'parts', resulting in an inextricability which negates the prescription of either a strict social determinism, or free will, as the engine motivating individual action. Instead, agency appears to be pure dispersion, suggesting that the acts of any one individual are never authored by her alone.

Within this reading, we could conclude Durkheim's thoughts with a seeming paradox concerning agency: that which motivates the intention of an individual is already an enactment of the collective of which the individual is a node. Similarly, we could conclude that human species being, or our experience of sociality, expresses a peculiar fact about human culture, namely, that encased within it are torrents of power and agency that are neither local nor collective, and yet both at the same time.

Intriguingly, the rehearsal of the very same set of questions that plagued Durkheim's imagination are observable when we return to biological riddles such as an individual cell's intricate consanguinity. As Durkheim specifically wanted to distinguish the parameters of sociology along with its object as distinct from any other discipline and phenomenon, it is striking that scientists are also struggling with this same dilemma which now appears peculiarly ubiquitous. Does the fact that this problematic is shared indicate that Durkheim misplaced the object of sociology, that he was unsuccessful in his attempts to provide it with a proper disciplinary boundary, or does it compel us to revisit the two cultures issue, as well as that of disciplinary identity more generally, as questions rather than givens? Could one think the ontological riddles *Physarum* embodies through Durkheim's methodologies? Would it be a projection, a mistranslation, a fortuitous fiction to see sociology at work in the cell? [4]

If the very theories that Durkheim recounts to complicate the integrity of human individual identity can be observed at the level of a single cell, a much more involved and convoluted notion of social ecology emerges. For one of the anchors of anthropocentrism is the general acceptance that the way human individuals and cultures act and respond is unlike that of any other animal. Against this accepted doctrine, what might Durkheim's social organism look like if its borders stretched beyond the human? It is surely remarkable that there is a comparable mystery of the 'conscious collective' in the slime mould just as there is in the human social organism. Perhaps what troubles us here is that its consequence lies precisely in its unsettling of the specificity of the social organism as *only and always human*. It seems that the specificities that Durkheim claimed for sociology cannot be cordoned off from the more comprehensive frame of the ecological as another incarnation of that same, collective sociality.

A close examination of two experiments conducted in Tanya Latty's laboratory returns us to our examination of biology *as* sociality and demonstrates the ways in which all the contentions *Physarum* embodies are managed in a precise, disciplinary setting. In 2011 Latty et al. devised an experiment which aimed to search for *Physarum*'s potential use of comparative valuation rules, a cognitive feature so far only demonstrated in humans, mammals and certain insects (Latty and Beekman 2011). Most models of animal foraging base their understanding of individual choice on the absolute value of items, which in turn defines what is considered economically rational. However, demonstrations of what is termed 'irrationality' remain frequent in human and animal studies (2011: 307). This illustrates that people may not judge an item by what might appear to be its inherent value, but instead determine its worth using comparative valuation rules. A simple example of this fact, often exploited by advertisers, can be seen in the example of the decision to buy a car. Provided with a choice between a $10,000 vehicle and another at $50,000, and if both are deemed reliable, the logical, or rational, choice is to select the cheaper option. Add another option to the choice set, in this instance, a $25,000 car, and the $50,000 car then appears less expensive: many people will change their initial value judgment and buy the $25,000 car (Tversky 1969). Operating in a similar way to the Saussurean sign, an item's value, then, is determined by the system of value within which it sits. This cognitive faculty requires one to compare, evaluate, analyse, and *then* choose. Latty's team wanted to discover if *Physarum*, too, could analyse value in comparative, not simply absolute, terms.

Latty et al. offered *Physarum* a choice between two food sources: one containing 3 per cent oatmeal, covered in darkness, and another with 5 per cent oatmeal, although brightly lit. As *Physarum* is photophobic, its choice was between a nutritious yet irritating and potentially dangerous menu item, or a less nutritious but more bearable option. Here one could argue that it is unclear which option is necessarily superior, and *Physarum*'s actions portrayed this very indecision. It didn't form a preference, but oozed toward both options with equal frequency. However, when Latty et al. added a third option – a food source containing 1 per cent oatmeal although placed in shadow, clearly the most inferior preference – it changed *Physarum*'s sense of equivalence between the first two options. With this simple addition, *Physarum* changed its initial decision and overwhelmingly chose the 3 per cent oatmeal disc in darkness. Even though the 3 per cent and 5 per cent options were unchanged, the presence of the 1 per cent option made the 3 per cent option more appealing.

What Latty et al. suggest from this finding is that *Physarum* is capable of making 'trade-offs between light exposure and food quality', inferring that 'poor values in one of an option's attributes (for example, light exposure) can be compensated by high values in another attribute (oatmeal concentration)' (2011: 311). This evidence underlines that *Physarum* must 'rank each attribute', or, use a 'comparative valuation process' in order to determine which option is preferable (311, 307).

Latty et al. continue, 'yet, despite lacking a brain *P. polycephalum* is capable of making consistent, transitive decisions when choosing between food sources that vary in multiple attributes' (311). Latty et al. then go on to question, 'given that they lack brains (or any form of centralized information processing), *how can* slime moulds make decisions?' (311, emphasis added). *Physarum* is referred to as an 'information processor' and a 'biological decision maker' in this article, and the conclusion states that 'it is remarkable that *P. polycephalum*, which belongs to an entirely different kingdom of life and lacks a central nervous system, uses the same comparative decision-making processes as do neurologically sophisticated organisms' (312).

Although it seems that this experiment squarely demonstrates choice, a degree of analytical ability, and what we would conventionally agree are decision-making capacities, the authority of the human and the presumptive centrality of the brain for decision-making are not problematised by the evidence. As we will see, if mould is not a brain then, by definition, its considerable achievements will prove more apparent than actual.

In 2012 Latty's colleagues, this time led by biologist Chris Reid, recreated an experiment to test *Physarum*'s ability to navigate intricate, dynamic environments (Reid et al. 2012). As *Physarum* travels, it leaves a gooey mat of thick, translucent extracellular slime in its wake. Reid et al. wondered what purpose this slime served, and whether it could increase navigational ability in unpredictable environments (17490). Beginning the experiment with the question, 'memory typically resides within the brain, but what if an organism has no brain?', the researchers gave *Physarum* a challenge: placing it in manufactured traps, they waited to see if, unlike a robot with a pre-programmed memory, it could escape.

Reid et al. first placed *Physarum* in a Y-shaped maze, with food sources at the top end of each arm of the 'Y'. If one arm was covered in slime, *Physarum* would always travel down the adjacent path. However, if both arms were covered in slime, it would move over the slime. In effect, while *Physarum* forages for food, it avoids areas that contain its slime, yet avoiding the slime is overridden in the absence of choice;

its avoidance is preferential. The researchers argue that this behaviour 'is a "choice" because when no previously unexplored territory is available, the slime mould no longer avoids extracellular slime' (17490). It is, however, noteworthy that this simple assertion, easily understood and described as if unexceptional, already assumes what is in question. How *did* it choose, and if choice is indeed an accurate description, one which does not obfuscate scientific objectivity, why is it suspended in inverted commas?

Continuing with this experiment, Reid et al. next created a miniature U-shaped trap. A classical test of navigational ability traditionally used in robotics, the U-shaped trap problem draws a robot into a U-shaped trap, and tests its ability to efficiently escape. To succeed, robots must have symbolic maps of their surroundings in their hard drive, and an ability to discern where they've been in the past. Fundamentally, they must have some kind of inbuilt memory system.

The experiment runs as follows: the trap consists of a petri dish full of agar with a 'U' formed out of plastic, creating a barrier the slime mould will not travel over. On one side of the 'U' is a well of glucose and water, which gradually disperses through the gel. Following the attractive chemical gradient of the food source, *Physarum* is lured to its location, rendering it effectively trapped within the 'U'. Reid et al. tested *Physarum* to see if it could solve the maze and reach the glucose goal on substrates of plain agar, and on a separate batch of agar that included fresh extracellular slime.

When *Physarum* was placed in a dish containing no extracellular slime, it escaped the maze and reached its goal within 120 hours, using slime trails to guide it in 96 per cent of cases, travelling short distances and travelling very close to the optimal path length. When the agar was pre-coated with slime, however, *Physarum*'s success rate fell to 33 per cent, the time it devoted to traversing previously explored areas increased almost tenfold, and it travelled a greater distance and considerably further from the shortest possible path.

Why did the control group far surpass the *Physarum* in agar with extracellular slime? Reid et al. had in fact demonstrated something incredible: *Physarum* can sense extracellular slime upon contact, and utilises its presence as an 'externalized spatial memory system to recognize and avoid areas it has already explored' (2012: 17490–1). *Physarum* was able to use its slime to circumvent the trap, instead of repeatedly navigating the same territory, thus actively using its slime as a mnemonic to avoid retracing its steps. Upon encountering its slime, it recognises that it has previously attempted that route and tests an alternative.

Just as ants place a trail of pheromones to inform collective decisions in the colony, *Physarum* 'constructs a map of its environment before constructing a solution' (Reid et al. 2012: 17492). When animals or insects forage for immobile resources, an organism's search efficiency generally increases with its ability to avoid previously visited areas. This reliance on memory is one of the hallmarks of intelligent foraging behaviour, and has been found to occur in organisms ranging from mammals to insects. The utilisation of this memory system isn't a chemical reaction to concentration gradients, or, what is termed, 'reactive navigation' (2012: 17490). If we take *Physarum* as an example here, it preferentially explores *before* deciding where to go. The quantifiable presence of this ability places *Physarum* in the same realm as a range of insects and mammals that have various ways of reading and symbolically mapping their environments in order to lessen their onboard cognitive load.

Reid et al. also describe *Physarum*'s use of environmental and chemical cues as 'the first step toward the evolution of memory in organisms with more sophisticated neurological capabilities than our slime mold' (2012: 17492). Reid et al. conclude that 'even an organism without a (central) nervous system can effectively navigate complex environments', thereby signifying that navigation does not necessitate 'learning or otherwise sophisticated' abilities (17492). *Physarum* is referred to as a 'nonneuronal, reactive organism', its 'spatial memory system' a 'simple behavioural mechanism' (17492). It is positively compared to robots, and the paper closes with the argument that externalised spatial memory systems are a 'functional precursor to the internal memory of higher organisms' (17492, 17490). In short, the evidence of *Physarum*'s use of choice and memory, or minimally, the evidence that these capacities and what informs its decisions might require further elaboration, is entirely discounted. For instance, one might query the status of 'precursor' in this concession (17490). What preconceived suppositions inhere within this term alone?

Such responses are thematic in this research, and they are not confined to the publications of this particular laboratory. The absence of terms such as 'consciousness' when describing *Physarum* is pervasive amongst researchers conducting experiments on this organism across disciplines. What is generalisable throughout the scientific literature is that 'programming' is used in place of cognition, 'signalling' instead of language, and 'anticipation' replaces forethought. 'Simple', 'primitive' and 'lower' repeatedly appear in the very papers in which the captivating results of these experiments are published.

Indeed, all terminology suggestive of intelligence, even impoverished definitions such as 'decision making', is placed in quotation marks. Recast as Cartesian automatons, *Physarum* are referred to as 'living computers', 'programs', and 'machines' (Marks 2013; Conover 2001; Adamatzky 2010). In both journal articles and media discussions of these experiments, the metronomic conclusion is always the same: *Physarum* is a primitive, mindless computer. Even Andrew Adamatzky, a computer science professor who has a considerable corpus of work on *Physarum*, including an article claiming it displays creativity (Adamatzky et al. 2013), states that '*Physarum's* intelligence is not higher than [the] intelligence of a stone rolling down a hill (the stone 'chooses' a shortest path downhill) or a plant orienting itself towards the sun. *Physarum* just obeys physical, chemical and biological laws' (cited in Yong 2010).

We are thus left with something of a puzzle. What the scientific evidence illustrates is quickly diminished, or poorly reflected, in the literature that represents it. Given that the production of scientific knowledge is said to be an evidence-based pursuit, why would scientists employ language that makes *Physarum's* cognitive feats appear so ordinary, indeed, unthinking? Compellingly, words like intelligence or memory never appear in the literature, or never appear free of inverted commas. Albeit more traditionally associated with the human, they are, in a sense, at least loosely synonymous with the terms that the scientists substitute. It is curious that specific expressions do not get used while their tempered counterparts certainly do. Yet, in both these experiments, despite the fact that there is a clear elision of consciousness, these larger questions surface, nevertheless. What is it that would be risked if the quotation marks were removed?

Interestingly, in my conversations with Tanya Latty her views of *Physarum's* capabilities, and her understanding of intelligence more generally, appeared far more open and nuanced than her published work would suggest. I asked her whether there were disciplinary constraints that prevented her from using certain language and making certain claims. She responded,

> when he [Chris Reid] presented that at a meeting, at a behavioural science meeting, someone stood up and said exactly the same thing, 'It's really interesting but I don't agree with the term "externalised memory."' It's tricky, but I find that neurobiology, people who work with brains, tend to be particularly resistant to anything that uses the words 'cognition', etc. . . . Like I never use the word 'cognition' . . . we even had debates about 'problem solving' and 'decision

> making'. . . . We've had arguments about whether you can have decision making
> without a brain. Can you have problem solving without a brain? . . . Saying the
> word 'intelligence' . . . you'll notice we don't say that in any of our papers. We
> quite consciously avoided that. I still don't think it's all that accepted, because
> when I write new talks I'm always very careful not to say that they're clever,
> they're intelligent, unless I'm doing it very kind of glibly . . . I'm not sure that
> they are or that they're not. I don't know that anybody is . . . I guess in a sense
> there is this censorship in that I would never say they were intelligent on paper,
> and part of that is because I know it wouldn't work. But the other part is I don't
> know what I really think. (Latty 2012, pers. comm., 14 September)

Commendably honest in her own hesitations, Latty's comments are
especially revealing. She undoubtedly acknowledges unease about how
to even describe the evidence she is observing, as well as an ambiguity
between what she thought and what she was willing or in fact able to
publish. There are strong disciplinary dictates that curtail what scientists
are able to say about living organisms, irrespective of whether it echoes
what the researchers actually think, or even what they recognise in their
data. It seems that while the question of intelligence has in a way been
predetermined, Latty herself is trying to manage the provocation truth-
fully and openly in her own work. For example, during conversation
it became apparent that in order to get published in A-grade academic
journals, potentially controversial issues were best omitted.

> There are certain financial realities (in relation to grants and funding) . . . if
> you want to get into *Nature* or *Science* or any of the good ones then it usually
> tends to help if you can have something in there . . . that says 'why is this so
> important beyond just being kind of cool.' There's so much emphasis getting in
> those journals [*Science, Nature, Cell*], because without that you really start to
> run into trouble. (Latty 2012, pers. comm., 14 September)

If attesting to the potential intelligence of microorganisms is a certain way to 'run into trouble', then the policing of this question in the
sciences is noteworthy. What emerges is a portrait of a disciplinary
culture in which anthropocentrism is not only enabled, but *required* in
order to function. In fact, specific disciplinary structures don't merely
stop certain questions being answered, they actively prevent them
being asked. These dictates are reiterated through, and in turn, drive,
what is deemed 'publishable' work, and subtly they set academic and
ideological standards which govern the determinations of what constitutes science, evidence, and here, how we define consciousness. It is
not then a case of the anthropocentrism of individual scientists, but
rather a scientific culture that has anthropocentrism as an institutional
reference point.

But do these orthodoxies reflect the personal views of those in the field? When Latty was asked whether her opinion of *Physarum*'s capabilities for intelligent thought had changed since her engagement with the organism, she answered,

> I think you have to work with the things to kind of get to that point [of seeing *Physarum* as some expression of agency] almost, because I don't think I would have said that before I worked with them . . . I even think . . . plants have behaviour and I remember thinking, 'Plant behaviour, that's stupid'. You just get a different opinion when you start working with them and when you are actually the one setting up the experiment . . . When you read them it's one thing but I know how they behaved, I know that I didn't lie, I watched them go in one direction or another, I watched them do it . . . We set up the experiments really well so that they weren't doing something strange . . . I'm a lot more open to that idea than I used to be. (Latty 2012, pers. comm., 14 September)

Here, Latty displays her own uncertainties in how to best imagine the potential for microbial intelligence. What is striking is her admission that the ability to re-evaluate hegemonic understandings of the capacities of single-celled organisms was provoked by intimate, close work with *Physarum*; watching it solve puzzles, escape mazes and develop a certain faith in its ability to do so.

Certainly, one of the crucial motives for what we might call the scientists' terminological restraint is that there is significant confusion as to where cognition might be occurring. The premise of this confusion is the apparent cerebral deficit of the organism, as scientists struggle to comprehend how what is essentially a mere bag of cytoplasm could be acting intentionally. In other words, because *Physarum* lacks a brain, neurons, a nervous system, a spinal cord – even a *body* as traditionally conceived – the assumption is that it simply cannot be cogitating. Further to this, scientists are working on an organism whose borders they don't even feel confident in defining. And yet, the practice of science relies on a sense of producing objective truths about a scientific object whose parameters are known and stable. Attributing consciousness, whether to an individual or location, is hindered by the fact that they can't circumscribe the borders of one individual with any conviction. Put otherwise, without establishing the periphery of 'a' subject, how does a scientist establish the periphery of a mind within it?

To further complicate this perplexity, *Physarum* could not embody the tropes of passive, unreasoning matter any more successfully. It is literally slime. And yet, this brainless ooze is able to listen to all of its 'individual' oscillators and form a response, interpret environmental cues, materialise the information, and flexibly respond to the unpredictability of its circumstances, all without what we might risk calling an 'intellect' that conforms to a sender/receiver model of information transfer. Distinguishing the part doing the thinking is problematic as there is no one part of *Physarum* that is not identical to every other part, as in a certain sense, there is no 'part'. There is no biological core that motivates its apparent periphery into action, no higher centre of intelligence as Cartesian arguments presume. This is not a case of mind controlling matter, as all of *Physarum is* matter. Perhaps one could argue that either *Physarum* has no cognising centre, organ or capacity, or it *is* its cognising capacity. To employ the scientists' terminology, if the term 'brain' acts as a synonym for thought, cognition, consciousness, then *Physarum is* its brain. In this case, and importantly for this argument, how does the possibility of 'thinking cytoplasm' reorient our understanding of consciousness? The political implications of seriously entertaining this question, given the way mind and body are routinely conceived, are weighty. It is perhaps unsurprising that scientists grapple uneasily with what they observe in the laboratory when their research could well displace the very how, where and what of consciousness.

Indeed, how do scientists juggle the cognitive dissonance, the necessary mental operations that one must perform when working with an organism displaying sophisticated abilities that will inevitably and predictably be labelled primitive? Negotiating what she thinks, what she has observed, how to accurately describe it, how to manage the question of evidence, how to maintain funding, to ensure publication success, to appear credible to her colleagues – these are all the corollaries of opening such contentious questions within a certain inherited legacy. Given the associational weave of interconnection here, debates over word choice are more than semantics, but are instead symptomatic of all the ideological, disciplinary and emotional complexity now enveloped within what we might call the sociality of the single-celled slime mould.

Why would the burden of such consequence come to bear on a series of modest experiments if the thinking cell was not, by implication, a disturbing provocation to what constitutes intelligence, and correspondingly, to what then secures the human's special authority in identifying it? It is possible that in not posing particular questions, scientists are displaying a certain perverse awareness of what might be at stake in asking them. Or, it may be that keeping within these accepted constraints by way of a more muted choice of vocabulary might provide an avenue for scientists to open those very questions which their disciplines have cordoned off as unruly. In other words, can we embrace this same scientific terminology to enable different conclusions?

In recent decades both the sciences and the social sciences have significantly recast concepts such as program and algorithm.[5] In light of these reinterpretations, one could read the scientists' use of such terminology as an acknowledgement of the complexity of computing. As a generalisation of the specific conceptual tenor of this field, however, algorithm, program, computing and biology are routinely understood as predetermined and comparatively inflexible. Nevertheless, what would happen if, instead of correcting and replacing these terms, we altered our interpretations of this vocabulary? For example, are scientists really misguided in their assertions that *Physarum* is an 'information processor' or a 'decision maker'? For it surely is one. The unease again pivots around the politics of terminology. The assertion that *Physarum* is a simple program relies on an assurance that a program is somehow diminished and automatic when compared against the human. We might concede that *Physarum* is certainly a program, although it is one that decides, mutates, rewrites itself, and responds with agility to spontaneous, unpredictable environmental information. Similarly, scientists have established that *Physarum*'s movements can be predicted by mathematics, that it acts in terms of algorithms, that it computes and behaves much like a machine. However, in acknowledgement that numerous scholars have called into question the apparent distinction between a generalised notion of language and that of mathematics, it is worth pausing over this notion of mathematics to query what it actually involves.[6]

Could we consider, for instance, if *Physarum*'s computation is a kind of communication? In this way, odd as it may sound, it could be said that *Physarum* practises mathematics; indeed, what would prevent us from saying that it *is* mathematics?[7] While scientists argue that *Physarum* embodies random thinking, here, an example of how sophisticated Nature's programs and patterns can be, it is worth pondering the consequences if such concessions included the human intellect. There is certainly a comparison between the eloquence of such programs and those complexities of the human brain at which we marvel. We could, for example, reorient our interpretation of this framing if we conceded that the stuff of human specificity *is* a chemical, biological, algorithmic expression. Could human biological machinations be akin to a stone rolling down a hill? Why *would* a reading of human agency as pro-grammatic offend?

In recalling the scientists' terminology I do not mean to assert that they are somehow mistaken, but rather to use this evidence to illus-trate that in order to sidestep an anthropocentric double standard, this same working definition of biology could productively be applied to the human. In this way, relegating *Physarum* to the realms of biological determinism may not require correction, as the hinge is rather what one understands biology or determinism to be. Read differently, behaviour could not be motivated or enacted if it wasn't determined biologically, and this needn't imply a simple, static prescription.

We should thus be critical of the naivety of desires to wholly reject terms like 'program', 'automaton' or 'computation', terms which humanities scholars would typically read as Cartesian. Nor can we undertake a project of simply replacing them, as that would only con-stitute another kind of rejection and oppositional standoff by those possessing the intellectual authority *to* redeem. Whether uncritically employed or uncritically discarded, what this juxtaposition forecloses is the question of why these terms evoke the antonyms that they so often do. If our project is to work *with* the myriad paradoxes in this work rather than to find ways of denying, or diluting their fascination, then perhaps we can question and reinvigorate the vocabulary that too cursorily adjudicates difference.

If *Physarum* is considered to be 'all matter' and, as such, 'brainless', is the distinction between mind and body actually necessary? *Physarum* undermines the temporal conventions that would insist on a cognitive centre, as it does not convert intelligent thought into a somatic or cor-poreal reaction or enactment, a thought that *then* propels a flood of cells to move this way or that. Rather, its 'decision-making' or 'infor-mation processing' is somatic in the most literal sense: its intelligence is immediately corporeal, its body directly cognisant. When observing *Physarum* in any of its distinct stages, whether as a spore, as slime, as pulsing cytoplasm, these particular morphologies are not channels *for* an intelligent agent – the very biology of their anatomy *is* already fully intelligent, literate, articulate. This is not so much a consciousness produced *by* the body, it is a matter of consciousness *as* the body. Con-sidering matter in this way, we see instead that intelligence is written into the repertoire of materiality, its biological possibilities, such that matter *is* the capacity to think, to cognise. Put differently, cognising is a material imperative.[8] If matter is always already thoughtful, and biology intellectually animated from its genesis, then mindfulness must appear through, and as, embodiment. If we could at least entertain such a possibility rather than censoring it axiomatically, then we could venture that *Physarum*'s body does not react to cognitive instruction but is rather its very corporealisation.

Gliding smoothly through the labyrinth at speeds of up to 10mm per second, seemingly intuitively, the shortest route is discovered the very first time (Lagzi et al. 2010: 1198). Momentarily pausing before the exit, as if hesitating, it elegantly resumes and solves the maze. The ability to decipher a maze is a common scientific test of intelligence. What, then, if this accomplishment is achieved by something considered inanimate? Much of the discussion surrounding *Physarum* frames it as a curious anomaly, although the above description is of the maze-solving acuity of a single drop of oil. Irrespective of their scientific interpretations, these kinds of examples force the conventional definitions of cognition to arrive at a strange place. If slime can cognise, can a drop of oil? Can a particle of light?[9]

Scientists may refuse to use certain words that they perceive as detracting from objectivity. For them, such terms refer to a particular semantic domain, a human context, whose specificity should not be abused. However, by providing us with different notions of potential or decision-making, these same scientists are effectively stretching the conventional parameters of these terms, suggesting, even if minimally, that they might not be kept intact. The fact that terms like choice and memory are used, even if in inverted commas, certainly suggests that cognition should be a question, and one on the agenda for all of us. Can we confidently justify the ways in which we attribute, but also censor, the use of these terms?

My own position is encapsulated perfectly in Tanya Latty's own words, when in relation to describing *Physarum* as intelligent, she states, 'I'm not sure that they are or that they're not. I don't know that *anybody* is' (Latty 2012, pers. comm., 14 September; emphasis added). Intelligence, here, is conceded its questionable and somewhat mysterious status. To acknowledge this hesitation and to take it even further, scientists must display the same uncertainty about how, exactly, intelligence might be elaborated. The problem is not one of choosing the right set of terms, but of acknowledging how a narrow understanding of intelligence, memory and creativity that rests on the presumed self-evidence of human cognition can exempt the latter from interrogation, leaving it poorly understood.

During my ethnographic work with Latty it became apparent that the very methodological paradox that gives sociology its definition equally inhabits scientific practice. Returning to Durkheim, in raising the inextricability of the individual from the social, he inadvertently raises questions of objectivity, methodology and disciplinarity. If the individual cannot be pried away from the social, then we are left with the methodological paradox whereby any subject is always already implicated in the object they are studying, thus forfeiting any possible grounds for objectivity. Implicit in this traditional divide between knowing subject and object known is a differentiation between the human and the natural world, a cut which ascribes an intellectual omnipotence to the human; our separation from nature thereby forming that outside or external point necessary to come up with an authorial source that guarantees objectivity. However, if we extrapolate Durkheim's logic that the individual is a manifestation of sociality, then in a similar way we might describe the human as an individuation of nature's ecological system. This would entail that there is no radical divide between the study of what is apparently the natural world and what constitutes, for example, the rhythmic pulse of human sociality. In that case, there can be no outside point from which to objectively judge the natural world. This is because, as Florence Chiew succinctly states, 'The *involvement* of the human with/in nature underlines the crucial point that the human is not only *of* nature; the human is nature's self-involvement' (2012: 40).

How sustainable is an argument that investigates intelligence if the one who determines its attribution is the one who perceives reflexively, as properly human? To argue for the intelligence of humans but the stupidity of amoebas would require an objective third party, an externality, to make that judgment, and this is the very juncture where, as Manuel DeLanda has argued, Cartesianism 'fades into Creationism' (cited in Dolphijn and van der Tuin 2012: 43). Any gesture, then, whose aim is to distinguish intelligence, gradations of it, where it rightly sits, or who/what lacks it, must rely on a conception of an objective outside (complete with theological pretension) – an anthropocentrism that figures the human as independent and impartial adjudicator of what counts.

The aim of this interrogation is not that of corrective, an arbitration on what should properly constitute intelligence and its measurement. Nor is the remedy akin to a Latourian gesture of accommodation – now, the slime mould too has agency and consciousness.[10] Rather, if we entertain these dilemmas we should be left with somewhat of a puzzle, as the implications of the aforementioned scientific work do not simply reconfigure the way the material is traditionally considered – as a corporeal shell containing a cognising agent – but it does perturb the foundations of a human identity that is reliant on cognition as its emblem of difference. To seriously entertain the question of intention and consciousness, as well as the possibility that intelligence may not be brain or species dependent, is what we risk if we remove the inverted commas. Studies like that of *Physarum* afford us the opportunity to open such inquiries in myriad new directions, as it is precisely the question of cognition that automatically makes those discriminations (of human/animal, mind/body, animate/inanimate) for us. If cognition is displaced, or dispersed, we are left with a very different set of questions to contend with. That is, what does it mean for the human if the location of consciousness appears to already inhere within/as its extended and diverse corporeality? Indeed, what *if* Nature thinks?

Notes

1. This gesture has been generalised within both posthumanism and animal studies, and is explicitly evident in works such as Latour (1993), Haraway (1991), Bennett (2010).
2. For another similar perspective on slime moulds (although discussing cellular slime moulds *Dictyosteliida* and social amoebas), see Barad (2012), in which she reflects on the moral unease often aroused by ontologically indeterminate organisms.
3. Although scientific investigation into *Physarum* is varied and interdisciplinary, most of the more intriguing work that has emerged in the last decade has come from three laboratories, and each has published numerous innovative studies on the organism. They are: Tanya Latty and her colleagues at The Social Insects Laboratory, Sydney University; Adam Adamatzky and his colleagues at the Department of Computer Science, University of the West of England Bristol; and Toshiyuki Nakagaki and his colleagues at the School of Systems Information Science, Future University Hakodate.
4. In 'Discovering the Ties that Bind: Cell-Cell Communication and the Development of Cell Sociology', Andrew Reynolds traces the shifting metaphors of cell theory whose distinct sociological flavour is evident from as early as the nineteenth century. He maps a fascinating shift in metaphors from atomistic, mechanistic symbolism to a growing understanding of the body as a 'society of cells' or a 'cell state' (Carrel in Reynolds forthcoming: 7). In 1931, biologist Alexis Carrel coined the term 'cell sociology' to describe his work on the behaviour of cell-cell interactions, and individual-group cell interactions, and in the 1970s embryologist Rosine Chandebois finally developed 'cell sociology' into a theory of biological development. Focusing on the expressly social behaviours

between and within groups of cells, she argued that 'development is a "social" phenomenon' and 'its study must be pursued from the viewpoint of a sociology of cells' (Chandebois in Reynolds forthcoming: 7). Currently used as a concept within cell and molecular biology, the term's founding presumption is that individual cells have different capabilities and behave differently alone than when in a group. Sociality, then, quite literally makes a cell: cells are ontologically 'transformed by their social interactions' (Reynolds, forthcoming: 18). Other scholars have referred to 'cell sociobiology,' 'socio-microbiology' and 'socio-bacteriological' approaches (forthcoming).

5. Commonly, conceptions of algorithms, programs or computation are aligned with notions of prescription, inflexibility, a lack of mind, agency and intention. Arguing against this position, from cybernetics and biosemiotics to systems theory and philosophy, certain thinkers have, in lieu of replacing these views, chosen to realise them very differently. See, for example the work of Derrida (1989), Emmeche (1994), Kirby (2003, 2005), Luhmann (1995), and Wilson (1998, 2010). These scholars have reinterpreted notions of consciousness and intentional behaviour, habitually thought to be distinctly human, by arguing that similar, if not synonymous displays of cognition, memory and agency more generally could be seen in machines, computers and non-human organisms.

6. Whether mathematics is its own language or whether it exceeds the parameters of language – indeed, the very question of what mathematics is, its identity and ontology – continues to be acomplex, ongoing debate across the humanities and the natural sciences. The divergence of opinion in this field is most evident in the question of mathematics' origins. Is mathematics a pre-given structure, a fixed prescription that humans stumble upon or unveil, a secondary technology objectively *re*presenting an already existing reality? Or, is it a cultural construction, one that can cleanly be hived off from the linguistic or semiotic, contingent on the arrival of the human and his calculating authority? For an entry point to begin to open the mired nature of the question of mathematics, see Barad (2012), Derrida (1974), Kirby (2003, 2005), Rotman (1997), Changeux and Connes (1995).

7. For example, plant transpiration, the complexity of root economics, or Fibonacci patterns are all exemplary of finessed mathematical formulas. A numerical sequence that is pervasive in Nature, decreeing the unfurling spiral of a fern, the branching of trees and the specific configuration of petals on a sunflower, Fibonacci numbers are generally understood as a mathematical constraint, pulling Nature into shape. Although ostensibly a self-evident, genetically set prescription ordaining correct form, one could instead contend that the performance of these equations are tantamount to the very *being* of a fern or a sunflower. In other words, plant ontology requires erudite mathematical calculation: nature counts.

See Livio (2002), Hodge (2004, 2008), and Trewavas (2003, 2009), for an introduction.

8. In her article 'Somatic Compliance: Feminism, Biology and Science', Wilson deftly builds a critique concerning the ways in which hysteria and conversion disorder are habitually narrated as a trauma experienced psychically which is *then* converted into a somatic fact, re-inscribing the traditional psyche/soma divide. Wilson's clever intervention into this Cartesian two-step, with its appeal to 'ontological addition', has been an indispensable influence on my own thinking (1999: 12).

9. Barad's musings on the complications of empirical scientific evidence, such as that which has emerged from quantum physics, offer insightful entry points to reconsider classical understandings of ontology. In 'Nature's Queer Performativity' Barad notes that perhaps the most routinely undisputed distinction within the humanities is that between the animate and the inanimate (2012). Signifying a subordination of physical matter to biological matter, with physical matter the inert underpinning of liveliness, Barad warns of the dangers of beginning analysis with this boundary left uncompromised. The pertinent point she stresses is that posthumanist intervention should not begin with this too easy bifurcation where a lack of animation grounds the difference of agency and decision. Such scholarship should instead take as its starting point a theoretical commitment that could never assume such cuts in any straightforward sense. Rather, thinking causality, temporality, identity and origin in terms of quantum entanglements enables a complication of the formulaic prerequisites necessary to hold the in/animate partition hygienically in place.

10. For a critique of Latour's notion of agency as distributed among a 'parliament of things', see Kirby (2010).

References

Adamatzky, A. (2010), *Physarum Machines: Computers from Slime Mould*, New Jersey: World Scientific.

Adamatzky, A. (2012), 'The World's Colonisation and Trade Routes Formation as Imitated by Slime Mould', *International Journal of Bifurcation and Chaos*, 22: 8, pp. 1–26.

Adamatzky, A., R. Armstrong and J. Jones (2013), 'On creativity of slime mould', *International Journal of General Systems*, 42: 5, pp. 441–57.

Barad, K. (2012), 'Nature's Queer Performativity', *Kvinder, Køn og forskning/ Women, Gender and Research*, 1–2: pp. 25–53.

Bennett, J. (2010), *Vibrant Matter: A Political Ecology of Things*, Durham, NC: Duke University Press.

Changeux, J., and A. Connes (eds) (1995), *Conversations on Mind, Matter, and Mathematics*, trans. M. B. DeBevoise, Princeton: Princeton University Press.

Chiew, F. (2012), *Systematicity: the human as ecology*, PhD thesis, School of Social Sciences, The University of New South Wales.

Conover, A. (2001), 'Hunting Slime Molds', available at <http://www.smithsonianmag.com/science-nature/phenom_mar01.html?c=y&page=1> (last accessed 2 March 2014).

Derrida, J. ([1967] 1974), *Of Grammatology*, trans. G. Spivak, Baltimore: Johns Hopkins University Press.

Derrida, J. ([1962] 1989), *Edmund Husserl's Origin of Geometry: An Introduction*, trans. J. Leavey, Lincoln, NE: University of Nebraska Press.

Dolphijn, R., and I. van der Tuin (2012), *New Materialism: Interviews & Cartographies*, Open Humanities Press. An imprint of MPublishing, Ann Arbor: University of Michigan Library.

Durkheim, É. ([1893] 1933), *The Division of Labor in Society*, trans. G. Simpson, New York: The Free Press.

Durkheim, É. ([1898] 1953), *Sociology and Philosophy*, trans. D. F. Pocock, London: Cohen & West.

Durkheim, É. ([1914] 1973), 'The Dualism of Human Nature and its Social Conditions', in R. Bellah (ed.), *On Morality and Society: Selected Writings*, Chicago: The University of Chicago Press, pp. 149–66.

Durkheim, É. ([1913] 1983), *Pragmatism and Sociology*, in J. B. Allcock (ed.), trans. J. C. Whitehouse, Cambridge: Cambridge University Press.

Durkheim, É. ([1938] 1996), *The Rules of Sociological Method*, in J. H. Mueller and G. E. G. Catlin (eds), trans. S. A. Solovay, 8th edn, New York: The Free Press.

Durkheim, É. ([1896] 2006), *On Suicide*, trans. R. Buss, London: Penguin Books.

Emmeche, C. (1994), 'The Computational Notion of Life', *Theoria*, 9: 21, pp. 1–30.

Haraway, D. (1991), *Simians, Cyborgs and Women: The Reinvention of Nature*, Routledge: New York.

Hodge, A. (2004), 'The plastic plant: root responses to heterogeneous supplies of nutrients', *New Phytologist*, 162: 1, pp. 9–24.

Hodge, A. (2008), 'Root decisions', *Plant, Cell & Environment*, 32: 6, pp. 628–40.

Jabr, F. (2012), 'How Brainless Slime Molds Redefine Intelligence', *Scientific American*, available at <http://www.scientificamerican.com/article/brainless-slime-molds/> (last accessed 13 October 2015).

Kirby, V. (2003), 'Enumerating Language: "The Unreasonable Effectiveness of Mathematics"', *Configurations*, 11: 3, pp. 417–39.

Kirby, V. (2005), 'Just Figures? Forensic Clairvoyance, Mathematics and the Language Question', *SubStance*, 34: 2, pp. 3–36.

Kirby, V. (2010), 'Anthropomorphism, Again', *The New Centennial Review*, 10: 3, pp. 251–68.

Lagzi, I., S. Siowling, P. Wesson, K. Browne and A. Grzybowski (2010), 'Maze Solving by Chemotactic Droplets', *Journal of the American Chemical Society*, 132: 4, pp. 1198–9.

Latour, B. (1993), *We Have Never Been Modern*, trans. C. Porter, Cambridge, MA: Harvard University Press.

Latty, T., and M. Beekman (2011), 'Irrational decision-making in an amoeboid organism: transitivity and context-dependent preferences', *Proceedings of the Royal Biological Sciences Society*, 278: 1703, pp. 307–12.

Latty, T., personal communication, 14 September 2012.

Lehman, J. M. (1993), *Deconstructing Durkheim: a post-post-structuralist critique*, London: Routledge.

Livio, M. (2002), *The Golden Ratio: The Story of Phi, The World's Most Astonishing Number*, New York: Broadway Books.

Luhmann, N. ([1984] 1995), *Social Systems*, trans. J. Bednarz, Stanford: Stanford University Press.

Marks, P. (2013), 'Slime mould could make memristors for biocomputers', *New Scientist*, 18 June, available at <https://www.newscientist.com/article/dn23713-slime-mould-could-make-memristors-for-biocomputers/> (last accessed 29 December 2015).

Reid, C., T. Latty, A. Dussutour and M. Beekman (2012), 'Slime mold uses an externalized spatial "memory" to navigate in complex environments', *PNAS*, 109: 43, pp. 17490–4.

Reynolds, A. (forthcoming), 'Discovering the Ties that Bind: Cell-Cell Communication and the Development of Cell Sociology', in L. Nyart and S. Lidgard (eds), *E pluribus unum: Biological parts and wholes in historical and philosophical perspective*, Chicago: University of Chicago Press.

Rotman, B. (1997), 'Thinking Dia-grams: Mathematics, Writing, and Virtual Reality', in B. Herrnstein and A. Plotnitsky (eds), *Mathematics, Science, and Post Classical Theory*, Durham, NC: Duke University Press, pp. 17–39.

Schmickl, T., and K. Crailsheim (2007), 'A Navigation Algorithm for Swarm Robotics Inspired by Slime Mold Aggregation', in E. Şahin and W. M. Spears (eds), *Swarm Robotics*, 4433, Springer: Berlin, pp. 1–13.

Tero, A., S. Takagaki, T. Saigusa, K. Ito, D. Bebber, M. Fricker, K. Yumiki, R. Kobayashi and T. Nakagaki (2010), 'Rules for Biologically Inspired Adaptive Network Design', *Science*, 327: 5964, pp. 439–42.

Trewavas, A. (2003), 'Aspects of Plant Intelligence', *Annals of Botany*, 92: 1, pp. 1–20.

Trewavas, A. (2009), 'What is plant behavior?', *Plant, Cell & Environment*, 32: 6, pp. 606–16.

Tsuda, S., K. P. Zauner and Y. P. Gunji (2006), 'Robot Control: From Silicon Circuitry to Cells', in A. Toshimitsu and M. Kusumoto (eds), *Biologically Inspired Approaches to Advanced Information Technology*, 3853, Springer: Berlin, pp. 20–32.

Tversky, A. (1969), 'Intransitivity of Preferences', *Psychological Review*, 76: 1, pp. 31–48.

Waugh, R. (2011), 'Slime that can "think" its way through a maze could turn our idea of intelligence upside down', *Daily Mail Australia*, 29 December, available at <http://www.dailymail.co.uk/sciencetech/article-2079394/Slime-think-way-maze-turn-idea-intelligence-upside-down.htm> (last accessed 18 July 2013).

Wilson, E. (1998), *Neural Geographies: Feminism and the Microstructure of Cognition*, London: Routledge.

Wilson, E. (1999), 'Introduction: Somatic Compliance: Feminism, Biology and Science', *Australian Feminist Studies*, 14: 29, pp. 7–18.

Wilson, E. (2010), *Affect and Artificial Intelligence*, Seattle: University of Washington Press.

Yong, E. (2010), 'Let Slime Molds do the Thinking!', *The Guardian*, 8 September 2010, available at <http://www.theguardian.com/science/blog/2010/sep/08/slime-mould-physarum> (last accessed 23 April 2015).

CHAPTER 9

Nature Represents Itself: Bibliophilia in a Changing Climate

Astrida Neimanis

The tongues of the glaciers are receding, the voices of our rivers are being dammed and clogged with toxic debris. Who are the scribes writing about our waters and where are the libraries that store their moist stories?

(Irland 2011)[1]

In *Antarctica as Cultural Critique* (2012), Elena Glasberg avers that 'ice is not to be written and not to be read. It is not to be captured within pages. It is not a book; certainly, it is not *like* a book' (xiii). Glasberg's aim here is to challenge the capture enacted by historicity and narrative, instead pointing to ice as 'inexpressible supplement to the historical process' (xiv–xv). Yet if ice resists being read '*like* a book', what are we to make of critical-creative interventions into the ecological imaginary such as Basia Irland's ice books, set adrift in order to reseed riparian habitats – 'read' by the currents and their congeries of multispecies life? Or Roni Horn's *Library of Water* (2013), where, in the Icelandic town of Stykkisholmur, Horn fills twenty-four floor-to-ceiling columns, each with water from a significant glacier in Iceland – and names it after a book repository? We might also puzzle over Glasberg's own photography that accompanies her claims of resistance to ice-as-book, where a cutaway of ice-and-earth striations appears, in the words of a glaciologist, 'like a book open on its spine' (Glasberg 2012: xiii). Here, Glasberg recasts her position, provocatively claiming that her own book is not a 'book on ice', but rather 'a book of ice that instead opens horizontally' (xiii).

Reading Glasberg (that is to say, with her book in hand), we might surmise that there are books and reading 'proper', and then there is a different sort of book – written of/with/by the ice, in another mode of material articulation. This tentative distinction brings to mind Katherine Yusoff's musings in *Bipolar*, a collection of textual archives on ice cores, polar knowledge, and climate change. 'From the beginning', writes Yusoff,

> I had this image in my mind of putting an ice core next to the central core of books in the British Library. This image of two cores – one cultural and one biophysical – set a lot of questions in motion about the possibilities of these two types of environmental knowledges. (Yusoff 2009: 34)

While their specific projects diverge, both Glasberg and Yusoff look to watery and icy matters as a way to destabilise any rigid boundary between nature and culture – one as passive, inert matter there to be consumed and rendered transparent; the other the consumer, the renderer. Similarly, both invite critical scrutiny of a human colonisation of nature and of our supposed arrival in the Anthropocene, whose dominant imaginary posits humans as again separate from the 'Nature' they are rewriting. The ecologically oriented (and culturally critical) impetus behind these queries, particularly in a context of rapid climate change, is to be urgently affirmed. Yet, at first glance, in positing 'two types of environmental knowledges' such proclamations might be interpreted as reinstalling the very bifurcation they seek to challenge. What if instead, this contiguous and overlapping placement of *ice/water* and *writing* – of *nature* and *culture* – were an invitation to literalise, to suspend the very cut that keeps these concepts, these spheres, apart? What if, in Vicki Kirby's words, 'Culture was really Nature all along?' (Kirby 2011: 68). What if it is all just a case of *Nature writing*?

If this is the case – that Nature just writes itself, all the way down – then what kind of representations are these matters that are like books, but aren't? This chapter aims to rethink representation through and with these aqueous libraries. Representation is neither a *re*-presentation that produces the illusion of presence, nor is it a (somewhat less felicitous) 'standing for' of some untouchable or purer nature. Representation is rather recast in posthuman terms, where it refuses the ontological break noted above. Similarly, these ice books and watery writings are posited not as cultural renderings of an ultimately inaccessible nature, but instead as always caught up in those same climates, waters and icy matters, reconfigured or written anew. Attending to the bibliophilic impulse of the artworks I think with here – an impulse that both suggests *and* contests the idea of water or ice as book-to-be-read – invites further reflection on the relationship between 'nature', representing, reading and writing, in the context of a proclaimed Anthropocene. In the end, we are left not with a human writing of this epoch, but with what Kirby calls 'originary humanicity' (2011: 1) writing itself, all the way down.

This critical recasting does not exonerate human bodies but rather asks for heightened responsiveness toward the way in which we take up Nature's pen.

Representation without Representationalism

The question of representation – what it is, whether it is even possible – has been recently revisited by posthuman feminist theorist Karen Barad in her critical exploration of representationalism, whereby things, or reality, are taken to exist independently from their representations. In Barad's helpful parsing, the representationalist view contends that 'the world is composed of individuals – presumed to exist before the law, or the discovery of the law – awaiting or inviting representation' (Barad 2007: 46). Importantly, such a view holds both for realist views that would claim scientific knowledge 'represents things in the world as they really are' (48) *and* for poststructuralist orientations that view representation as always a form of violent and distancing mediation that structures reality itself. In other words, even hegemonic views of language, text or representation ('outside of' which nothing can purportedly exist) implicitly hold on to a pre-representational reality that ultimately evades capture.

In representationalism, Barad notes, the distinction between 'representations and entities to be represented' (46) is cast as thoroughly *ontological*. Not unrelated, as we shall see, is the ontological cut between nature and culture. This conceptual bifurcation has been theorised with considerable nuance within ecologically oriented material and posthuman feminisms.[2] A key concern, as Alaimo and Hekman note, is that this dichotomy generally keeps nature in a subordinate position, as 'the inert ground for the exploits of Man' (Alaimo and Hekman 2008: 4), while also inhibiting an understanding of nature as agentic, changing and transformative (5). While Barad does not explicitly take up the history of representationalism within feminism in terms of nature/culture, the basic resonance between the material or posthuman feminist indictment of the nature/culture divide, and the quarrel with representationalism, as parsed by Barad, deserves a closer look. As Barad notes (drawing on the work of philosopher of science Joseph Rouse), representationalism suffers a Cartesian hangover, whereby the representation – that which we control, master and direct – becomes the privileged site of investigation. According to Rouse, we presume 'that we can know what we mean, or what our verbal performances say, more readily than we can know the objects those sayings are about'

(Rouse in Barad 2007: 49). Meanwhile, 'reality' becomes oblique, rarefied and ultimately inscrutable. Not only does representationalism, like the nature/culture cut, posit an ontological hierarchy of value, but these two frameworks evidence a very cosy overlay: language aligns with culture, while some (often unacknowledged) pre-discursive 'reality' aligns with nature or matter.[3] In other words, these are not just analogous couples. In a quiet conflation, nature (oblique, rarefied) comes to be that which is unrepresentable, and representationalism becomes an alibi for the nature/culture divide.

Donna Haraway, already decades ago, argued explicitly against 'a political semiotics' or a 'politics of representation' (Haraway 2004: 87). Insisting that the question was never one of 'power to represent at a distance' (85) even if the fantasy of a whole-earth perspective led us to believe this was possible, Haraway suggests that representation must instead cede its position to 'a possible politics of articulation' (86). This politics recognises a 'constitutive social reality' where representations are ever-emerging in the entanglements of the represter and what she purports to represent. Barad develops this lead in her own proposed solution to the problem of representationalism: namely, a posthuman performative 'realism without representationalism' (Barad 2007: 50). In this account, reality is not figured as 'beyond representation', nor is it simply given. What is real are not a priori 'things' ('realness', she stresses, 'does not necessarily involve "thingness"' (56)); rather, phenomena come into being through intra-actions. Eschewing representationalism, Barad argues instead for a realism that is an entangled engagement of matter, apparatus of knowledge, and she who represents. Such entanglements do not re-present what is 'there', but constantly, in their ongoing entanglement, elaborate and *perform* the reality that is purportedly represented. If we recall the close overlay of representationalism with the nature/culture split, then we can also see how Barad's account contributes to the release of matter and nature from a prison of brute inertia. Nature is not to be 'represented' by culture; rather, both are becoming together; both are entangled in the coming-to-matter of the world.

Yet, while Haraway and Barad move away from talking about 'representation', other posthuman feminist thinkers still feel the need to think with and within it. Feminist theorists Stacy Alaimo and Catriona Sandilands both, for example, insist on asking after the representability of nature. They acknowledge, on the one hand, the important ethico-political impetus for recognising the *un*representability of nature, or its ultimate unsubsumability within Culture's tight embrace. This would be a necessary counter to the mastery and colonising impulse that serves as a structuring element for both nature/culture and reality/representation. In Sandilands' words, 'Nature cannot be entirely spoken as a positive presence by anyone; any claim to speak of or for nonhuman nature is, to some extent, a misrepresentation' (Sandilands 1999: 180). Similarly, Alaimo insists that a 'cut' between human and non-human nature might be ethically crucial.[4] Yet, on the other hand, the 'perpetual failure' of representation for Sandilands 'does not absolve ecofeminist politics from the responsibility of producing alternative conversations about human and non-human nature' (1999: 180). Alaimo, referencing Sandilands' work, also notes that environmental politics demand that we speak for nature, not only in spite of, but *because* of, the impossibility of the task (Alaimo 2010: 23). In other words, from an ethico-political point of view, there is no way out of representation, even if it is always destined to fail. This failure is not a problem to be overcome, but a crucial part of a radical politics whose promise lies in its very unfinishedness.

My question then is: is there a way to hold on to representation, but as a posthuman representation without representational*ism*? That is, a representation that recognises the political necessity of this endeavour, but in a way that rejects a privileging of either 'things' or 'words', that refuses the ontological split between 'reality' and 're-presentation', and even more importantly, leaves behind the nature/culture divide altogether? Given the ethical significance of these questions (for bound up within the quandary of representation is the question of what makes some beings, bodies or ways of life unthought or unthinkable, violated and violable – a point on which Alaimo, Sandilands, Haraway and Barad all agree), it seems crucial to give such an articulation a try.

In *Quantum Anthropologies: Life at Large*, Vicki Kirby suggests just such a possibility. In asking, 'What If Culture Was Really Nature All Along?' Kirby implicitly entertains the possibility that *everything is representation*. In a generalisation of human (cultural) capacity, Kirby might also suggest that representation has been there all along, in what she refers to as an 'originary humanicity' (Kirby 2011: 20–1). This is not to place the human at the beginning or centre of it all, but rather to suggest that the assumed capacities of humanness are generalised 'in a way that makes us wonder about their true content; after all, what do we really mean by agency . . . or by intentionality and literacy?' (87). Neural plasticity in brains; natural selection in evolutionary biology; or the 'code-cracking and encryption capacities of bacteria as they decipher the chemistry of antibiotic data and reinvent themselves accordingly' (Kirby 2008: 219) all attest to creativity and 'language skills' always already there. 'Life at large', has always been 'reading and rewriting itself' – representing itself – in a 'universal genesis and reproduction' (Kirby 2011: xii).

To put Kirby's offerings in the context of our discussion above, her target is also a view of cultural production or construction that would seemingly separate itself out from natural 'life'. She is explicitly uninterested in cultural constructivist arguments that would understand Nature as 'the dissembling of Culture' (Kirby 2008: 93). Even as Kirby is determined to find a way to think of nature as agential and intelligent, this cannot be accomplished by a reversion 'to the logic of assemblage, Nature *and* Culture' (93) – in other words, a 'simple sense of "and" that necessarily recuperates an uncritical understanding of identity even as it claims to interrogate it' (2011: xi). Kirby shares a poststructuralist conviction 'that there is "no outside of language"' (83), insofar as she is interested in an expansive 'interiority whose articulating energy is the entire system' (xi) – a flat ontology, if you will. But in a bid to get out of the problem where such a view of culture still relies on a prediscursive nature that is always *before* it, Kirby flips the axiom to suggest 'there is no outside of Nature' (87). For Kirby, 'the point is not to take away the complexity that Culture seems to bring to Nature but to radically reconceptualise Nature "altogether"' (88). Culture – cultural texts, human capacities, writing, neural pathways in human brains – are all also instances of *Nature writing itself*.

We note here the close kinship between Kirby's position and Barad's performative realism, where what we count as real is in fact a citation, or an iteration. Such intra-actions share a sense of phenomena 'reading and rewriting' themselves. Kirby, moreover, explicitly acknowledges Barad's key contributions to thinking 'ontoepistemological entanglements' as alternatives to the temerity of binary and copular logics. But at the same time, Kirby also underlines that such alternatives are 'most difficult to think because thinking presumes cuts and divisions of simple separation' (2011: xi). In other words, Kirby's quarry – an attempt to think without an underlying dependence on these separations – can be read as an implicit development or further pushing of Barad's thought beyond its potential reliance on an image of nature *and* culture as two, even if intra-active and co-constitutive. Let me be clear: Kirby's proposition is not fundamentally different from Barad's. What Kirby offers us is a different thought-image – a new figuration of terms that affords the possibility of imagining what we call 'nature' and 'culture' as truly consubstantial.

Kirby thus proposes a way to hold on to representation without representationalism. Instead, it might be figured as an instance of originary writing. In Kirby's words, 'could the generalised origin of re-presentation . . . be thought as the Earth's own scientific investigations of itself?' (Kirby 2011: xi). Not only the non-human scribblings of plastic brains, hungry microbes and eroding coastlines, but even – and especially – 'the tiny marks on this page' (xi) all become a rendering, an iteration, a re-presentation of various natures finding ways to contract and offer life anew. For Kirby, the question is not one of solving the 'problem' of representation but more importantly: 'What do we forfeit and what do we gain by claiming Nature's "textuality", its literacy, as our own?' (xii).

Another question follows: with nature always already representing itself, and representation by humans included within these natural scribblings, how can we acknowledge nature's own withholding of itself, as Alaimo and Sandilands might implore? 'Nature writes itself' certainly troubles the Cartesian privileging of language and representation over 'reality itself', but Kirby's shepherding of us into the 'expansive interiority' of an 'originary humanicity' might nonetheless raise concerns of a backdoor anthropocentrism, where nature is splayed out before us, the human once again taking up all of the oxygen in the planetary room. Put otherwise, is nature's unknowability what we are asked to 'forfeit'? Kirby recognises something akin to this danger: in rethinking humanicity as always already there, we risk affirming the world as human-shaped, or as modelled on human being – the 'purported error and pomposity of anthropomorphic projection' (Kirby 2011: 20). But it is just as possible, she suggests, that 'originary humanicity' might 'refute' or even 'entirely redefine what we mean by "anthropomorphism"' (20). Really, it is a question of '*how* we approach this phenomenon (which includes us)' (21, emphasis added). To take Kirby's suggestion and weave it back into my own problematic, we might say that where nature is representing itself always already, in myriad ways and to varied effect, the question is no longer: 'what is representation?' or even 'is representation possible?' but: 'what does (this) representation do?' What are the effects of specific writings/representations on bodies, polities, discourses, imaginaries, times? What bodies and knowledges come to matter? In other words, a flat ontology does not presuppose a flat ethics. We are not exonerated from representation's ethical quandaries. Nature writing itself does, however, recast them. To work this through, let's return to the specific question with which this chapter began: ice, or water, as book.

Bibliophilia, Frozen and Adrift

At dusk in January, along the muddy-red waters on the Rio Grande near Albuquerque, New Mexico, a daughter wades in a river, fishing with her father. A piece of ice floats by.

> He says it appears to be an open book. Made of ice? Inscribed with lines of text? Another translucent volume appears, twirling in the current . . . Rows of seed script embedded in the ice sculpture form calligraphic paragraphs. Father and daughter look at the indecipherable text. She decides it is a language of the land, one that the birds can read from their cottonwood perches, and she speculates about where the seeds might end up. (Irland 2011)

This volume is one of US-based eco-artist Basia Irland's ice books. Collaborating with local communities, Irland freezes water into blocks of ice, each of which is then carved into the shape of a book – open or closed, some paperback-size, others worthy of massive lecterns. These books are studded with nourishment (mostly seeds, seed pods, or in one case krill) for the riparian communities into which the books are then launched. In Irland's words, these books emphasise 'the necessity of communal effort, scientific knowledge, and poetic intervention to deal with the complex issues of climate disruption and watershed restoration' (Irland 2011).

The book occupies a special position in questions of nature representing itself. On the one hand, we imagine books as quintessential cultural objects, as deliberate vehicles to shuttle the human reader from reality or 'the thing itself' into a necessarily once-removed cultural interpretation. The book could easily be said to mark an entrance *into* culture. No longer the animal that is 'like water in water' (Bataille 1992: 19),[5] the human writes or reads a book in a deliberate act of human self-awareness. On such a view, Irland's books would be nothing more than metaphor, icy replicas of cultural text. Irland's own use of inverted commas seems to signal that her creations are not quite real books, but more 'like' books: these books are 'embedded with an "ecological language" or "riparian text" consisting of local native seeds, and placed back into the stream' (Irland 2011). A photograph of one specific book shows the carved ice resting between two large rocks, the flowing water visible below its icy translucence, with 'three students standing in the river as they "read" the seed text on the book' (Irland 2011). The seeds are not quite 'language', this book is not quite to be 'read'. Recalling the Cartesian hangover Barad invokes via Joseph Rouse, we might get the sense that the watery nature invoked here – the 'real thing' – comes full circle: at first unreliable and inaccessible, then turned into privileged text, and finally recast back into or as the 'real world', but with even further diminished standing.

Environmental matters read through bibliophilic metaphors are actually rather ubiquitous. We read the autobiography of a felled tree in its ringed writings (the book jacket now removed), or the traces of past epochs, climates and earth inhabitants in the fossil records we might also legitimately call archives. But water, and ice specifically, stand out in the world of nature books and libraries. For example, in a choro-graphic meditation on Montreal's Lachine Canal and from the vantage point of a footbridge, Peter van Wyck comments on this 'post-indus-trial river's' various 'inscriptions' and 'traces': 'A reader then am I', he notes, 'of this dilatory place, sifting and gleaning through the remains' (van Wyck 2013: 263). He insists he is not gathering information from archives *about* this historical site (although he does that too), but 'the site as archive' itself must be acknowledged. Elsewhere, anthropolo-gist Julie Cruikshank reminds us that 'culturally significant landforms' such as glaciers – 'with their charges and retreats, may provide a kind of archive where memories can be mentally stored' (Cruikshank 2005: 11). Stephan Harrison similarly notes that glaciers are 'archives of envi-ronmental information' and 'libraries of past change' (Harrison 2009: 77). Kathryn Yusoff, we recall from the introduction to this chapter, suggests that ice cores might be an 'alternative' library, analogous to 'real' ones hosting paper and leather-bound tomes. Yusoff also quotes Richard Alley, who muses that 'to read a record of past climate shifts, we have to find the right history book. Fortunately', Alley notes, 'there is a sort of "library" in ice sheets' (Alley in Yusoff 2009: 35). Each of these readings potentially figures nature 'like' a book, anachronistically mimicking the culture which will follow it. The question is thus begged: if metaphor is a mode of linguistic representation, what kind of rep-resentation represents in advance – in anticipation of the language or humanicity that supposedly comes later?

To push this line of questioning further, if on the representationalist view the text is already a stand-in, then Irland's ice books are a stand-in for a stand-in: ice before the book, represented metaphorically as book, now passing through the book to return as a literalised material metaphor – that is, a repetition both before and after the textuality it re-presents. On the one hand, yes, we might be lured into a funhouse of ever-receding and anachronistically enfolding simulacra, where 'real nature' disappears entirely. And here, we might risk the anthropomorphic affirmation of which Kirby warns us above, in our reinstatement of the human's centrality, always there already. Or conversely, we might take up Kirby's invitation to read Irland's books as anthropomorphism entirely 'reinvented'. Nature as already always anthropomorphic – not as human per se, but as an originary humanicity, writing, reading and rewriting itself.

This shift might begin by asking about the readers of these texts. In each of the above examples of water or ice books, we find human sensory apparatuses turning to these material matters to decode their languages. For Yusoff, this is one of the main points about ice cores: these archives are not *only* 'read', but deliberately curated by humans, thus asking questions about the 'cultural contexts in which scientific knowledge is produced', and the ends to which it is directed (Yusoff 2009: 35–6). At the same time, the reading community of these texts is more expansive, and more-than-human. As van Wyck notes, the Lachine Canal's 'archive of toxicity' is 'legible to biochemical transactions and curious academics' – scholars sharing these texts with the canal's (necessarily) hearty life forms that decipher its toxic messages as a matter of life-and-death. Irland's ice books beg the question of the reader even more explicitly. While on the one hand it is students and father-daughter couplings attempting to read these icy chapters, the daughter also points out that this is a 'language of the land', the seeds a braille for the water. The pods will read the currents as they find new niches; the herring will read the krill as part of their own metabolic stories. And most notable perhaps are the haptic decipherings of the river's own watery fingers, caressing the books, carrying them, and consuming them altogether.

The title of Irland's essay about these ice books is 'Receding/Reseeding' – the first word being a direct reference, in Irland's explanation, to the retreat of glaciers that are pivotal as both stabilisers and indices of a changing planetary climate (a point to which I return below). But might we also take 'receding' as a reference to a human writer or reader relinquishing her claim to textuality's origins? If these books are texts and their writings are language, the linguistic community is larger than the human, while incorporating it too. The second 'reseeding' refers of course to the dispersal of seeds from the icy pages as a 'replicat[ion of] the way seeds get planted in nature' (Irland 2011). This reminds us that such a writing – of habitats by krill and seeds – and such a reading – of nourishment by riparian flows – was there in 'nature' all along – but this does not imply that human writings/readings are a second order textuality. Even if the human 'recedes' from a place of primacy, our entanglements in these writings are simply further articulations and modes of nature's self-representation. Our reading of these texts is also a further writing – a representation of the earth, but only insofar as it is also its further writing of itself. On such a view, Irland's sculptures strongly *resist* a representationalist metaphorisation of ice as 'book' or river and riparian lives as literate. Instead, Irland configures representation in language as a material process that unfurls us all; these sculptures suggest an originary literacy that makes our human textual capacities intelligible and even possible.

'The seeds transcribe an international ecological text', she notes. 'Since it is not a specific language – neither Hindi nor Spanish, Swahili nor Russian – the ice books can be read as a universal invocation of the earth' (Irland 2011). In our postmodern, postcolonial, posthuman moment, 'universality' surely joins representation among the ranks of those least trusted of words. Alongside a well-founded scepticism of one-for-all, however, flows the fact of our communal implication in and as hydrocommons: every living body on earth is at least 50 per cent water, and most considerably more than that. Shimmering in the eddies of this literate ecological community gathered (really, imaginatively) around Irland's ice books is thus also the reminder that we are all bodies of water, reading and writing ourselves, all the way down. Joining the promiscuous scribbling of our bodily fluids, or the protective imprint of an amniotic bath, these rivers write us, too, in a slow-moving cursive script. And our buoyant fleshy selves will continue to read, and rewrite, their messages.

Vatnasafn and Situated Literacy

Vatnasafn (Library of Water) is a permanent installation by Roni Horn housed in a former library in the town of Stykkisholmur, on the west coast of Iceland – the place where, in 1845, Iceland's weather was first monitored and recorded. Horn's *Library* is actually made up of several dimensions, together evidencing a pronounced slipperiness around the idea of representation, books, and their repositories: an apartment for visiting writers-in-residence; a nook that houses many of Horn's book projects, including 'The Weather Reports You' (gathering local reflections on the weather) and 'You Are the Weather' (a portrait series); a viewing room that includes tables and chessboards; and a massive (specifically installed) window that overlooks the bay and the rocky, icy geologies that rise up out of it. The floor of the largest room (which housed the books in this former 'real' library) is rubber, engraved with Icelandic and English affectively oriented words for the weather. The dominant element of the installation is also in this room. 'Water, Selected'[6] includes twenty-four floor-to-ceiling glass tubes filled with water collected by Horn from some of Iceland's glaciers. If this is all library, are all of these elements books? Who wrote them? And how should we read them?

Ice is not a book. This, we recall, was Elena Glasberg's admonition that opened this chapter. Then, tempering her position: 'certainly, it is not *like* a book'. Now, we can surmise that Glasberg, like both Barad and Kirby, is suggesting that ice is not to be written and read in a representationalist sense; its primary task is not as stand-in (whether more authoritative or less) for text. Its purpose is not merely 'detection of data and truth' (Glasberg 2012: xii). And if it *is* a book, we must read ice against these dominant metaphors – that is, we must read it 'open on its spine' – as 'an assemblage of nested ecologies within the hard limits of the material earth' (xiii). This is a different kind of book where, in Glasberg's citation of Deleuze and Guattari, 'writing is one flow among many others, with no special place in relation to others, that comes into relations of current, countercurrent, and eddy, and other flows – flows of shit, sperm, words, action, eroticism, money, and so on' (Deleuze in Glasberg 2012: xiv). Kirby's suggestion – that nature writes itself – carries Deleuze and Guattari's ontological levelling even further, proposing that this all is flow, and this all is writing. Ice books in these terms, according to Glasberg, would 'indicate . . . the blankness or un-storied-ness that is not actually blank but rather its obverse, the inexpressible supplement to a historical process' (2012: xiv–xv). There is always something in excess of the information that such non-representationalist books provide us.

If we stay for a moment with this excess, we are brought back to the questions provoked by Alaimo and Sandilands above, namely, concerning the possibility of representation that can also speak to nature's unrepresentability. It should already be clear that 'unrepresentability' is not the term we need here. There is no excess or remainder that is somehow beyond translation, for within the transformative translations of nature writing itself, nothing escapes, insofar as all matters participate in a general entanglement.[7] But it does not follow that the meaning of these translations would be self-evident to all bodies engaged in such decipherings (namely human ones), or that the modes or machinations of this transformativity are transparent at every situation. We need to insist, however clumsily, that even as human reading and writing are part of nature writing itself, 'life at large' (Kirby 2011) is not an open book! Humans participate in an originary literacy, but reading is not mastery; it is engagement and implication in specific mixtures in particular contexts. This is not a case of human culture versus inaccessible nature. Rather, we might call this *situated literacy*[8] – not relativism, but an acknowledgement of partial perspective,[9] not only among differently situated human bodies, but among all of life's readers. No translation is adequate, no text is perfectly captured, but some books and some libraries are particularly resistant to our human reading skills. While we must be wary of such distinctions, the limits I invoke here are not ontological, but epistemological and ethical.

Vatnasafn calls us to attend to the challenges of a facile human literacy, even when these texts engender, flow through, and sustain us too. Horn herself notes that the idea of a repository of water is 'completely absurd' but also 'hideously, painfully apt' (Horn 2007: 66). While water, with its shapeshifting capacities and wily escape-artist know-how, could never really be contained by these glass houses, this seems to be precisely the work of these 'stacks'. In a co-authored article on ice, art and data, Lisa Bloom and Elena Glasberg point out that the columns of *Vatnasafn* mimic the shape of ice core samples – 'the major form of glaciological research' (Bloom and Glasberg 2012: 131). The library is thus brought into the frame of other scientific practices that strive to 'ensure the purity and even reproducibility of the data and result' (131). Re-presented as data and transformed into 'stacks', Iceland's glaciers are exactly the sort of ice book that Glasberg resists in her Antarctica book – the kind employing 'languages and methods of mapping and measure' in a bid to 'predict the unknown, or to manage a future that by definition cannot be predicted' (Glasberg 2012: xiii). This seems to be, on first glance, *Vatnasafn*'s offered critique: not only do archives of ice re-present the human perspective, but they also maintain that ice – *and specifically, the absurd but all-too-real project of creating libraries of ice* – in the end, (literally) boils down to this. This absurdity is rendered all the more palpable when the columns are read beside the outside world – also deliberately framed and magnified by Horn in the design of the Viewing Room bay window. An almost invisible membrane, the window draws us to the bay, the water, the ice beyond . . . Meanwhile, the stacks of melted glaciers are drawn into line, organised, subdued (in all the connotations of that word).

Yet these columns offer neither a blunt critique of anthropocentric representationalism, nor one that is comfortable simply pointing the finger at the reductions enacted by science. Ultimately, *Vatnasafn* resists a bifurcated nature/culture set-up, where the glaciers in the library are 'turned into' culture, unable to be compared with 'the real thing'. Dwelling in a relation of contiguity rather than contrast, the water columns alongside the books, the view, the water outside, suggest that no book is sufficient; all undertake different kinds of work. For one, data as representation is also a book we need to write for deliberately political reasons. Recalling the sometimes political necessity of representation as 'speaking for' nature discussed above, Bloom and Glasberg also remind us of the deliberate silencing of scientific data on climate change under the George W. Bush regime in the US (Bloom and Glasberg 2012: 122), a muzzling of climate science that in 2016 is still very much at play in Canada, the UK and Australia. And at the same time, these stacks are also the material evidence of love and care for these waters (each sample also collected by Horn by hand), and a testament to Horn's deep relationship with the landscape and the people of Iceland. So if these columns are a reduction, they are also an amplification, suggesting a kind of scientific data that exceeds itself. In Bloom and Glasberg's parsing, the melted glaciers create 'an affective possibility for the data' (133); they create a space not only for Horn, but for Icelanders and other visitors to 'recognise themselves in the data – or, *as* data' (132–3). The words of weather-feeling carved into the floor; the portrait series of the subtle ways in which weather also swirls within us; a room for playing chess protected from the wind and the sea by a portal of glass: these all attest to the fact that the nature of glaciers is continuous with our own embodied selves. 'When you talk of the water, are you talking of yourself, or the weather?' asks Horn (2013). *We are all bodies of water.* And if we are data, as Bloom and Glasberg suggest, then like data we – our saltwater blood, our intercellular fluids, our humours and biles and various other lubrications – are the writing outputs of a scribbly nature. As Horn says of a different project, but so apt in this context: at the heart of her work is the idea of the book, or rather 'a series of books, each one of which adds to the whole in a way that alters the identity of it retroactively' (Horn, n.d.). And in *Vatnasafn*'s 'nested ecology' (that congery of nature's flows, writing and representing as water contained, as portraits on paper, as floor, window, light, view) we are book-bodies among other books, each gesturing to still other books, other representations, none of them fully legible by humans, even as they write themselves as and through us.

Climate Change Represents Itself, or an Ethico-Onto-Epistemology[10] Against the Anthropocene

Irland notes, 'the tongues of the glaciers are receding, the voices of our rivers are being dammed and clogged with toxic debris. Who are the scribes writing about our waters and where are the libraries that store their moist stories?' (Irland 2011). Irland would likely agree that the 'about' in her question should just as well be an 'as', a 'with' or removed altogether – but leaving it there for the moment stresses again the ethico-political urgency of speaking for nature. Irland, too, recognises that representation or textuality is not only an ontological question hovering at a presumed nature/culture divide. While nature is always writing and reading itself, this acknowledgement must rest alongside a recognition of the ways in which anthropogenic incursion is also muting and mutilating riparian writing. To be sure, this is a contradictory claim. On the one hand, even a toxic damming and clogging is an iteration – the next inscriptions onto a palimpsest of watery natures. On the other, do we not have an obligation to answer for our human failure of 'good literacy', as the toxic waters rise? And, just as Irland's ice books 'depict a problem – receding glaciers – and a suggestion for action – reseeding riparian zones to reduce some of the effects of climate change through plants' (Irland 2011), so too does Horn's *Vatnasafn* draw attention to 'the menace of anthropogenic climate change' (Bloom and Glasberg 2012: 133). As Bloom and Glasberg wonder, will Horn's insistence that *we are water* instil as well a sense of 'the story [we] are collectively writing: that the end of the Earth is already legible?' (134).

If we, as nature, are to be read, then we also, as nature, are writers. A growing chorus indicates that we have entered a new age of the Anthropocene, where human incursion into planetary geological, meteorological and biological systems has become a determining factor in its evolution, and in climate change specifically. As Jeanette Winterson comments in relation to Horn's *You are the Weather*, 'weather affects everyone and everything on the planet, but now, for the first time in evolutionary history, humans are affecting the weather in return' (Winterson 2009). There is good reason to be cautious about such proclamations, not only because of the sense of human mastery they reify, but also because of their installation, once again, of the nature/culture split as a matter of ontology. The Anthropocene, in the words of Eileen Crist, 'blocks from consideration the possibility of abolishing a way of life founded on the domination of nature' (Crist 2013: 129). But even if 'nature writes itself' suggests a different ecological imaginary than 'Man-Made Nature', the question of responsibility still looms large: if nature is always a writing-becoming, and humans are but one instance of that process, how do we hold ourselves responsible in the context of the Anthropocene? To attribute all authorship to nature cannot be an easy getaway; 'Nature writes itself' offers no absolution.

In the case of her ice books, Irland notes that part of their significance 'is that they melt away. Time and energy that has gone into the carving of the books vanish in the current of a stream' (Irland 2011). In one sense, the disappearance of these tomes is meant to invoke glacial melt and the urgent environmental questions begged by anthropogenic climate change. How are we, as nature's scribes, writing these events into being? At the same time, the melting books aren't disappearing at all; they are lapped by the rivers and the fish and the grasses; the seed-texts they harbour spread their stories through the currents. This is *also* the human as nature writing, but in a very different way. Irland signals the ambivalence of this writing by noting that 'everything is actually in existence for only a period of time. Instead of dust to dust, here we have water to water' (Irland 2011). Nature always writes itself; water's phase changes will happen. But how, where, for whose benefit, and precipitated by what? How are we, as natural agents among myriad others, taking up nature's pen?

If Irland's ice books float toward questions about anthropogenic incursion into the writing of these riparian habitats, Horn's *Vatnasafn* magnifies these questions in ways both familiar and uncanny as we stare into our own distorted self-image in the massive cores of melted waters: the glaciers, at once definitive of Iceland's 'nature', are in Horn's installation rendered unrecognisable. As we slalom through these library stacks, we want to know: who wrote these tomes? Or perhaps more to the point: what was *un*written in their writing? In Horn's library, the idea of glacier as always already book, where 'nature writes itself' in the story of the earth and its temperature fluctuations, is folded claustrophobically into the idea of book as a human cultural scribbling, our version of the world. If Iceland's glaciers are indeed a book to be read by us, the messages are becoming illegible. Like Irland, Horn offers no easy comforts: writing goes both ways. Writing seems also to be an unwriting in this case. The melting away of Irland's ice books is also a gift to the river, a reminder that these books have meanings for bodies and beings that aren't human. But for whom is Horn's glacial library written, or unwritten? If *we are water*, might this also be an unwitting unwriting of ourselves?

Yet, in a context of 'nature writes itself' there is no such thing as unwriting. That Irland's dissolving books and Horn's melted glaciers gesture to such a possibility underlines this very point: the promise, or dread, of an ultimately impossible unwriting that haunts these artworks. Taking the Anthropocene's microphone in hand, climate researcher Stephan Harrison notes that we now recognise the 'alarming implications of our present and future predicament' of climate's high sensitivity to anthropogenic changes. 'With the melting of these archives go forever these libraries of past change' (Harrison 2009: 77). In the shadow of the Anthropocene, unwriting looms large . . . but it may be something of an empty threat. Apocalyptic imaginaries may still have some useful power of persuasion (Gabrys and Yusoff 2011: 521), but so much focus on the eraser might miss the fact that the pen still moves across the page. To 'unwrite' only makes sense in a non-durational temporality where something is not yet done, done, or undone. In the thickness of deep time, creeping into gathering presents and possible futures, nothing is delible, and all of these intra-acting times pool and puddle without the security of linear conviction. Like the multiple hydrological cycles that water our planet, writing is always translation, transubstantiation – all phenomena reading and rewriting themselves in new ways.

This realisation might arrive with alarm, or relief. Everything remains, but everything changes: a word, a font, a sentence shifted, or an entire language disintegrated – yet writing is inescapable. In these terms, an 'ethics of representation' inhabits an altered territory. Representation is not a way of capturing or speaking for that which is ontologically separate, but instead always a case of iteration of the matter of writing; an ethics of representation is thus about our own adventures in writing as attending to what J. K. Gibson-Graham (2011) calls the project of belonging. How will we, as nature, water and climate *contracted*, continue to inscribe attunement, listening, partial dissolution, collectivity, care, curiosity, wonder, grace, gratitude or other modes of becoming-with, instead of writing against them, dazzled (numbed?) by a myth of separateness? This question does not romanticise belonging, as if it were all benign, pleasurable or even just. A project of belonging is a necessary experiment and improvisation, and hence always a risk.

As Karen Barad writes, 'we (but not only "we humans") are always already responsible to the others with whom or which we are entangled' (Barad 2007: 393). Against the Anthropocene, an ethics of 'nature writes itself' similarly suggests we are all water, all climate change, all the way down; representation must also be responsivity. 'Ethics is therefore not about right response to a radically exterior/ised other, but about responsibility and accountability for the lively relationalities of becoming of which we are a part' (Barad 2007: 393).

Notes

1. I express thanks to Vicki Kirby for her generous engagement with the ideas articulated in this chapter, as well as to both Basia Irland and Elena Glasberg for sharing with me texts that deeply inform my analysis here.
2. See, for example, the extensive writings of Stacy Alaimo (2000), Rosi Braidotti (2002, 2013), Greta Gaard (1997, 2001), Val Plumwood (1993), and Catriona Sandilands (1999), among many others.
3. As Alaimo and Hekman note, 'far from deconstructing the dichotomies of language/reality or culture/nature', postmodern theorists have problematically 'rejected one side and embraced the other' (Alaimo and Hekman 2008: 2–3) – thus explicitly connecting the language/realist split to the nature/culture binary as bound up in one another.
4. 'It may still be best', Alaimo writes, 'to embrace environmental ideals of wilderness, or the respect for the sovereignty of nature (as Plumwood puts it), both of which work to establish boundaries that would protect nature from human exploitation and degradation' (Alaimo 2008: 258). Neither Alaimo nor Sandilands advocates a nature/culture split – in fact, both deliberately eschew it. Yet 'unrepresentable nature' still figures in their work, begging the question with which this chapter grapples. My own argument appreciates Alaimo's call, but seeks a parsing that would not rely on 'unrepresentability'.
5. See Bataille (1992), who distinguishes between humans and other animals on the grounds that humans are aware of their separation from their environment.
6. This title invokes both a human curation and natural selection – another instance of nature writing, reading and rewriting itself!
7. My appreciation to Kirby for pressing this point to me, and suggesting a more careful formulation of this position. Kirby and I may still disagree on my arguments concerning excess.
8. This phrase is after Donna Haraway's (1988) concept of 'situated knowledges' – always emerging from embedded and embodied entanglements between the knower and what she knows.
9. See Haraway (1988).
10. This term is used by Karen Barad (2007) to stress the inseparability of these three terms.

References

Alaimo, S. (2000), *Undomesticated Ground: Recasting Nature as Feminist Space*, Ithaca: Cornell University Press.

Alaimo, S. (2010), 'The Naked Word: The Trans-corporeal Ethics of the Protesting Body', *Women and Performance*, 20: 1, pp. 15–36.

Alaimo, S., and S. Hekman (eds) (2008), *Material Feminisms*, Bloomington: Indiana University Press.

Barad, K. (2007*)*, *Meeting the Universe Halfway: quantum physics and the entanglement of matter and meaning*, Durham, NC: Duke University Press.

Bataille, G. (1992), *Theory of Religion*, New York: Zone Books.

Bloom, L., and E. Glasberg (2012), 'Disappearing Ice and Missing Data: Climate Change in the Visual Culture of the Polar Regions', in J. Marschine and A. Polli (eds), *Far Field: Digital Culture, Climate Change and the Poles*, Bristol: Intellect, pp. 118–39.

Braidotti, R. (2002), *Metamorphoses*, Cambridge: Polity Press.

Braidotti, R. (2013), *The Posthuman*, Cambridge: Polity Press.

Crist, E. (2013), 'On the Poverty of Our Nomenclature', *Environmental Humanities*, 3, pp. 129–47.

Cruikshank, J. (2005), *Do Glaciers Listen? Local Knowledge, Colonial Encounters, and Social Imagination*, Vancouver: University of British Columbia Press.

Gaard, G. (1997), 'Toward a Queer Ecofeminism', *Hypatia: a journal of feminist philosophy*, 12: 1, pp. 114–37.

Gaard, G. (2001), 'Women, Water and Energy: An Ecofeminist Approach', *Organization and Environment*, 14: 2, pp. 157–72.

Gabrys, J., and K. Yusoff (2011), 'Climate Change and the Imagination', *WIRES (Wiley Interdisciplinary Reviews, Climate Change)*, 2: 4, pp. 516–34.

Gibson-Graham, J. K. (2011), 'A feminist project of belonging for the Anthropocene', *Gender, Place & Culture*, 18: 1, pp. 1–21.

Glasberg, E. (2012), *Antarctica as Cultural Critique*, New York: Palgrave MacMillan.

Haraway, D. (1988), 'Situated Knowledges: The Science Question in Feminism and the Privilege of Partial Perspective', *Feminist Studies*, 14: 3, pp. 575–99.

Haraway, D. (2004), *The Haraway Reader*, London: Routledge.

Harrison, S. (2009), 'Glaciers: Icons of Snow and Ice', in K. Yusoff (ed.), *Bipolar*, London: The Arts Catalyst, pp. 76–7.

Horn, R. (n.d.), 'Interview' in *Journal of Contemporary Art*, available at <www.jca-online.com/horn.html > (last accessed 29 March 2016).

Horn, R. (2007), 'The Master Chameleon', *Tate Etc.*, 10, pp. 62–7.

Horn, R. (2013), 'Saying water,' video, ed. Kamilla Bruus and Troels Kahl, Louisiana Channel, Louisiana Museum of Modern Art, <https://vimeo.com/67051609> (last accessed 29 March 2016).

Irland, B. (2011), 'Receding/Reseeding', *Downstream: A Poetics of Water*, Vancouver, Canada (transcript of talk).

Kirby, V. (2008), 'Natural Convers(at)ions: Or, What If Culture Was Really Nature All Along?', in S. Alaimo and S. Hekman (eds), *Material Feminisms*, Bloomington: Indiana University Press, pp. 214–36.

Kirby, V. (2011), *Quantum Anthropologies: Life at Large*, Durham, NC: Duke University Press.

Plumwood, V. (1993), *Feminism and the Mastery of Nature*, New York: Routledge.

Sandilands, C. (1999), *The Good-Natured Feminist: Feminism and the Quest for Democracy*, Minneapolis: University of Minnesota Press.

van Wyck, P. (2013), 'Footbridge at Atwater: A Chorographic Inventory of Effects', in C. Chen, J. MacLeod and A. Neimanis (eds), *Thinking with Water*, Montreal: McGill-Queens University Press, pp. 256–73.

Winterson, J. (2009), 'Roni Horn – Entering the Flow-World', *Art World Magazine*, available at <http://www.jeanettewinterson.com/journalism/roni-horn-entering-the-flow-world/> (last accessed 29 March 2016).

Yusoff, K. (2009), 'Core Histories', in K. Yusoff (ed.), *Bipolar*, London: The Arts Catalyst, pp. 34–6.

CHAPTER 10

Climate Change, Socially Synchronised: Are We Really Running out of Time?

Will Johncock

Concerns regarding the industrialised Earth's changing climate explicitly represent ecological transition as a planet 'running out of time'. Implicit within this concern is the realisation that it is humans that could be 'running out of time', in that climate change threatens to render the planet uninhabitable for our species. This seems to combatively oppose ecological/climate change from human existence, as well as characterising time as an adversarial force whose source transcends humans.

This characterisation of time as both a transcendent source, and as something against which we battle, permeates our everyday experiences. Time provides a regulatory and adjudicatory framework via which we are assessed. This governs short-term intentions such as doing enough work in a day, arriving at social commitments without being late, and making the right bus, as well as longer-term ambitions such as career development or having children. Here we see that time is always apparent, yet there is often not enough of it when we feel we need it. Or in other words, we often feel like we are racing against it.

The clocked and calendared forms of time through which these responsibilities are assessed seemingly derive from an already existing temporality. That is, time is an inherently worldly phenomenon that humans then represent via clocks and calendars (to facilitate social coordination and synchronisation, amongst other uses). What this assumes is that the social construction of time is separate from the phenomenon of time itself. The above paragraph briefly lists situations where we 'run out of time' at a social level. What will be considered in this chapter though, is whether climate change discussions that demand time is something of which humans are 'running out' indicate that humans are involved in an adversarial relation with time at an existential level. Are we running out of time to get to work on time, or are we running out of time, our time, entirely?

Ecological/Climate Change Represents a Planet 'Running out of Time'

The argument that the earth is 'running out of time' has had no more prominent champion than Denis Hayes, renowned for having dropped out of Harvard Law School to organise *Earth Day*, the 'event which gave birth to the environmental movement in modern America' (Quade 1990: 16). Hayes, described as North America's most prominent environmentalist,[1] is joined by Donald Brown, Associate Professor of Environmental Ethics, Science and Law at Pennsylvania State University, who similarly proclaims, in response to the *Copenhagen Accord*,[2] that scientific evidence concerning climate change reveals the 'world is running out of time' (Brown 2010). Nick Hansen, introduced as the world's leading climate scientist in *Storms of My Grandchildren* (2009), equally observes that contrary to efforts to regulate the human contribution to ecological/climate change, 'short-term special interests' neglect that 'we are running out of time' (xi). Interestingly, this characterisation of ecological/climate change is not a recent trend. Over forty years ago the prominent geoscientist, Albert Engel, in an *American Scientist* article titled 'Time and the Earth' (1969), warns that 'man, if not the Earth, is running out of time' (460). Furthermore, when David Runnalls, President of the International Institute for Sustainable Development, declares that 'the world is running out of time to deal with seemingly overwhelming environmental threats' (2008: 19), it is apparent that both human *and* earthly existence is implied by the phrase 'the world'.

Also warranting attention are the assumptions that underpin the temporality of environmental threats. The interpretation of the source of time as an adversarial externality frames our presumption of the futility in trying to change it. In this regard, sociologist Barbara Adam's 'Time and Environmental Crisis' (1993), in engaging the 'consensus that we are facing an environmental crisis', notes that 'while the spatial dimension has been brought to the fore in a number of disciplines, the temporal equivalent has stayed implicit' (1993: 399). I am interested in this evaluation of climate change discussion, given the insight it provides into the belief that we can affect the spatial realm/world, while situating time as objectively separate and beyond human influence. It seems that humans, having changed the world's spatial/material ecological constitution via processes of industrialisation, believe that potentially 'recuperative' changes can be made via spatial/material resources. Conversely, time is simply there to be used or lost, and there is nothing we can do about that except to race faster against it. Adam again illustrates this common interpretation in stating that 'we are running out – not of resources, but of time' (1993: 401).

Given that time manifests in the spatial/material realm, however, it is worth asking whether time's source is actually an adversarial, invariable parameter in determining if a changing material climate means that humans are 'running out of time'. To frame this interrogation, the presumption that the source of time is objectively separate from humans must be clarified.

Why is it Presumed that the Source of Time is Objectively Separate from the Human?

Social systems are able to regulate their subjects because of something regular and consistent about the time they represent on calendars and clocks. German sociologist, Georg Simmel, observing that a society would be 'derailed' if all the watches and clocks within it 'went wrong in different ways' (1997: 177), argues that social time only functions because of its objectively common conditions. This interpretation presumes that social time represents, and is conditioned by, an objectively separate rhythm that transcends individual idiosyncrasies. Abiding by an objective temporality, subjects conform to, and cohere with, the social collective. Consequently, social time, as well as the time it represents, 'transcends all subjective elements' (177).

There is no more ubiquitous representation of time than international time zones, which seemingly divide an already occurring global time-source to which the world collectively adheres. The assumption duly emerges that global synchronisation is conditioned by a worldly temporality, which Adam describes as the international coordination of social action via a global standard (1995: 20). Global standardisation demands that 'one hour of clock time is one hour wherever we are' (24). Here we see that the social construction of time is presumed to be separate from, because it is subsequent to, the actual phenomenon of time.

The physics of Isaac Newton informs this interpretation, positing a time-source that is objectively outside human interference (Newton in Barrow 2009: 160). This objective separation gives 'true, absolute time' uniformity, as it 'flows equably without relation to anything external' (Newton 1978: 77). True, absolute time can consequently explain the social synchronisation of human subjects. Subjects synchronise by collectively using a representation of this objectively uniform temporality. While Albert Einstein's theory of relativity (2006) problematises the notion of an absolute objectivity of time, the assumptions derived from Newton's model remain relevant for this particular inquiry. This is because it captures something that humans almost inevitably take for granted; namely, that time is separate from human influence, which means that via common representations of it, time can be used as the objective source upon which social synchronisation depends. Here the recognition that humans can affect social representations of time, but not the actual source of time that they represent, means that regarding the material, spatial effects of ecological climate change, only space, but not time, can be affected by humans.

The conceptual separation of the supposedly real phenomenon of time from its social construction(s) installs a curious divide between reality and representation that will be interrogated at various points in this chapter. If it is posited that time, real time, is a phenomenon that is removed from the human, social representation and construction of it, what must be asked is how such representations actually end up working as time at all? Because these representations certainly do seem to work in terms of social temporality. The regularity of social organisation and function is conditioned by such 'representational', social time. However, if there is a gap between the necessary reality of time, and any such contingent, social, human representation of it, then what must be asked is how representation traverses an ontological gap in order to access the real source from which its function is conditioned. This curious ramification will come under justifiable scrutiny here.

Compared to the relatively visible, material effects of changing climates, the temporality framing our fear concerning climate change is harder to locate. Barbara Adam, noting this mysterious quality of time, brings our attention to the typical characterisation of time as invisible. While space is visible as worldly substantiality, time is everywhere but nowhere. Or in Adam's terms, 'time is everywhere, yet it eludes us. It is so deeply implicated in our existences that it is almost invisible' (1990: 9).

Philosopher Elizabeth Grosz also recognises this characterisation of time as a mysterious, hidden, 'silent accompaniment, a shadowy implication' (1999: 1). This is consistent with the earlier observation that while the spatial/material ramifications of climate change can be potentially manipulated, thereby remaining open for debate, time is invisible, objective and outside human influence.

The focus in this argument on the relation of time to environmental, ecological change is, in this regard, novel. Adam's inquiry, while problematic in ways that will soon become apparent, does recognise that an 'explicit focus on time . . . illuminates the shadow side of environmental phenomena, aspects which are normally ignored' (Adam 1994: 110). In attempting to *not* ignore this aspect of environmental phenomena, we will first try to locate where, or when, time occurs, in the same manner that we are able to with material space.

States of Time are Produced in the Present

Assuming that the origin of time occurred in a distant, transcendent past, installs time's source as pre-existent and exterior to humans. This assumption can be interrogated via the provocative insights of philosopher George Mead (1863–1931), who addresses the relation of the present to the past. In *The Philosophy of the Present* (2002), Mead firstly, rather unprovocatively, recognises that the past 'irrevocably conditions the present' (36). This correlates with the everyday interpretation that time moves forward from past to present. Counter-intuitively however, Mead also characterises the past as 'revocable' (36), a description attributable to the novelty of a new present. As the present emerges, the past that conditions it must also, in a certain fashion, be present. Interestingly for Mead, this re-produces the past, rendering it 'a different past' (35) because the past-present relation is a new development that the past did not already constitute. The past's constitutive participation in a novel/new present re-constitutes the past as that which will have become this present's past. Or in Mead's terms, it is 'what it was' of the past 'that changes' (37). Given that the past only becomes past in relation to a present, it is not that this past was once a present and is now a past; 'we orient ourselves not with reference to the past which was a present' (46). Rather, the past which has conditioned the present is as novel/new as the present, because the past only emerges as 'past' concurrently with its relational present.

After such a knotty description I anticipate that the response to this explanation might be, understandably, that all that changes is our *impression* of the past, while the 'past in itself' remains as it was. However, let us note that a past 'in itself' is not a 'past', nor a state of time. It is only via its relation with the present that the past state of time/ temporality *becomes* – concurrently produced as both 'what it was' and 'what it is'. This problematises the notion that the origin of any state of time is permanently fixed and sealed off. Mead, indeed, demands the perpetual alterability of a state of time such as the past, and argues against the shared and unquestioned belief in 'an ultimate unchangeable past spread behind us in its entirety' (58).

Past, present and future are contingent human descriptions for time. Nevertheless, the point to be taken from this discussion with Mead is that what constitutes time has perpetually reproduced origins. The source of time is not simply via an origin fixed in a distant past, away from which new presents are increasingly distanced. This insight will inform our interrogation of the belief that what is spatial, such as embodied humans or climate change materialities, is governed by an untouchably transcendent, preceding temporality.

Perception Incarnates, rather than Simply Observes

The phenomenology of Maurice Merleau-Ponty (1908–61) can assist here in terms of analysing the temporality of what is spatially or materially observable about climate change. Of particular note is Merleau-Ponty's interest in blurring the relation between the observing subject and the observed object-world. In *The Visible and the Invisible* (1968), Merleau-Ponty posits the 'singularity' (7) of perceptual relations between observer and observed. These relations are posited as being embodied, whereby a spatial, 'corporeal component' (8) conditions perception.

It is the bodily, and therefore the spatial/material, focus of Merleau-Ponty's phenomenology that is of most relevance to our current inquiry. This distinguishes this version of phenomenology from the work of other influential phenomenologists such as Edmund Husserl (1859–1938) and Martin Heidegger (1889–1976). Husserl focuses on a transcendent consciousness as the condition of worldly experience, an 'infinite world of absolute mental processes – the fundamental *field of phenomenology*' (Husserl 1983: 114; emphasis in original). The body accordingly sits tenuously in Husserl's phenomenology, caught in dichotomous relations as a 'thing inserted' (1990: 169) between the transcendental consciousness/subject and the spatial/material realm.

Heidegger's phenomenology conversely neglects to specifically address the body. His most important work, *Being and Time* (1962), is notably criticised by the French existentialist, Jean-Paul Sartre, who claims that Heidegger does not make the 'slightest allusion to it [the body] in his existential analytic' (2003: 405). Sartre's critique of why Heidegger 'only wrote six lines on the body in the whole of Being and Time' (231) is later acknowledged by Heidegger himself in the *Zollikon Seminars* (2001). Here Heidegger argues that his ontological model *implicitly* assumes the body, inasmuch as humans could not participate in the 'world-openness' of subjectivity if they were not constituted by 'bodily nature' (Heidegger 2001: 231–2). This world-openness relates to Heidegger's later explication that the body is not a 'thing which stops with the skin' (86). There are consistencies between Heidegger's conception here and Merleau-Ponty's understanding of the body, which will be addressed when we consider bodily limits. Nevertheless, given that for Merleau-Ponty the perceptual, spatial body is the primordial condition (1962: xvi) of all experience with perceptual temporality, it will be this chapter's conceptual ally.

In *Phenomenology of Perception* (1962), Merleau-Ponty argues that a subject never transcends their body (103). This idea is extended in *The Visible and the Invisible* in developing an Husserlian insight that when touching one's hand with the other, a subject simultaneously *touches* and *is touched*. The point being made here is that the subject is a part of the world it touches at the same time as the touched world is a part of the subject (1968: 133). Perception conditions not only the hand-as-subject touching itself-as-body/thing, but also the self-as-body touching the world-as-bodies/things. Body-world borders are perpetually (re)produced because the body experiences itself, and the world, from the inside of, and also as, the world. Given this profound sense of implication, subjectivity is described by Merleau-Ponty as a 'chiasmic' (130–55) production, where worldly things and the self are co-constitutive (123).

The timing of this subject-world co-constitution is of special interest to our inquiries. In problematising the notion of an autonomous subject that perceives a pre-existing, separate world, perception, according to Merleau-Ponty, shifts from a communication between a discovering subject and an already existing worldly thing, to instead being an event 'formed in the midst of the world and as it were in the things' (134).

Perception is not simply a capacity the embodied subject possesses in order to access pre-given, pre-fabricated objects, for perception is rather a world-incarnating process by which subjects and worldly objects manifest concurrently with/in each other. Merleau-Ponty describes these conditions as essential, because perception of the world is only possible if the perceiver '*is of it*' (134–5; emphasis in original). Perception that incarnates subjects and objects co-constitutively problematises the notion of separate, pre-existing things that are *then* perceived by a perceiver. Instead, in perceiving, the human body is *among* such objects/things, where 'among' does not simply mean intermingling with, side by side, like marbles jostling for position, but instead suggests that the body is implicated in and through the constitution of other objects/things. Or as Merleau-Ponty eloquently states, 'I do not see it [an object] from the depths of nothingness, but from the midst of itself' (1968: 113). Heidegger's aforementioned *Zollikon* seminars similarly evoke the plastic liveliness of bodily limits. What was implicitly contained in *Being and Time* is in *Zollikon* articulated more directly, whereby 'when pointing with my finger . . . I [as body] do not end at my fingertips. Where then is the limit of the body? "Each body is my body". As such, the proposition [bodily limit] is nonsensical' (2001: 86).

What can be concluded from this section is that embodied perception, conditioned by what is spatial and material, incarnates subject and object in/as a singular phenomenon instead of connecting a subject to an already existing spatial, material object. This conception of spatial/material co-constitution will have ramifications for the supposedly oppositional relation that environmentally concerned discourses install between materially embodied humans and climate change materialities.

The Relation between Spatial/Material Incarnations and the Space/Matter of Being

What we will now consider is why this worldly co-constitutive, perceptual (re)production of spatial/material subjects and objects means that all are simultaneously localised *and* globalised. With the help of Merleau-Ponty the idea has been developed that the body manifests through a general process in which the world distinguishes itself *from* itself as a *particular* spatiality/materiality. The body-as-space/matter and the world-as-space/matter materialise each other, where, as the world incarnates the body, the body's incarnation (re-)produces the world as this world that has materialised this body. This is worldly perception (what Merleau-Ponty calls *the flesh of the world*), a world perceiving itself through distinguishable, spatial/material forms of itself (such as bodies). Without this self-distinguishability, Being, or what is, would not manifest, whereby every entity is the condition of Being's internal reflex.

Against this backdrop of Being's all-inclusiveness, we should now consider more carefully how we might approach the question; what *is* climate or ecological change? It is now routine to conceive such environmental change in terms of its disastrous ramifications for the human species, not to mention other species. Increased global heat, the melting of polar ice caps, rising seawaters, polluted air and contaminated soils represent a changing environment that threatens human life. However, while these scenarios describe the dramatic ways in which ecological/climate change manifests, it does not address their fundamental constitution. The fundamental constitution of embodied humans is space/matter. What, then, is the fundamental constitution of ecological/climate change?

Raymond Pierrehumbert, co-author of the United States National Research Council report, explains in *Climate Change: A Catastrophe in Slow Motion* (2006) that 'human-induced' changes to Earth's ecology and climate are attributable to modern industrialisation. The most significant change has occurred via global warming, 'wrought by industrial carbon dioxide emissions' (573). While 'several other gases' contribute to the 'human-induced' aspects of global warming, carbon dioxide is 'by far the biggest player' (274). Albert Engel, whose work we engaged earlier, also commentates in 1969 on the destructive influence of industrial, carbon emissions, pouring 'millions of tons of carbon dioxide into the air from the irresponsible destruction of fossil fuels' (1969: 480–1).

Humans are attributed with most responsibility, or blame, for Earth's changing environment, however carbon dioxide itself was of course not a human invention. Rather, it is an atmospheric constituent that has played a repeatedly prominent role in the Earth's climatic changes. This includes the Ice Ages, the warmer dinosaur era seventy million years ago, and the Earth's collapse into deep freeze in the Neoproterozoic era six hundred million years ago (Pierrehumbert 2006: 574). However, human industrialisation has increased the atmospheric carbon gas levels by about fifteen times their pre-industrial levels (574). In fact, global news in recent years has been dominated by this theme. *The Atlantic* magazine describes carbon dioxide as 'the great engine of climate change' (Meyer 2015), and that the dangerous level it reached on 11 November 2015 means that 'Earth's atmosphere just crossed an epochal threshold' (Meyer 2015). The United Kingdom's *Guardian* newspaper reports that the amount of carbon dioxide gas in the Earth's atmosphere is more than it has experienced in five million years (Carrington 2013). Consistent with the earlier observation that climate change discourses typically characterise the world as 'running out of time', Australia's *Sydney Morning Herald* newspaper describes the same story as a worldly 'clock running down' (Hannam 2013).

Rather than joining the global chorus identifying carbon as the destructive villain against which the Earth must battle, what I am attempting to acknowledge here is that this fundamental constituent of climate change is also a spatial/material form of Being. Carbon dioxide, a worldly substance, a chemical compound, is constituted by a space/matter that is *of* the world as much as it is *in* the world. This is interesting, because according to the phenomenological conception of space/matter developed above, every spatiality/materiality, in being distinguished *from* Being, thereby enacts the *productive* iterability that is internal to Being, a worlding that is always a specific expression of Being's space/matter.

We have seen climate change discourses install an adversarial relationship between humans and climate change, and between the Earth and climate change. As climate change materialities such as carbon dioxide proliferate, the world and humans are described as running out of time. However, if climate change materialities are forms of worldly spatiality/materiality, and every spatiality/materiality co-conditions the being of Being, then the notion of an ontological opposition between spatial/material embodied humans and spatial/material climatic change requires attention. A phenomenological conception of space/matter would argue that embodied human subjects do not merely observe or perceive specific examples of climate change. Rather, all such spatial and material manifestations condition each other's becoming.[3] It is in this co-conditioning of Being's becoming that we might suspect that the materialities of climate change have a more primordial relation to time than simply symbolising that a species or a planet is running out of time.

The Spatial/Material Production of Time?

In the previous section we have encountered the notion that Being is produced via self-distinguishable, spatial/material forms *of itself*. If this is the becoming of Being, or in other words, if this is the condi-tion of there being Being, what can be asked now is whether such a generalised, incarnating ontology is also the condition of Being's time. To consider this, let us revisit our engagement with Mead in which it emerged that every state of time perpetually, co-constitutively, (re) manifests relationally with other states of time. According to Mead, a state of time is never 'in-itself'. Rather, states of time only manifest *with* other states, whereby the past only becomes the past in relation with its co-constitutive present.

What is now apparent is that this logic correlates to a phenome-nological conception of space/matter. No spatial/material state exists separately 'in-itself', but instead, each spatiality/materiality manifests co-constitutively with other spatial/material states. If this co-constitu-tive ontology is the condition not only of the becoming of Being, but also of there being Being, that is, of the origin of Being, then how could this be anything but Being's time? If every spatial/material state con-ditions the being of Being, it follows that every spatial/material state conditions Being's time.

A particular spatiality/materiality would originate Being's time because Being only becomes, or originates, as the Being that has manifested this particularity via this particularity's manifestation. Consequently, if there is Being, worldly space/matter, then there is never a point at which time, as something extraneous, is introduced. Wherever there is Being, wherever there is anything, there is always already time. This is consistent with Merleau-Ponty's characterisation of time as 'a general flight out of itself' (1962: 419). If we think of Being as internally self-distinguishing, then every spatiality/materiality/ecology temporalises what would otherwise be what Merleau-Ponty describes as the atemporal, 'unbroken fields of presence' (423). However, this is not to say that time dismantles an anterior plenitude that *subsequently* becomes temporal. Instead, time is Being's self-distinguishability, a process which is always already occurring in order for there to be existence/Being. Without time/temporality there is no plenitude, there is no Being.

The external objectivity of time in Newtonian physics can seemingly account for social synchronisation. Subjects collectively conform to the same representation of a time-source that is outside the interference of any subject. Within such a conception, every human subject is *inescapably temporal* in that time governs our transience and our inevitable demise. The phenomenological argument developed in this chapter however, characterises human subjects, and all other spatialities/materialities, as also inescapably entwined in temporality, but not because of an unavoidable finitude that a transcendent time-source imposes. Rather, all spatialities/materialities are inescapably temporal because they are temporalising, whereby from their intersubjective, co-constitutive incarnation, time and/as Being is made manifest. According to this, a changing spatial/material ecology does not indicate that time is running out. There is either time, or there is not.

A potential contradiction has now emerged, however. If each individual manifestation is the incarnation of time, would these seemingly *subjective* and specific qualities of time contradict what is *objectively* common about the time which conditions social synchronisation? If every spatial thing incarnates time, how do any spatial things ever experience the *same time*? More specifically, in the case of the spatial 'things' that are human, how is a social consensus about time ever reached or produced if each human's very possibility and animation involves a certain individual time which is somehow, also, a common time? The notion that the social construction of time is contingent and separated from what is inherent and real about time will come under scrutiny here. If, as has just been explained, the ontology of time has intersubjective, co-constitutive conditions, then there seems to be something inherently social about time's construction or production.

Spatial, Material, Ecological Synchronisation

It should first be emphasised that according to the understanding just developed, no subject wills time in a manner where they pre-exist the time they then decide to source. In other words, this isn't an argument that posits time as a transcendental frame of reference, outside human control and being, nor is it a representational, social contructivist argument of human exceptionalism that installs the human as the exclusive author of time's model. Instead, time manifests with/as manifestation generally. What is general is simultaneously, inescapably, particular in this regard, whereby Being's time is inherent to being a subject, and therefore inherent to subjectivity. Merleau-Ponty describes this in *The Visible and the Invisible* as a 'universal dimension' (1968: 142) of subjectivity. The nature of this universality will be this section's focus, addressing how the process of individuating identifiable things, subjects, events *in* time and *from* time renders them, and time – *objective*. This will accommodate the reality of our everyday lives, in which something objectively common about time is required for social function and synchronisation.

Subjectivity *is* a living temporality. Being, in perceiving itself through myriad forms of itself, self-incarnates. If Being's self-incarnation is a perpetual *self*-perception, then spatial/material subjects incarnate Being's 'own' self-awareness/self-consciousness. Merleau-Ponty also describes the becoming of consciousness in self-self terms, where the upsurging of the flesh of the world becomes 'aware of itself, for the explosion or dehiscence of the present . . . is the archetype of the relationship of self to self, and it traces out an interiority' (1962: 426). Every spatiality/materiality, including each embodied human subject, involves a living consciousness that is resonant with, and as, the flesh of the world. Merleau-Ponty agrees; 'every thought known to us occurs to a flesh' (1968: 146).

Given this sense that consciousness is, and has, a worldly resonance, the assumption that humans are the only material incarnations with self-awareness of their place in ecological/climate change deserves interrogation. This consideration of the universal conditions of consciousness will frame a discussion that will explain why the incarnation of time by spatial/material subjectivities does not jeopardise the objectively common conditions of social synchronisation. After all, social synchronisation seems to occur because subjects share consciousness of the same time.

Pierrehumbert characterises humans as an environmental force, causing 'practically irreversible changes in global conditions' (2006: 573). However, this is not to say that humans are the only worldly incarnations to cause globally significant ecological, climate change. The evolution of oxygen-generating photosynthetic algae between one billion and two and a half billion years ago 'changed one fifth of the atmosphere, poisoned much of the previous ecosystem, and terminated the dominant role of methane as a greenhouse gas' (573). The colonisation of land plants half a billion years ago had similarly momentous repercussions, by increasing 'the rate at which atmospheric carbon dioxide is converted to limestone in the soil, leading to severe global cooling' (573). However, despite how different worldly incarnations, different forms of life, have changed ecologies and climates, Pierrehumbert separates 'human induced' changes from all others. What makes current climatic change unique according to Pierrehumbert is that 'the causative agents – humans – are sentient' (573).

It is debatable, as explored in the field of object-oriented ontology, whether plants, algae and other nonhuman forms of life are sentient.[4] But if sentience is, as a dictionary definition informs us, 'being conscious of sense impressions' (Merriam-Webster 2015), it could certainly be argued that plants and algae *are* aware of their sense impressions, and thus *are* sentient.[5] Rather than enter this particular debate, we will use our earlier exploration into the worldly, material constitution of consciousness to structure an interrogation of the commitment that only humans are really aware of the Earth's changing climate, and of the possible relevance of their activities to this. Being's consciousness, or awareness, manifests by perceiving itself through spatial/material/ecological forms of itself. Worldly spatial/material/ecological incarnations *are* Being's self-consciousness. This approach reconfigures what is typically captured by the term 'consciousness'. All spatial/material/ecological subjects such as plants, algae, carbon dioxide and humans are self-conscious of their participation in (re)producing Earth's changing climate/ecology, given that the incarnation of each conditions (Being's) consciousness in general.

The previous section has explored how Being's self-incarnation, as a diversity of individuations, *is* time. It is now argued that Being's self-incarnation is also Being's self-consciousness/self-knowledge. Every spatial/material/ecological subject whose incarnation conditions there being Being, the Being of time, the general entirety of Being/time, can never be outside time-consciousness. Importantly, time's singularly subjective constitution is equally evoked by Merleau-Ponty, who states that 'time must *constitute itself* – be always seen from someone who *is of it*' (1968: 184; original emphasis).

Let's review the argument so far:
Premises

1. The incarnation of every spatiality/materiality conditions the very possibility of there being Being, the entirety of Being generally.
2. The incarnation of every spatiality/materiality conditions there being consciousness, Being's self-consciousness.
3. The incarnation of every spatiality/materiality, as Being's becoming, conditions there being time, the entirety of time generally.

Outcome

If every spatiality/materiality conditions; (1) Being, (2) consciousness (as self-consciousness) and (3) time, then every spatial/material subject is always conscious of all time(s).

Every spatial/material subject is concurrently, ambiguously, a subjective time and the objectivity of time in general. This ambiguous, worldly co-constitution means that no particular spatial/material subject is ever separate from, or out of sync with, any other subject. Ambiguity conditions the co-consciousness/co-knowledge of every thing, for it produces and yet confounds the limit of what one can absolutely know. This interpretation coheres with Merleau-Ponty's description of 'know[ing] myself as I am inherent in time and in the world, that is, I know myself only in my ambiguity' (1962: 345).

If we are to pursue this line of thinking, then a key claim made by Barbara Adam in 'Time and Environmental Crisis' (1993) requires more attention. In reiterating the common fear 'pervading climate change debates' of 'time running out for effective action' (401), Adam's concern is that political and legislative responses are too slow. This is typically attributable to political and economic interests failing to prioritise 'the exigency of the crisis' (401). What eventuates is a world of 'out of sync' relations. It follows that humans are out of sync, not only with each other, but also with the changing ecology/climate, whereby 'the time-frame of the perceived danger is out of sync with the time-frame for action' (401).

In 'Running out of Time: Global Crisis in Human Management' (1994), Adam further discusses how all human-induced environmental, ecological and climate changes are characterised by dissonant time frames (98). Nowhere is this dissonance more apparent, as Adam's 'Time and Environmental Crisis' (1993) informs us, than in the 'depletion of the ozone' (1993: 401). Ozone depletion is significantly increased by chlorofluorocarbons (CFCs); synthetic gases found in appliances in most Western households (401). Consequently, the speedy removal of CFCs from the market would significantly assist in arresting ozone depletion. That this has not occurred exemplifies for Adam the aforementioned 'out of sync time-lags' (402).

Given this chapter's developments, it must be acknowledged that CFCs, as instantiations of worldly spatiality/materiality, and therefore, of worldly ecology, are also inherent to the process distinguishing Being from itself. CFCs, like any individuations, condition/produce Being. It must therefore be said that CFCs, humans, and other material manifestations, are each concurrently a particular spatiality/materiality/ecology/temporality, as well as a general worlding. Crucially for our current discussion on social synchronisation, this means that all worlding expressions or manifestations are always already in sync, because they inhere within these ambiguous, shared, co-conditioning ontologies.

Adam claims that if our 'contemporary environmental crisis exhibits global features', then they are the characteristics of 'ecologically networked interconnectedness' *and* 'out of sync time-frames' (401). However, I argue that in order to recognise an 'ecologically networked interconnectedness', spatial/material entities such as CFCs cannot be positioned outside, or out of sync with, spatiality/materiality generally. We should not assume that CFCs are *externally introduced* to a worldly setting, as it ignores spatial/material co-constitution. This chapter has attempted to problematise such inside/outside modes of analysis, where time's source is a pre-existing, distant origin that clocks and calendars represent in social frames. The latter assumes a disjuncture between time as a worldly phenomenon, and time as it is socially represented/constructed, an assumption we will soon address. Notably, Adam actually criticises this 'linear-perspective and clock time' by describing both as 'powerful externalisers that separate subject from object' (1994: 97). Yet Adam's interpretation of out of sync time frames *does* externalise subjects from objects. It does this by assuming an already existing, ecological/environmental scene of objects into which human subjects enter and perpetrate a disturbance. From this manifests the aforementioned supposition of an adversarial relation between humans and climate change.

Conversely, in my inquiry the intent is to suggest that all material incarnations, inasmuch as they are of the world and its ecological involvements, are co-constitutively in sync. Spatial/material/ecological subjects and spatial/material/ecological objects manifest simultaneously. Not only does this contest the notion of an 'out of sync time-lag' between humans and CFCs, it also reconceptualises what is implied by social synchronisation.

Social synchronisation is typically defined as subjects meeting by using the same socially derived representation/construction of a pre-existing, universal time-source. Because such time is common for all subjects *and* outside the interference of all subjects, its objectivity can be *utilised* for synchronisation. This chapter's characterisation of synchronisation, however, is of an imminent, simultaneous co-incarnation that comprehends diversity. Spatial/material subjects are inescapably synchronous because their 'arrival' is characterised by the way that they originate concurrently with, and co-constitutively/intersubjectively as, each other (socially) as time.

It is conventionally presumed that social constructions/representations of time are not time itself. Rather, a social constructionist understanding of time assumes that the human representation is contingently variable and separate from the worldly phenomenon of time itself. However, if what is inherent about time is that it is produced through spatialities, including human beings, and that such spatialities are inter-subjectively, socially, conditioned, constructed and produced, then the time of social constructionism remains within, rather than excluded from, the worldly phenomenon of time itself. Time *is* an intersubjective, and therefore a social, construction and production, however one wherein what is implied by 'social construction' is not separate from the 'actual', worldly phenomenon. Synchronisation between subjects is not conditioned by constructions or representations of a separate, worldly source. Instead, the subject *is* time, manifesting as Being's self-synchronous, self-social construction/production. Here, the social construction of time can still be considered a representation of time, whereby this re-representation is executed from, by, and as Being.

Adam astutely recognises that as 'sociologists we need to overcome the clock-maker's reductionist view of nature and society' (1993: 411). However, to frame the 'time-lags' as Adam does between 'out of sync' spatialities/materialities, she installs an externally objective, pre-existing time-source that transcends all such materialisations, and which humans can then only represent from afar. Adam's thesis duly adheres to the clock-maker's frame of time that she contests. The argument this chapter presents instead, where each subject is the condition of time generally, means that no subjects are out of sync. Subjects synchronise because each already is the time of other subjects, each already is a social time.

Monistic, Social Time

If every subject, as time, incorporates time generally, then what must now be asked is whether this monistic sense of time and subjectivity contradicts the notion of *social* time? Can the *singularity* of a monism also constitute and comprehend the *plurality* of sociality?

Mead can assist this inquiry via his discussion of an animal's physiological reaction when eating, which he describes as not simply an internal response to external objects. Rather, in recognising that objects such as food constitute a subject's/animal's/organism's physiology, and that this physiology concurrently constitutes the world of objects, the animal emerges with/as the spatial/material/physical world of those objects (2002: 93). This *singular* co-constitutive relation between physiology and the physical world (re)produces the animal organism and the ecology/environment simultaneously. Or in Mead's terms, the event comprises 'both the difference which arises in the environment because of its relation to the organism . . . and also the difference in the organism because of the change in the environment' (2002: 37). This ambiguity of corporeality, organism and subjectivity evokes Heidegger's aforementioned contestation of the notion of finite bodily limits. For Heidegger, the organism does not occupy a separate 'position in space' (1962: 420), but instead emerges as an aspect of 'the equipmental whole' (420). It is from a singular, worldly whole that organism and environment simultaneously co-emerge, as equipmental features of what Mead describes as 'an ongoing living process that tends to maintain itself' (2002: 37). This process of becoming evokes the singularity and synchronicity which this chapter has described in terms of Being producing itself via spatial/material/ecological forms of itself, whereby climate change materialities world the world; their vitalism being Being's changing perpetuity rather than the destruction of Being.

Having conjured something of this spatial/material *singularity*, Mead then acknowledges a spatial/material *plurality*. Due to the co-constitution of particular animals/subjects/organisms, and general, physical, worldly environments, particular animals/subjects/organisms are dispersed across many spatial/material 'boundaries'. For example, according to Mead, an animal is an individual 'system of distribution of energies which makes its locomotion possible' (2002: 75). Simultaneously, however, this particular spatiality/materiality comprises 'part of the jungle system which is part of the life system on the surface of the inanimate globe' (75). This chapter describes all such entities as ecological individuations whereby carbon dioxide, or human beings, simultaneously constitute a particular materiality *and* participate in conditioning worldly spatiality/materiality/ecology generally. Mead's characterisation here of the globe as 'inanimate' must consequently be questioned, given that it positions the Earth as a passive stage upon which activity occurs. Conversely, if all individuations, or incarnations, condition Being, then the Earth is one such materiality whose ecological identity (re)emerges with/as all others.

What is monistically singular *and* systemically plural can be characterised as 'social' via Mead's definition of systemic plurality as sociality. Systemic plurality refers to something's concurrent presence in more than one system, and for Mead, 'sociality is this capacity of being several things at once' (2002: 49). Interestingly, we have seen that time exhibits this capacity. The past conditions/constitutes the present, *as* the present conditions/constitutes the past that *will have* produced this present. Present and past are simultaneously, systemically plural. If states of time are thus co-constitutively plural, and such plurality is sociality, then co-constitutive spatialities/materialities – which are states of time according to the argument just developed – must equally be social. Time is this intersubjective, social plurality.

Our frame of reference then regarding synchronisation is not circumscribed by what it is to be human, for material time socially synchronises *as* this comprehensive generality, where synchronisation is the concurrent co-incarnation of *all* timings. The materialities of climate change, in systemically-plurally co-constituting all other spatialities/materialities (as time(s)), duly manifest as socially implicated with, rather than adversarially opposed to, embodied humans. Mead broadens the definition of socialisation via pluralisation similarly, as what 'belongs not only to human organisms' (46). In this sense, sociality is unrestricted: every thing, every entity, is a social constituent, an implicated ecology (177).

This concept of a monistic, limitless, social mechanism from which nothing is excluded is consistent with the earlier accommodation, rather than the exclusion, of social constructionism. Time is a monistically self-social construction, internally differentiated, concurrently represented *and* produced via spatial forms of itself such as bodies-as-spaces. Social constructionism defines worldly time's ontology, instead of indicating how humans alone represent something unreachable about the world. The social construction/representation of time is Being's self-representation, in spatial forms of itself, dissolving representation and production into the one, simultaneous, worlding phenomenon. This dissolution of the reality of Being with the representation of Being into a singular ontological process speaks directly to the earlier concern regarding the characterisation of time as a real phenomenon that is removed from its contingent, human, social representations. The curiosity was noted that despite such supposed ontological separation, representational time still works or functions. How could it happen that representational time works as time while facing an ontological gap from the very source that is responsible for its function? This contradiction of representation having to traverse some phenomenal abyss to access the conditions of its own reality has now been reconfigured, whereby what is representational is always already the real, for indeed, what is the world representing in the form of worldly phenomena but itself, as itself, as time?

A novel way to address the relation of humans to climate change can now be suggested. David Runnalls' work at the International Institute for Sustainable Development, discussed earlier, imposes the typical, adversarial relation between humans and the rest of Earth's ecology when he describes human activity as *disturbing* 'three quarters of the Earth' (2008: 20). Celebrated environmental author and journalist, William McKibben, takes this supposition of an opposition between humans and climate change to its extreme point. In McKibben's most popular work, *The End of Nature* (2006), he argues that 'true nature' exists independently of human influence on it. Indeed, it is because of the adversarial human-nature relation that true, in-itself nature, upon encountering humans, became an 'artificial nature' (115). According to McKibben, nature became artificial because human intervention 'deprived nature of its independence' (50).

In responding, we can turn to this chapter's focus on time, in which no time-state pre-exists any other, for all co-originate with/ as each other. Accordingly, the notion of a past, in-itself, a natural/ environmental state of primordiality, that was ever independent from subsequent, present, human incarnations, is reworked. The 'what it was' of anything is always already (re)emerging, meaning that past environmental and climatic conditions, and present environmental and climatic conditions, co-manifest. Time, as Being, perpetually re-originates, problematising the assumption that the source of time is simply an origin eternally fixed in the past from which new presents are increasingly distanced.

Characterising the common constitution of humans and climate change as time becomes important when considering the human relation to Being and the world in general. Rather than presuming that the human relation to time is a futile battle against an omnipresent, relentless, external force that is 'running out', the human-time relation, and indeed the human-world relation, become defined by a sense of self-responsibility. In the context of the argument just explored, what matters about the parameters of self-responsibility are their inescapability, expressed in this chapter as the always already of self-production. A responsibility in, or for, environmental care is duly portrayed not simply as something humans are ethically obliged to recognise and subsequently act upon, but rather as something about being human that cannot be avoided.

The argument presented thus does not preclude political concerns around environmental change. The world whose climate changes is the same world that manifests political action to 'deal with' such climatic change, whereby consistent with the dissolution of representation and reality that has been presented in this chapter, it must be said that the political representation of environmental issues is the worldly reality of environmental issues. What is reconfigured here, however, is the notion that any such political action is an intervention into a passive, unthinking, oppositional worldly scene.

Notes

1. See biographical interview, *Saving the Earth Since 1970* (Quade 1990: 16).
2. A document produced by the *United Nations Framework Convention on Climate Change* demanding that global warming be arrested by cutting industrially induced emissions (McKibbin, Morris and Wilcoxen 2011).
3. The argument that the observation of worldly objects is not simply a case of a perceiving subject overcoming an oppositional distance, separation or gap *between* it and the object being observed emerges in Karen Barad's interpretation of the conditions of quantum mechanics in *Meeting the Universe Halfway* (2007). In considering the experimentation undertaken by physicist Niels Bohr, Barad illustrates that 'in the face of quantum nonseparability', the objectivity of object manifestation is not based 'on an inherent or Cartesian cut between observer and observed' (339). In this regard, laboratory experiments reveal worldly phenomena, its objective materiality, as manifesting concurrently as observing and observed entities, each involved in, and as, the constitution of the other. The apparent borders of an entity, rather than being straightforwardly attributable to its exteriority from other entities, manifest due to 'the condition of exteriority-within-phenomena', the consubstantiality of *all* phenomena, whereby '"observer and observed" are nothing more than two physical systems intra-acting' (339–40) as the one system. As Barad further notes, this is not a model that is exclusively dependent upon human observers, given that *all* phenomena emerge in this fashion. However, the emergence of humans is as implicated in this ontology as any other phenomena (340). For more on the relations and differences between quantum and phenomenological ontologies of observation and manifestation, see Johncock 'The Experimental Flesh: Incarnation in Terms of Quantum Measurement and Phenomenological Perception' (2011).
4. Recent discussions in object-oriented ontology explore the possibilities of non-human consciousness and sentience. For a recent source of papers discussing these issues, see Richard Grusin's *The Nonhuman Turn* (2015).
5. The notion of plant sentience is also considered by authors Peter Tompkins and Christopher Bird in *The Secret Life of Plants* (1973). Here Tompkins

and Bird discuss how Cleve Backster, an interrogation specialist for the CIA, applies polygraph instruments to plants in the 1960s in order to develop a theory that accredits plants with primary perception and the capacity to feel pain, whereby 'plants appear to be sentient' (4). Also of interest in this sense is the work of Anthony Trewavas, professor in plant physiology and molecular biology at the University of Edinburgh, which considers the intelligence of plants. As Trewavas states in his article, 'Aspects of Plant Intelligence' (2003), 'intelligence is not a term commonly used when plants are discussed. However, I believe that this is an omission based not on a true assessment of the ability of plants to compute complex aspects of their environment' (1).

References

Adam, B. (1990), *Time and Social Theory*, Cambridge: Polity Press.

Adam, B. (1993), 'Time and Environmental Crisis: An Exploration with Special Reference to Pollution', *Innovation: The European Journal of Social Science Research*, 6: 4, pp. 399–413.

Adam, B. (1994), 'Running out of Time: Global Crisis in Human Management', in *Social Theory and the Global Environment*, ed. M. Redcliff and T. Benton, London: Routledge, pp. 92–112.

Adam, B. (1995), *Timewatch: The Social Analysis of Time*, Cambridge: Polity. Press.

Barad, K. (2007), *Meeting the Universe Halfway: Quantum Physics and the Entanglement of Matter and Meaning*, Durham, NC: Duke University Press.

Barrow, I. ([1735] 2009), *Geometrical Lectures*, trans. J. Child, Charlestown: BiblioBazaar.

Brown, D. (2010), *A Comprehensive Ethical Analysis of the Cophenhagen Accord*, available at <http://blogs.law.widener.edu/climate/2010/01/31/a-comprehensive-ethical-analysis-of-the-copenhagen-accord/> (last accessed 20 July 2015).

Carrington, D. (2013), 'Global carbon dioxide in atmosphere passes milestone level', in *The Guardian*, Friday, 10 May 2013, <https://www.theguardian.com/environment/2013/may/10/carbon-dioxide-highest-level-greenhouse-gas> (last accessed 16 October 2015).

Einstein, A. ([1920] 2006), *Relativity: The Special and the General Theory*, ed. N. Calder, trans. R. Lawson, London and New York: Penguin.

Engel, A. (1969), 'Time and the Earth', in *American Scientist*, 57: 4, pp. 458–83.

Grosz, E. (1999), 'Becoming . . . An Introduction', in *Becomings: Explorations in Time, Memory and Futures*, ed. E. Grosz, Ithaca, NY and London: Cornell University Press, pp. 1–11.

Grusin, R. (ed.) (2015), *The Nonhuman Turn*, Minneapolis: University of Minnesota Press.

Hannam, P. (2013), 'Global Carbon Dioxide Levels Hit Landmark High', in *The Sydney Morning Herald*, Saturday, 11 May 2013, available at <www.smh.com.au/environment/climate-change/global-carbon-dioxide-levels-hit-landmark-high-20130510-2je8u.html> (last accessed 17 May 2015).

Hansen, J. (2009), *Storms of My Grandchildren: The Truth about the Coming Climate Catastrophe and Our Last Chance to Save Humanity*, London: Bloomsbury Publishing PLC.

Heidegger, M. ([1927] 1962), *Being and Time*, trans. J. Macquarrie and E. Robinson, New York: Harper Collins.

Heidegger, M. (2001), *Zollikon Seminars*, trans. F. Mayr and R. Askay. Evanston: Northwestern University Press.

Husserl, E. ([1913] 1983), *Ideas Pertaining to a Pure Phenomenology and to a Phenomenological Philosophy: First Book: General Introduction to a Pure Phenomenology*, trans. F. Kersten, The Hague, Boston and Lancaster: Martinus Nijhof Publishers.

Husserl, E. ([1952] 1990), *Ideas Pertaining to a Pure Phenomenology and to a Phenomenological Philosophy: Second Book: Studies in the Phenomenology of Constitution*, ed. and trans. R. Rojcewicz and A. Schuwer, New York: Springer Publishing.

Johncock, W. (2011), 'The Experimental Flesh: Incarnation in Terms of Quantum Measurement and Phenomenological Perception', in *Phenomenology & Practice*, 5: 1, pp. 140–54.

McKibben, W. (2006), *The End of Nature*, New York: Random House.

McKibbin, W., A. Morris and P. Wilcoxen (2011), 'Comparing Climate Commitments: A Model-Based Analysis of the Copenhagen Accord', in *Climate Change Economics*, 2: 2, pp. 79–103.

Mead, G. ([1932] 2002), *The Philosophy of the Present*, New York: Prometheus Books.

Merleau-Ponty, M. ([1945] 1962), *Phenomenology of Perception*, trans. C. Smith, New York and London: Routledge.

Merleau-Ponty, M. ([1964] 1968), *The Visible and the Invisible*, trans. A. Lingis, Evanston: Northwestern University Press.

Merriam-Webster Online Dictionary (2015), available at <http://www.merriam-webster.com/dictionary/sentient > (last accessed 10 December 2015).

Meyer, R. (2015), 'Earth's Atmosphere Just Crossed an Epochal Threshold', in *The Atlantic*, 24 November 2015, available at <www.theatlantic.com/science/archive/2015/11/november-11-2015-the-last-day-of/417378/> (last accessed 10 December 2015).

Newton, I. (1978), *Unpublished Scientific Papers of Isaac Newton: A Selection from the Portsmouth Collection in the University Library*, ed. A. Hall and M. Hall, Cambridge: CUP Archive.

Pierrehumbert, R. (2006), 'A Catastrophe in Slow Motion', in *Chicago Journal of International Law*, 6: 2, pp. 573–96.

Quade, V. (1990), '20 Years of Saving the Earth: Barrister Interview with Denis Hayes', in *Barrister Magazine*, Fall 1990.

Runnalls, D. (2008), 'Our Common Inaction: Meeting the Call for Institutional Change', in *Environment*, 50: 6, pp. 18–29.

Sartre, J. ([1943] 2003), *Being and Nothingness*, trans. H. Barnes, London and New York: Routledge.

Simmel, G. ([1903] 1997), 'The Metropolis and Modern Life', in *Simmel on Culture*, ed. D. Frisby and M. Featherstone, London: SAGE Publications, pp. 174–86.

Tompkins, P., and C. Bird (1973), *The Secret Life of Plants: A Fascinating Account of the Physical, Emotional, and Spiritual Relations Between Plants and Man*, New York: Harper & Row Publishers.

Trewavas, A. (2003), 'Aspects of Plant Intelligence', in *Annals of Botany*, 92: 1, pp. 1–20.

CHAPTER 11

A Sociality of Death: Towards a New Materialist Politics and Ethics of Life Itself

Peta Hinton

New Materialist Ontologies

Introducing the new materialisms in the seminal anthology of the same name, the editors, Diana Coole and Samantha Frost (2010), provide us with a sense of the sociological import of this contemporary field. Materiality, they contend, is everywhere. It is the very stuff of the quotidian: the dependence of our existence on 'diverse species', our bodily and cellular reactions, 'the material artifacts and natural stuff that populate our environment', and the 'socioeconomic structures that produce and reproduce the conditions of our everyday lives' (2010: 1). Such reckonings with materiality demand an analysis commensurate with the ubiquity and complexity of its myriad relations and processes. Thus, as the editors outline, new materialist perspectives emphasise matter as a way to both identify and to address some of the most 'urgent challenges' in contemporary society (2010: 3). Their aim is to return our focus to 'material phenomena and processes' that have been de facto neglected by the 'dominance of analytical and normative political theory' and the styles of 'radical constructivism' that characterise Anglophone and Continental traditions associated with 'the cultural turn' (2010: 3).

With this focus, new materialism should not be regarded as a neo-positivist approach that might take materiality for granted as the mere foundation of sociological concerns. Matter does not presuppose the 'baser desires of biological material' or the 'inertia of physical stuff' that is inferior to a 'host of immaterial things' (2010: 2). Nor can it be reified for the purposes of critical interventions that aim to *think* its processes differently.[1] On the contrary, new materialism opens the dualisms that would insist on matter's separation from mind, cognition, language, representation, and so on.[2] Instead, it offers a different, we could say broadened, ontology that puts into question the nature of materiality itself, as well as the status and shape of the human actors who would ordinarily comprise our conventional understandings of 'the social'. It is this non-dualist (Dolphijn and van der Tuin 2012, Coole and Frost 2010) and posthumanist (Irni 2013; Coole and Frost 2010; Thiele 2014) orientation within new materialism that redefines material activity beyond 'substantialist Cartesian or mechanistic Newtonian accounts of matter' (Coole and Frost 2010: 12–13), and it requires that humans, 'including theorists themselves, be recognised as thoroughly immersed within materiality's productive contingencies' (Coole and Frost 2010: 7).

Matter thus opens up in new materialist inquiry as emergent, generative and dynamic. No longer consigned as the inert and dead weight that sits underneath the lens of human interpretation or manipulation, it constitutes 'an excess', or 'force', that renders it 'active, self-creative, productive', and 'unpredictable' (Coole and Frost 2010: 9). The emphasis here lies with the indeterminate and autopoietic nature of materiality, dimensions that prominent feminist and (new) materialist scholar, Rosi Braidotti, underscores in her account of matter as *potentia* – a way of understanding its transformative capacities as the political and ethical action of matter. Comparing this to *potestas*, or the 'negative or confining' (Braidotti in Dolphijn and van der Tuin 2012: 22) operations of power, understanding matter as *potentia* helps to shift the way the social is perceived and engaged. Conceived in terms of a systemic liveliness, materiality, or life itself, offers a different political and ethical vision premised on ecologies of becoming that may help to produce 'alternative subject positions and social relations' (Braidotti in Dolphijn and van der Tuin 2012: 22).

A significant element of Braidotti's argument for material agency is her attempt to rework negativity through this attention to *potentia*. This gesture is particularly evident where she recasts *Zoē* as an affirmative life force in order to advance an 'approach that starts with asserting the primacy of life as production, or *zoē* as generative power' (2006: 110, cited in van der Tuin and Dolphijn 2010: 156). Such a move necessarily draws death, or 'new and subtler degrees of extinction' (Braidotti 2010: 203), into discourse with life. However, this approach cannot sustain a dualist separation of life and death through which death is conceived as a horizon for life, or as 'the inanimate and indifferent state of matter'

(Braidotti 2006: 147) that supports instrumentalist, consumerist and patriarchal renderings of 'Nature as resource'. Instead, with her emphasis on material vitality, death constitutes for Braidotti a point or an event that transpires *within* the broader generativity of life itself, at the same time that it underscores and opens to address the inhuman capacities of the vital ontology that she proposes (2006: 2010).

With this focus, Braidotti does not simply abandon death to a problematic and negative 'outside' of the autopoietic wanderings of life. Her alternative is to offer an affirmative politics and ethics that take a complex route *through* death in order to establish some understanding of the generative mechanisms of life that foreground ethical sustainability and the possibility for different modes of existence, or sociality. Nevertheless, the way that Braidotti positions death within her affirmative reading of *Zoē* raises another, related question about the priority that materiality, or life itself, is given in her argument, and the consequences of granting this priority. The concern that will be discussed here is whether Braidotti's new materialist analysis tends towards an affirmative reading of life itself that, in emphasising an 'ontology of presence' (Braidotti 2010: 202), or the continuity of life, privileges *potentia* as the active force that makes political and ethical change available. In doing so, it may be the case that she has displaced, rather than reworked, a robust sense of negativity. Concurrently, we are pressed to ask whether this approach circumscribes the way politics and ethics are conceived as only particular types of projects or processes of intervention – specifically, progressivist and humanist. In other words, Braidotti's project prompts the questions of where political and ethical agency is presumed to reside, and in which direction(s) it is expected to work.

The aims of this chapter are therefore modest and specific. I propose to explore Braidotti's reworking of *Zoē*, or life itself, via her explorations of death, to consider how the neo-vitalist and affirmative commitments contained in this approach orient the forms of social transformation with which she is concerned. With Braidotti, I want to ask what happens when we account for death as politically and ethically *constitutive*, however, contra Braidotti, my aim is to try to sustain (without delimiting) *potestas* in and for political and ethical (im)potentiality. An important part of this exercise will involve excavating the ontology of presence to which Braidotti is faithful. And it will also demand an engagement with Karen Barad's more recent work in quantum field theory. My premise is that the generative possibilities of life itself may already be found in and with death (or nothing), indeed, as life's own 'dynamic interiority', to use

Vicki Kirby's terms (2006: 125). From here I will make some preliminary suggestions for what a sociality of death might mobilise within (and as the provocations of) a new materialist politics and ethics of life itself.

'Life' Addressing Anthropocentrism

As Braidotti astutely comments in her most recent monograph, *The Posthuman*, 'one's view on death depends on one's assumptions about Life' (2013: 131). Much of her engagement with life, spanning a number of texts including this most recent one,[3] concentrates on what she perceives to be the problematic separation of *Bios* and *Zoē* that supports Giorgio Agamben's interventions into biopolitical govern-mentality. Where Agamben defines '"*bios*" as the result of the inter-vention of sovereign power which is capable of reducing the subject to "bare life"' (Braidotti 2010: 206), or *Zoē*, two contentions arise for Braidotti.[4] First, this dualist separation situates *Zoē* as that which is 'mindlessly material' and devoid of agency – a familiar (Cartesian) rendering of matter that aligns it with nature (Braidotti 2006: 138). The naturalisation of political asymmetries is rendered automatic as a consequence, and this process of denigration implicates all 'others' that help to define 'the classical vision of the subject', including 'the sexual other (woman), the ethnic other (the native) and the naturalised other (earth, plants and animals)' – while *Bios* demarcates 'intelligent life' (Braidotti 2006: 138). With a Nature/Culture split operating, *Zoē* is reduced to 'the constitutive vulnerability of the human subject, which sovereign power can kill; it is that which makes the body into disposable matter in the hands of the despotic force of unchecked power' (Braidotti 2013: 120), 'or *potestas*' (Braidotti 2006: 211).

Braidotti's second concern is to take issue with the separation of *Bios* and *Zoē* as it corresponds with a distinction between life and death that figures finitude or mortality to be 'the trans-historical horizon for discussions of "life"' (2013: 120). Here, finitude is understood in terms of *Thanatos*, life's tendency *towards* death. This translates into an approach to the governmentality of life that is 'inherently linked to death' (2013: 118). And yet, with death positioned outside or beyond the scope of lively generation, its marginalisation also works to under-play, or to leave under-examined, its productive role in engineering and orienting forms of sociality. Specifically, political efforts gather around a shared sense of vulnerability – our mortality – that work in the direction of *avoiding* death. What this evokes is a notion of bio-ethical agency that culminates in, among other things, 'taking adequate care of one's own genetic capital' (Braidotti 2013: 116). Within this mode of governmentality, the bio-ethical subject 'takes full responsibility for his/her genetic existence' (Braidotti 2013: 116). This may include, for example, such things as risk reduction through self-managed strategies for a healthy lifestyle, and these expressions of bio-ethical agency strongly correlate with a 'neo-liberal normative trend' of 'hyper-individualism' (Braidotti 2013: 116).

We find another example of this point in Braidotti's (1994) more concentrated analysis of biotechnologies, presented in her earlier monograph, *Nomadic Subjects*. Here, a distinction between biology and technology is aligned with the sexual differential, nature/culture, and dismantled through Michel Foucault's approach to biopolitics as it finds technologies – even those that fulfil techniques of control, or the less agreeable functions of bodily regulation – to be continuous with biology. According to Braidotti's read, this inextricable connection of organic bodies and technologies suggests that patriarchal relations with technology, defined by those means of regulation and control, enable not so much a death-driven socius, but one that remains blind to death in its focus on forms of life. In this approach the body is both that which must be preserved (in its aliveness), but also that which is exploited in the process: the body is 'raw material, destined to be socialised into purposeful productivity' (Braidotti 1994: 45), or bound into a set of relations that extend 'the commerce of living bodies' (1994: 52). The discourse of the biosciences provides one such example of the way bodily material has been cast as object and resource (*Zoē*). According to the directionality of this logic, the bioscientist becomes the 'very prototype of the instrumental intellectual' (Braidotti 1994: 47), (*Bios*), the modern knowing subject under whose gaze living organisms 'lose all reference to the human shape and to the specific temporality of the human being' (Braidotti 1994: 47). What this separation between *Zoē* and *Bios* effectively achieves, as Braidotti explains, is a freezing out of time. 'All reference to death disappears in the discourse about 'biopower' – power over life' (Braidotti 1994: 47), and instead living matter, now cast beyond death and outside time, becomes abstracted and utilisable. The anxiety that this produces is clearly marked out: biopower denies death at the behest of its capacity to master life, and, in doing so, it produces a sanitised, technologised and alien relationship with bodies, for example, with reproduction and maternity.

While death figures in this logic as a silent and somehow latent force for forms of bodily regulation and social organisation, the tendency to avoid it has resulted in what Braidotti regards as a lack of robust engagement with the necro-political dimensions of contemporary life, including an adequate address to those ways of dying that are a product of our posthuman condition (Braidotti 2013). A main concern that opens *The Posthuman* is how to address the potential loss of value for human life that the decentering of the human seems to anticipate, along with the capacity for the posthuman condition to 'engender its own forms of inhumanity' (Braidotti 2013: 3); 'aberrations', 'abuses of power' (2013: 4), and inhuman(e) technologies that configure and reproduce hierarchies of value and violence. From this position, Braidotti argues that what is central to the task of 'an affirmative posthuman theory of death' (2013: 110) is the capacity to identify and to respond to the reality of 'horrors, violence, and destruction' (2013: 122) – those negative products of global capitalism as they mutate and potentially overwhelm in the posthuman era.[5] What this requires is an even more devoted analysis of death, a suggestion that follows William Connolly's point that critical theory 'needs to engage with the present', '*including* the horrors of our times', in order to bring about transformations in 'existing social and political givens' (Braidotti 2013: 129, emphasis added).

Braidotti finds that the best way to both account for and respond to these potential forms of inhumanity is to rethink the relation of life and death, and this involves reworking the distinction between *Bios* and *Zoë* as it orients both this relation and the way that life, or matter, can be valued. To this end, her task becomes one of reconfiguring *Zoë* through those autopoietic powers of life (Braidotti 2013: 115) that emphasise the 'vital, self-organizing and yet non-naturalistic structure of living matter' (2013: 2). This emphasis on *Zoë*'s vitality does not re-situate death on the brink of life, nor does it re-invest in some notion of dead matter as that which stands in contrast to *Zoë*'s lively capacities. On the contrary, in a move that configures death in terms of immanence, or its inseparability from life, Braidotti expands on the implications of this thinking.

> Death is not a failure, or the expression of structural weakness at the heart of life: it is part and parcel of its generative cycles. As such, it is a 'zero institution', in Levi-Strauss' [*sic*] sense: the empty shape of all possible time as perceptual becoming which can become actualised in the present but flows back to past and future. It is virtual in that it has the generative capacity to engender the actual. Consequently, death is but an obvious manifestation of principles that are active

in every aspect of life, namely: the pre-individual or impersonal power of *poten-tia* ... It is a temporal brand of vitalism that could not be further removed from the idea of death as the inanimate and indifferent state of matter, the entropic state to which the body is supposed to 'return'. Death, on the contrary, is ... part of the cycles of becomings, yet another form of inter-connectedness, a vital relationship that links one with other, multiple forces. The impersonal is life and death as *bios-zoe* in us – the ultimate outside as the frontier of the incorporeal. (Braidotti 2006: 147)

It serves us to pause for a moment over Braidotti's suggestions, because the terrain she opens is quite convoluted. Death is recast as something active and generative, the potentiality of what life becomes. In other words, what appears outside of life here becomes an interiority that engenders all life forms, including what is inhuman, or indifferent to anthropocentric concerns. What this quotation starts to make apparent, then, is that reworking death in terms of its productive capacities also involves shifting the priority given to human-centred conceptuali-sations of life and death. It also suggests that quite different forms of sociality will be enabled through this shift.

As Braidotti (2013: 115) explains it, 'a focus on the vital and self-organizing powers of Life/*zoe* undoes any clear-cut distinctions between living and dying' because it draws death from the brink of life into its centre.[6] Importantly for Braidotti, death is never final because 'life carries on relentlessly' (2013: 131). This does not deny the individual experience of death 'in the form of the physical extinction of the body' (Braidotti 2013: 133), nor as 'the inhuman conceptual excess: the unrepresentable, the unthinkable, and the unproductive black hole that we all fear' (2013: 131). But nor can death be maintained as 'a human prerogative' (Braidotti 2013: 130): its commandeering of the value of life cannot be solely located with the privilege of the rational subject. Because death is *also* the 'creative synthesis of flows of energies and perpetual becoming' (Braidotti 2013: 131), it exceeds 'the demands and expectations of the sovereign consciousness' (Braidotti 2010: 208). It becomes 'larger than life' in the sense that its tie to the thinking/reflec-tive subject is diminished. In view of Zoē as *potentia*, death cannot be parked in 'the specific slice of life that "I" inhabits'; instead, it is dissolved 'into ever-shifting processual changes' (Braidotti 2013: 137).

This 'post-anthropocentric shift' (Braidotti 2013: 121) opens death as an 'event' (2013: 133), but it is not an event that can be specifically located, for example, as an occurrence or an encounter. Rather, Braidotti (2013: 132) insists that 'death as a constitutive event is behind us'. Because our mortality, the transience of life, is 'written at our core' – it is 'ever-present in our psychic and somatic landscapes' (2013: 131–2) – death, 'in the sense of the awareness of finitude, of the interrupted flow of my being-there . . . has already taken place' (2013: 133). What this creates, then, is a strangely inverted temporality. Death does not lie ahead as a 'teleological destination' (2013: 133), instead it structures our sense of time as well as 'our becoming-subjects, our capacity and powers of relation and the process of requiring ethical awareness' (2013: 132). Death 'is the event that has always already taken place at the level of *consciousness*' (2013: 133, emphasis added).

I will return to this claim that death registers at the level of consciousness at a later point, but for now I want to expand upon the productive potentialities of death that earn Braidotti's attention here. In particular, for Braidotti, finding death *within* life forces us to think *with* death, rather than against it. More specifically, it carries a critical valency that works in hand with a political and ethical eco-logic that acknowledges the impersonal and inhuman capacities of Zoē, and therefore opens the way to their acknowledgement and hoped-for response. As Braidotti insists, in stressing the 'productive differential nature of *zoe*, which means the *productive* aspect of the life-death continuum' (2013: 132, emphasis added) its 'threatening' *and* 'generative' force(s) (2013: 112) must be emphasised. What this means is that 'the negative face of current socio-political power relations' (2013: 119) – the inhuman – can be recognised and resisted, rather than avoided or denied. Even more strikingly, on the basis of death's inculcation within life, Braidotti is able to assert that her 'vitalist notion of death is that it is the inhuman *within* us, which frees us into life' (2013: 134, emphasis added). Accordingly, death is not an obstacle or bystander to social change, but of the order of inhuman intensities that propel life in(to) its sustainability.

This, for Braidotti, establishes the political and ethical imperative of Zoē in its full potential – a potential which is firmly tied to, or, more significantly, *enabled by*, its post-anthropocentric qualities as 'a nonhuman yet affirmative life-force' (2010: 203). With the displacing of the human, ethics is not confined to 'mutual recognition' (2010: 214), an attempted egalitarianism that is enacted as a form of reciprocity on the part of one subject towards another. Instead, and in line with its posthumanist disposition, it is broadened to that of a 'mutual codependence' (2010: 214), where the emphasis appears to shift to forms of relation that both exceed and include the human. Thus, subjective intention is no longer the sole precursor to living an ethical life. Rather, life engenders an ethics that forges a different sense of community through hybrid forms of kinship with the more-than-human (such as 'animals, insects, machines') (Braidotti 2006: 138), and this attests to the vulnerability that *is* life and the tendency towards dissolution that life involves. This acknowledgment prompts an 'affirmative' politics and ethics that 'strives for freedom from the burden of negativity' (Braidotti 2010: 215). It is 'the process of transmuting negative passions into productive and sustainable praxis' in a mode that 'does not deny the reality of horrors, violence and destruction. *It just proposes a different way of dealing with them*' (Braidotti 2013: 122, emphasis added). Specifically, we are called upon to rework the inhuman capacities of the posthuman predicament 'so as to assert the vital powers of healing and compassion' (2013: 132). More broadly, we are provoked to 'actively work towards a refusal of horror and violence – the inhuman aspects of our present – and to turn it into the construction of affirmative alternatives' (2013: 130). These alternatives include 'social cohesion, the respect for diversity, and sustainable growth' (Braidotti 2010: 207), ethical goals that constitute 'social horizons of hope' (2010: 215) grounded in 'mutual and respective accountability' (2010: 204) and 'responsibility for future generation' (Braidotti 2013: 113).

The Matter of Death

Braidotti's attention to life itself insists upon a complex matrix of sociality that does not preclude death. Rather, it makes some surprising assertions about the nature and position of death in its relation to, and within, life, and the political and ethical formations that this inspires. In a very important sense, what Braidotti is able to mobilise is a notion of death that is *constitutive*. The shadow of finitude is firmly inscribed into life and 'into the script of our temporality' (Braidotti 2013: 132). It is 'a condition of possibility' (2013: 132) of sociality and its myriad, potential transformations. Further, death appears to be intrinsic to the somatic, or material: it is 'the unsustainable, but it is also virtual in that it has the generative capacity to engender the actual' (2013: 138). We might then understand death as *radically* interior to life, as its (material) potentiality. It is the tendency for life's dissolution at the same time that it also makes possible life's myriad forms and processes: in effect, death registers as life's/matter's necessity, as much as its contingency.

As provocative as this argument is, however, there are problems, and a clue to these can be found in the way that Braidotti differentiates her own brand of vitalism from the life/death binary that she finds so problematic.

> Life and death can occur simultaneously and even overlap, thus they do not follow the 'either/or' scheme, but rather the 'and/and/and' scheme ... Death in such a framework is merely a point, it is not the horizon against which the human drama is played out. The centre is taken by *bios-zoe* and its ever-recurring flows of vitality. In and through many deaths, *bios-zoe* lives on. (Braidotti 2006: 150)

Although the dichotomous either/or logic that separates life from death is contested within this formulation, moving to a *sequential* logic – the 'and/and/and' that supplements dichotomy – raises further questions about the complex life-death relationality that Braidotti aims to achieve. First, if death figures in the self-negating capacities of life in a sequential format, this emphasises its *inter*-relation with life. Strangely, as much as it exists *within* the broad schema of life – as an internal rupturing that simultaneously makes death necessary to life's complex performances – it also needs to be separated off from life in order that the imbrication of life *and* death will be possible.[7] In the quotation above, this appears to reduce death to a series of multiple events that all take place within, and in the service of, life itself.

Thus, Braidotti's (2013: 134) claim that 'Life as *zoe* always encompasses what we call "death"' now appears to be in terms that privilege life and its capacity for 'self-perpetuation', in which death, conventionally considered to be 'the ultimate subtraction' from life, becomes just 'another phase' in *Zoë*'s 'generative process' (2013: 134). While Braidotti (2010: 202) gestures to the neo-realism that this ontology of presence presumes, she does not do this circumspectly, and this has consequences for both how she positions matter (and therefore the *substance* of death) as well as how she expects social transformation to take place. In the first instance, if death is found within life's circuit in the way she presents it here, she runs the danger of invoking a view of life, or matter, as self-evident substance, even in its dynamism. In other words, Braidotti may be translating an ontology of presence (that wants to account for death) into a metaphysics of presence in which life's *self-presence* is in some way assumed. With death co-opted into life, Braidotti can then promote a vitalism that ultimately refuses failure and entropy as either horizon *or* condition of existence: a reminder that 'life carries on relentlessly' (2013: 131). The upshot of this is that *potentia* takes on a specific ethical and political trajectory in her argument. To the point, the *affirmative* nature of *Zoë*'s generativity works to absorb negativity into a life-affirming or sustainable ontology. Specifically, this politics and ethics is expected to offer 'a thin barrier against the possibility of extinction', a capacity to rework the pain and indifference of *Zoē* in order to actualise 'sustainable forms of transformation' (Braidotti 2006: 139). However, if this ethics (and politics) is aligned with the dynamism of life that both supersedes and exceeds death, then death in the form of negativity is significantly circumscribed within this vision of life's ethical (and political) administrations.

There is a real challenge in making clear what is at stake here because with her troubling of the life-death distinction Braidotti rethinks the usual associations that the term 'affirmative' carries. In her hands, 'affirmative' does not negate negativity, nor is her move to read death in terms of immanence the same as sublating death/negativity into life as a form of totalisation or negation in itself. However, inasmuch as she is reworking the terrain of the affirmative, and therefore the negative, then by bringing death into life's fold (in the manner that she has done), negativity, too, cannot run the full gamut in her argument. Hence, while negativity's 'productive' potential as *potestas* is not sidelined in her call for an affirmative ethics, its role in the ethical inventiveness of life itself is contained, and ultimately superseded, by *potentia*. This clears a way for Braidotti to identify what it is that needs to be counteracted, resisted or refused as the inhuman (deathly) capacities of contemporary posthuman culture, and, along with the way that it constrains ethics, this move carries a twofold implication for how the human is positioned within this ethical programme. First, it appears that 'humanity' corresponds with a capacity for compassion and responsiveness as it differs from the monstrous indifference of inhumanity. At the same time, the inhuman aspects of our times (horrors, violence, devastation) can be separated out from their response, whether this is performed analytically or via forms of activism. More precisely, it appears that it is humanity's efforts that constitute the ethical.

The problem I am trying to raise here asserts itself at another point in Braidotti's argument, namely, in her aforementioned emphasis on the ability for death to be registered at the level of consciousness in a way that finds it already within the scope of life. Braidotti's claim is significant: by interrupting the temporal dimensions of death she can respond to the problematic positioning of finitude that she finds in Agamben's argument. Thus, in saying that death is not in front of us, but already behind us, it appears that the event of death exceeds its reduction to that of individual bodily extinction. Such a claim goes so far as to position death as a condition of possibility for and within life. However, in suggesting that this disruption happens at the level of consciousness without further elaboration upon what or how consciousness constitutes, Braidotti diminishes the impact of her assertions about death's productive capacities *as* immanent, ontological force. Instead, death appears to be generative in narrowly psychological terms; as that which is acknowledged through, and transparent to, human consciousness.[8] When it comes down to it, then, there is a materiality/ideation split at work in Braidotti's claim for death's immanent efficaciousness that sets death up, *and supports death as*, specifically human apprehensions of mortality. The by-product of this move is that death's self-presence is retained at another level: the event of death in material and individual terms always takes place at the end of life.

A potentially similar problem arrives with Braidotti's agreement with Connolly on the need to deepen the engagement with death in our *critical* work, while we work to avoid or refuse the inhuman *realities* of the posthuman condition. In the absence of an explanation for what else participates in performing this conceptual and political undertaking, the distinction made here between inhuman realities and the analysis required to address them appears to rely upon a human subject as critical interlocutor to the potential by-products of the posthuman era. Thus, even with the post-anthropocentric dimensions of a life-death ontology underlined, again, a human subject is returned as the foundation for Braidotti's affirmative project: the human is the one who gets to choose how to respond differently to the horrors of our times. To clarify, it would be unfair to insist that on this point Braidotti is altogether wrong. With more space it would be possible to demonstrate how this recuperation of human privilege is accommodated in the complex ethico-political ontology that Braidotti's own work has helped to develop. For now, though, I want to ask what happens if we stay with her provocations about the material(ising) and temporal dimensions of death without falling into the grey area of retaining, at least at some level, its dichotomous, humanist and progressivist interpretations.

Nothing Matters: Ontological In/determinacy and the Quantum Vacuum

Karen Barad's (2012a) recent discussions with quantum field theory assist greatly in this endeavour to reconsider negativity. With her outline of the quantum vacuum, Barad enters into questions of life and death, yet in a way that confounds any rehabilitation of life or matter

in self-present terms. In particular, Barad demonstrates how nothingness can be understood as the seething potentiality of life itself, and her
move is not so very far from Braidotti's representation of death as the
virtual. However, there is an important distinction here. Barad's claims
pivot on Niels Bohr's understanding of ontological indeterminacy as a
'radical openness' at 'the core of mattering' (2012a: 18); a condition
of possibility for what takes shape that is at one and the same time
the dynamic in/stability of this form. The salient provocations of this
argument for ontological indeterminacy can be traced through Barad's
earlier explication of Bohr's interventions into our usual framing of the
empirical, especially in the comparison that she makes between Werner
Heisenberg's uncertainty principle and Bohr's notion of complementarity (Barad 2007: see for example pages 18–20). As is now well known,
what quantum experimentation has helped to reveal is that matter
changes according to the type of experimental apparatus being used
in its measurement. In other words, how a particle performs is contingent on the specific material arrangement being used to measure its
performance: a material arrangement from which the observer cannot
be separated. As Barad outlines it, for Heisenberg, this indicated that
the observer cannot *know* the behaviour or position of matter prior to
experimentation. For Bohr, the stakes were higher. What he surmised
was that the nature of matter is *itself* indeterminate and dynamically
contingent. There are no pre-measurable properties of matter that precede their experimentation, and this indicates that matter is inherently
indeterminate.

   This suggestion for ontological indeterminacy contains another
provocation, and it concerns how it is that different identities such as
particle, observer and apparatus gain their coherence in view of their
fundamental lack of fixity. For Barad, this comes down to the nature
of phenomena as Bohr conceived it. What we might call the different
components of phenomena can only become determinate and meaningful through and within the apparatus, their identities and relations are
again entirely contingent. Thus, the relations between observer, what is
observed, the concepts that shape the measurement, and the measuring
apparatus itself, are produced *intra-* rather than inter-actively. Nothing
precedes these identities in relation/creation: the apparatus is, in a more
general sense, the phenomena to which Bohr refers. With all boundary
and meaning-making taking place intra-actively, what resolves itself as
an identity and set of behaviours also implicates that which has been
excluded in its (temporary) resolution. Actualisation always involves
the play of presence and absence in/as phenomena: it is this which

makes identity and behaviour possible, and which attests to its ongoing dynamism. In this register, phenomena are essentially posthuman
in that human identity is always entangled with and as its other in its
intra-active production.

Thus, when Barad brings ontological indeterminacy to bear upon
the question of 'nothing', something extraordinary emerges. Indeterminacy becomes 'key not only to the existence of matter, but also to
its *non*-existence, or rather it is the key to the play of non/existence'
(Barad 2012a: 15, emphasis added). Materiality, then, is *also* other
than matter; what materialises at the same time as what is absent, or
what does not materialise. To put it another way, the 'other' of matter –
'no matter' (Barad 2012a: 12), no meaning and no/thing – is entangled
in and as the differentiating nature of phenomena. This works in the
other direction too: there is an ontological indeterminacy at the heart of
the quantum vacuum that renders the void neither absolutely nothing,
nor specifically something, and this gives the vacuum an *infinite* capacity to create finite form (that is never intrinsically finite, and certainly
not singular in any bounded and atomistic sense). As a result, 'nothing'
can be understood as the generativity of what matters rather than the
opposite of life as transparent and positive substance.

Accordingly, through the quantum vacuum we can arrive at an enlarged
understanding of the 'un-ending dynamism' (Barad 2012a: 11) of materiality that new materialist ontologies proclaim. Matter's dynamism does
not crystallise in the ongoing production and expiry of 'things', but is in/
determinacy itself, where the slash between 'in' and 'determinacy' represents the constitutive inclusions as well as exclusions that cannot be sub-
tracted from processes of (im)materialisation. The diffractive un/doings of
materiality account for the 'un/doings of no/thingness' at the same time
(Barad 2012a: 12). Death, in this sense, is not *only* something that eventuates, marking a temporal limit within the broader calculus of life (that,
in an implicated way, somehow faces off with life). Nor can our materialist engagements with death congregate in figures such as the corpse,
the crypt, the memorial, or in practices of dying, in terms that might still
favour an understanding of life that is required to converse with death in
its reductively empirical, or symbolic (from the vantage point of human/
social consciousness), forms. Instead, with Barad we find that death is
entangled *with* and *as* life itself in a way that fundamentally contradicts
an ontology of presence *in its self-presence*. Life is constitutively nothing,
immobility, non-actualisation, originary failure, just as nothing, or death,
is the potential for all life forms.

The Matter of Death Redux: Life/Death

Barad's thinking upon nothing presents us with a different way of understanding the relation of life and death, and therefore with a different set of considerations for how we might think social transformation. In short, what it starts to take account of are the incapacitations, absences and ruptures to continuity or the presumed self-evidence of the social and the empirical (and their political and ethical trajectories) that challenge an understanding of life or matter in its full presence. This opens a different line of inquiry: how are we to proceed if we acknowledge that life's autopoietic structurings perform themselves through stutterings, errors, insensibilities, and the like? If we return to the earlier discussion of Braidotti with this different perspective, what might it mean, for example, to suggest that (*Zoë's*) *in*difference is the work of social morphogenesis that cannot simply be addressed or overcome by a different way of dealing with it? And the still broader question remains; what purchase might there be in exploring death *in these terms* in new materialist approaches to life itself?

Admittedly, this line of thinking through death (and nothing) is demanding; both for the way it challenges us to persist with its subtleties, and for its counter-intuitive take on the life-death relation. At the risk of repetition, however, it serves to underline again a point that I need to emphasise: if we are to rethink the (presumed) self-evidence of life or matter, as Barad's thinking through nothing prompts us to do, then death is constitutive in a more substantive, and a more implicated sense than Braidotti has allowed for. One way of putting this, with the help of Barad, is that death is constitutive as the very im/possibility of life itself.

To develop this point a little further, we might turn to the resonances between Barad's argument for the entanglement of life and death, and Jacques Derrida's designation of 'life/death' as it is explored in the work of Cary Wolfe and Vicki Kirby. In his introduction to *What is Posthumanism?*, Wolfe underscores what the life/death relation evokes for Derrida, namely, life's *in*ability to be fully present to itself. In the philosopher's own words: 'the living present springs forth out of its *nonidentity* with itself' (Derrida 1991: 26–7, cited in Wolfe 2010: xxi, emphasis added). Life/death, then, is the 'relation of the living present to its outside, the opening to exteriority in general' (Derrida 1991: 26–7, cited in Wolfe 2010: xxi), which, if I could phrase it in the terms relevant to this argument, is the *nothing* outside of the text, or death. Even 'self-referential autopoiesis', as Wolfe (2010: xxii) puts it, cannot at any point remain self-enclosed,[9] as its very closure is in the same paradoxical moment its inexorable openness. Kirby explains this a little differently as a 'superposition of states that does not divide into the either/or of mortality/immortality' (2009: 121), but rather follows the suggestion thrown forward by quantum physics that these states, as they apply to the 'one' entity, are available at the same time.

Granted, Braidotti also points to the simultaneity of life and death, so stepping into Kirby's argument in a little more detail may make the logic informing this claim, and its difference from Braidotti's own position, clearer. In her investigations of Derrida's notion of the bio-gram, we find that, like Braidotti, Kirby, too, is committed to an idea of 'Life's enduring reproduction of itself' (2009: 119). This commitment arrives with her suggestion that '*différance* is Life Itself' – life's ongoing reinvention and differentiation (Kirby 2009: 118). But, as she argues, although it may appear to be the case, arguing for life's enduring reproduction of itself should not be interpreted as a claim that 'death has been entirely overcome' (Kirby 2009: 119). Approaching that question of how we might understand the divisibility of life and death, Kirby discovers in the logic of *différance* a very different and contaminated relationality. This is divisibility that involves internal movement and displacement, difference itself fractured and dispersed (Kirby 2009: 110) such that the presence of identity or origin is fundamentally unsettled. Accordingly, if *différance* is life itself, then it is 'an epigenesis of infinite mutation' (Kirby 2009: 118), dividing itself 'originarily (*urteilen*) in order to produce itself and reproduce itself' (Derrida 1975: 3, cited in Kirby 2009: 118). With this sense of reproduction, death does not stand outside of an entity called Life. Instead, 'death would be internal to the very possibility of an entity's being itself, not simply at its birth, but throughout its ongoing re-production/othering of itself' (Kirby 2009: 120). Thus, at no point can life/death be reduced to an 'amalgam or conjunction' (Kirby 2009: 121), and we can consider both 'the either/or of mortality/immortality' (Kirby 2009: 121) as well as Braidotti's (2006: 150) 'and/and/and' in these terms. Instead of aggregation, it is 'the torsional differential that is becoming' (Kirby 2009: 121) – the materialising/immaterialising of life itself as the very nature of death.

As Kirby has argued elsewhere, it is this divisibility, not counter to death (at any level) but as the very non/presence of death as life itself, that is the constitutive energy of the social.[10] In an interview with Judith Butler, Kirby (2006: 150) figures this divisibility in terms of a sociality that encounters, in its (re)production, its own self-negating capacities (here figured in terms of suicide).[11] Again, while this claim may carry some proximity to Braidotti's argument (see for example Braidotti 2006), the difference is clear. For Kirby, these self-negating capacities constitute an 'internal relationality' (2006: 125) that cannot sustain a notion of affirmation in purely self-present terms, but that understands negation and nothingness to be *essential* to the socio-ethical operations of life itself.

In/Different Politics, In/Human Ethics

If this thinking through life/death, or life's non-coincidence with itself, is brought to bear upon how we conceive of life's potential (as *potentia*), then it significantly complicates what we regard as the scope of politics and ethics, as well as any claims around their hoped for directions. Indeed, if we return again to the comments about inhumanity raised earlier through Braidotti's argument, we are forced to reconsider whether its eventual resistance or potential repair really are the political and ethical gestures of life par excellence. Barad's exploration of the quantum vacuum and its im/materialising capacities significantly complicates Braidotti's neo-vitalist circumscription of life. Barad's argument now confronts us with a more difficult question regarding ethicality, namely, how can we respect 'the inhuman that therefore I am' (Barad 2012b: 206) without transmuting *potestas* into a 'more productive' ('positive') outcome? Barad's broader point, explored in her 2012 essay 'On Touching', is worth quoting in full here because it provokes us into a very different understanding of what ethical practice involves, at the same time that it underscores some of the limitations of Braidotti's argument already outlined above. Ontological in/determinacy, as Barad points out, suggests an ethics that takes account not only of what matters, but also of nothing(ness), with significant implications.

> For all our concerns with nonhumans as well as humans, there is, nonetheless, always something that drops out. But what if the point is not to widen the bounds of inclusion to let everyone and everything in? What if it takes sensing the abyss, the edges of the limits of 'inclusion' and 'exclusion' before the binary of inside/outside, inclusion/exclusion, mattering/not mattering can be seriously troubled? What if it is only in facing *the inhuman – the indeterminate non/being non/becoming of mattering and not mattering* – that an ethics committed to the rupture of indifference can arise? What if it is only in the encounter with the inhuman – the liminality of nothingness – in all its liveliness, its conditions of im/possibility, that we can truly confront our inhumanity, that is, our actions lacking compassion? . . . How would we feel if it is by way of the inhuman that we come to feel, to care, to respond? (Barad 2012b: 216)

Barad's refusal to revoke the inhuman certainly meets with Braidotti's claims for its generative capacities. In a footnote to her reference to the inhuman Barad (2012b: 222) clarifies that it differs from the nonhuman in a specific regard: it is 'that which holds open the space of the liveliness of indeterminacies that bleed through the cuts and inhabit the between of particular entanglements'. In other words, it is the register of finitude as the very possibility of/for life. Thus, 'the inhuman in us', for both Barad and Braidotti, is a 'putting in motion of our finitude' (Geerts and van der Tuin 2016: para. 46). But with Barad there is a difference that makes a difference. As I have suggested above, the problem within Braidotti's mobilising of the inhuman is that while it contains that double movement of evoking finitude while stretching the human beyond its previously conceived limits, when this recognition of finitude is registered exclusively in human consciousness, the human remains the foundation to, and proper political and ethical agent of, social change. Accordingly, an implicit separation of human and inhuman is enacted in the mode of addressing the negativity of the latter, and this move invalidates Braidotti's more sophisticated claims regarding its entanglement with/in, indeed *as*, life (in the guise of death, broadly construed). And further, that this politics and ethics is expected to work with a specific directionality suggests that it is, at heart, a corrective to exactly that which enables it: in other words, the inhuman in Braidotti's read may very well be a self-negating tautology, leveraged for the purposes of advocating a neo-vitalist ethics of sustainability and broadened (read: inclusive) political ontology.

For Barad, however, (the) negativity (of/as the inhuman) is not presented as something in need of an affirmative analysis or address conceived in terms of a 'positive' critical agenda or transformation of social practices, and this is because her view of materiality cannot at any point sustain a metaphysics of presence (in a 'pure' sense). The way that nothing constitutes as *also* the impossibility of mattering itself – materiality as already im/materiality, or, an im/potentiality that radicalises ontology – means that, for Barad, the inhuman does not simply stand in relation to the human and its capacity for compassionate response, nor can it be wholly accounted for in terms of the differentiating exuberance of life (in its neo-vitalist dressings). Inhumanity, in the sense that Barad reserves for it, marks a limit – finitude as a form of sensibility – *and* it registers the im/possibility of this limit – life's insensibility – in a way that scrambles any separation of positive (life/*potentia*) from negative (death/*potestas*). Further to this, it also disturbs the assumption that both are productive forces (working to different ends) that constitute the continuity, and therefore the self-presence, of life.

Thus, if we return to Barad's suggestions above, *in*sensibility looks to be *essential* to the gesture of compassion that ethics is supposed to perform.[12] Along these lines, 'we subjects' do not merely confront the inhuman horrors of our time in order to forge alternative coalitions for ethical livelihood. Nor can we reduce ethics, couched in terms of an 'affirmative' response, to specific avenues for action that, although it won't be phrased as such, can constitute as 'more ethical' in that they fulfil something of the common (collective and generational) good. What Barad directs us to with her suggestion that we respect 'the inhuman that therefore I am', is the possibility that 'we' have always, and irrevocably, been inhuman(e). Accordingly, the inhuman cannot be resisted or refused. It *is* our entangled ontology. In fact, we could say that it is the way that life performs, ethically.

Finally, what can we now say about 'the political'? How are we to work with that statement that Barad (2012b: 216) makes about '*the indeterminate non/being non/becoming of mattering and not mattering*', or what I have flagged above in the brief excursus into Barad's thinking on the quantum vacuum as the immobility, non-actualisation, and originary failure that is also, constitutively, life? In other words, what might it mean to suggest that this entangled sense of life/death that Barad conveys for us also carries the implication that power is at once *impotent*? My preliminary thought is that it makes politics quite a curious affair because automatically it puts into scrutiny its goal driven, or agenda-making, potential. It provides a response to notions of political futurity when the full impact of ontological indeterminacy is taken into account. It inscribes error in the sense of *errans*, or *errare* – to wander (Kirby 1999), at the very heart of political production. And this suggests that there is always an incalculability to politics: it conveys both an incapacity for direction as well as the potential for an error to 'always infect its correction' (Kirby 1999: 28). It makes *no* meaning part of what makes meaning, and in such a way that *potentia* is also *in*different in the sense of it making *no* difference at all. Along these lines, we could say that indifference takes the post-identitarian emphasis in a new materialist politics to its *furthest* degree. Additionally, *potentia* and *potestas* cannot be automatically allocated their status as productive forces when productivity or production itself is found to be fundamentally self-disrupting. It suggests instead that the stuttering impossibility of transformation – the 'impotentiality'[13] of our political

endeavours or the indifference of differentiation – is also constitutively
political. Thus politics cannot be confined to the work of correcting the
error of injustice and inequality. It is the failure of this address as well
as the failure for life to materialise differently. That is, there is an incalculability to politics that will both generate and undercut that capacity
for change and for anticipated outcomes, at the same time that it is
the capacity to continue to reproduce the presumed error – injustice,
inequality – that any political agenda sets about to address.

These are not kind suggestions. They do not immediately deliver
hope for a better future. A politics that factors in/difference and im/
potentiality cannot promise emancipation or redemption. But at the
same time I would point out with Barad that the possibility for justice is
never simply lost if we are to foreground negativity in thinking through
a politics of life itself. In the same way that it will fundamentally complicate the nature of 'the affirmative', Barad's logic of life/death as
entanglement admits that negativity is also never simply *pure* negation
in the uncontaminated sense. As she points out, if life is constitutively
nothing, just as nothing, or death, is the potential for all life forms,
then finitude and infinite possibility are 'infinitely threaded through one
another' (Barad 2012a: 19). Thus, with the claim that 'nothing matters' what we have to contend with is an im/possible politics – that all
boundary-making is the work of negativity that is at once creation.
Death itself is also the *already* and *ontological* opening of life. And so,
to conclude as Barad (2012a: 19) concludes, we find that 'the possibilities for justice-to-come reside in every morsel of finitude'.

Notes

1. The clarification is important in the context of Sara Ahmed's (2008: 35)
   insistence that Karen Barad, for example, has chosen to reify matter as the
   missing object and theoretical category of (feminist) new materialist analysis. In her response to Ahmed, Noela Davis (2009: 75) defends Barad
   by explaining that her engagement with matter as 'active process' and
   'entangled agential becoming' confounds matter's identity as an object, as
   something that can be isolated within theoretical practice.
2. From across the broad and divergent contributions to new materialist
   inquiry one can draw upon a host of examples that demonstrates how the
   distinction between abstracting, theorising, and representing, on the one
   hand, and material foundations, on the other, cannot be sustained in substantive terms. See, for example; Karen Barad's exploration of quantum
   physics detailed in *Meeting the Universe Halfway* (2007) and discussed in
   this chapter; Sari Irni's (2013) exploration of the material-discursive and

affective economies of sex hormones; and Noela Davis's (2014) account of epigenetics and stigma as social processes and histories that manifest or materialise at a molecular level. Rick Dolphijn and Iris van der Tuin (2012) make a clear argument for the way new materialism does not so much reject dualism as it pushes it to an extreme to demonstrate its unsustainability. Diana Coole and Samantha Frost (2010) also provide a number of examples of the way dualism is contested via new materialist analyses in their introduction to *New Materialisms*. See page 17 of their text for an outline of these.

3. For the purposes of this argument, I have drawn primarily from three key texts through which Braidotti sustains her engagement with life and death. Although the emphasis within each text differs – an earlier interest in promoting a (non)subject-oriented ethics of sustainability (2006) shifts into a detailed consideration of a posthumanist politics and ethics that take up with the inhuman (2013) – the general argument concerning death and its various citations is sustained, indeed it is repeated in part, across this *oeuvre*. I have thus attempted to synthesise Braidotti's arguments to present a coherent position, and where possible I have marked out some of the developments and tensions that this approach introduces.

4. A brief note on inconsistencies in the presentation of the terms *Zoē* and *Bios* across this chapter: the proper noun form is used throughout as it is consistent with Braidotti's deployment of these terms in her earlier (2006) text, and the diacritical mark is retained in *Zoē* as it appears in her 2010 text. However, all direct quotations keep the form with which these terms appear in the original text.

5. Here, Braidotti (2013: 2) makes specific reference to 'robotics, prosthetic technologies, neuroscience and bio-genetic capital' as well as the aspirations of 'trans-humanism and techno-transcendence'.

6. Interestingly, Braidotti's more recent comments on the ethical formulation of death in the age of the Anthropocene appear to concentrate on forms of potential extinction, for example, with climate change as a *horizon* – 'a death horizon' (2013: 11) – that is now extended to most species, not only human. This horizon of extinction both 'recomposes humanity around a commonly shared bond of vulnerability, but also connects the human to the fate of other species' (Braidotti 2013: 111). As such, 'death and destruction' emerge as 'the common denominators' for a 'transversal alliance' (Braidotti 2013: 111), or extended form of community. What is unclear about this shift in emphasis upon a horizon of shared extinction (as ethical opening) is whether it is a recuperation of the very *Thanatos*-oriented notion of finitude that Braidotti seeks to disassemble with her suggestion that death is already internal to life, or whether she is angling towards a notion of death as a limit that 'effects'; that haunts the inside of life too, much like a spectre of mortality that she suggests motivates a different ethical approach to life itself. If it is the latter, this move is consistent with the complex terrain

of death that her argument has so far advanced. However, the question becomes one of precisely *how* death haunts. That is, what is the substance of death, as a limit, in this formulation?

7. This and/and/and logic has further implications for the forms of community, or hybrid ecologies, that Braidotti champions, and this is most clear where she draws a connection between the nonhuman and the inhuman in her vitalist politics. As she explains it, 'viewing a politics of life itself as a relentlessly generative force' requires 'an interrogation of the shifting interrelations between human and *nonhuman* forces. The *latter* are defined both as *inhuman* and posthuman' (Braidotti 2010: 206, emphasis added). From this clarification, Braidotti appears to draw a clear difference between what constitutes as human, or inhuman, and this raises two points for contention. First, despite her claim that it is the inhuman *within us* that frees us into life or a different ethicality, she is suggesting here that the human can only stand *in relation to* the inhuman. Second, it is unclear how this separation of human and inhuman can be retained or even achieved in view of the overwhelming and generative nature of *Zoë*. In other words, if *Zoë* is the inhuman indifference of life itself, then in a sense it 'saturates' all being, including human being, and to the point of confounding whether we can claim, with any certainty, the human as properly itself. The alternative, separating the human from the inhuman, both retains the integrity of human identity and results in an implicit recuperation of the human as *Bios*. Given that it is her specific aim to turn the anthropocentric tide within social theory, Braidotti's separation of the human from posthuman here is also unusual. Yet it is also somehow inevitable given that the logic of relationally operating in her argument is that of interconnection. On the basis of this intervention, what she appears to be supporting is a posthuman sociality that sets the human subject into a dynamic economy of connection and relation with the more-than, or other-than, human – the very definition of anthropocentrism. This leaves Braidotti's political and ethical efforts vulnerable to the same (anthropocentric) risks that she wants to ameliorate in opening the social terrain to its posthuman inhabitations.

8. Margaret Schwartz makes a similar move in her contribution to a recent online collection titled 'Communication and New Materialism' (2013). Here, with her analysis organised through Jane Bennett's (2010) notion of assemblage, Schwartz situates the corpse as a mediating figure because it is caught between its organic materiality and 'the symbolic power of death' (2013: 1). It 'functions as an archetypal symbol of human finality', embodying 'the power of death as something that always threatens subjectivity from *elsewhere*' (Schwartz 2013: 2, original emphasis). What is introduced here is a spatial separation between a subject and its actual death, with death being that which cannot inhabit subjective life per se except in a symbolic capacity (narrowly conceived). Schwartz attempts

to bridge this separation by troubling the temporal distinction between life and death. The corpse 'destabilizes the present with the threat of flux, decay, disappearance and oblivion' (Schwartz 2013: 2). On this basis she claims that there is nothing straightforwardly here or there about the corpse, it is a 'figure of relation' between life and death (2013: 2). Nevertheless, it is positioned as such from the vantage point of life. Its active capacities congregate in the symbolic function that it carries for subjective life, and which originate in and with that subject. Aside from this symbolic function, the corpse itself is understood as an object in (reductively) evidentiary terms – it is dead matter.

9. While Wolfe explores self-referential autopoiesis in the context of first and second order systems theory, the argument that he advances here is also relevant to attempts to read life or materiality in terms of an enclosed autopoietic system (inadvertently, or not).

10. Krzysztof Ziarek (2011) offers a different view of Derrida's argument in connection with his critique of the human sovereignty that underlies formulations of ethical relation. For Ziarek (2011: 24), Derrida offers an ethics that 'coincides with the realm of the living, no longer affording priority to human beings' but which is 'nonetheless, operative within the sphere of the living'. To further Derrida's project, Ziarek suggests that what is required is an ethics that can also account for the non-living. However, in terms of the argument I am making here, Ziarek's move to draw the non-living into the space of ethical encounter, as if it is, indeed, outside and other, awaiting his intervention, still subscribes to an ontology of presence that may not privilege life per se, but which retains its focus on what can substantively or tangibly be accounted for. Here, the non-living is described as 'mineral', 'things', 'earth, air, water, sky, etc.' (Ziarek 2011: 24). In other words, what might interrupt life, conceived in its self-presence – absence, failure, stasis or void, for example – does not figure in Ziarek's delineation of 'non-living'.

11. Although it would be very useful for this analysis, I do not have space here to enter into a comparison of Kirby's suggestions regarding suicide and Braidotti's own explorations on this theme. One point worth noting, though, is that Kirby's take on suicide, following Émile Durkheim, differs from the emphasis that Braidotti lays on the volitional subject, whose decision to defer death works in the ethical register of sustaining life.

12. Barad (2012b: 217) puts this another way in her essay when she claims that 'responsibility extends to the insensible as well as the sensible'.

13. I have drawn this word from Claire Colebrook's reading of Giorgio Agamben in the introduction to her 2014 monograph, *Death of the Posthuman*. Here, she refers to Agamben's notion of human impotentiality as 'our essential capacity not to actualize that which would distinguish us as human' (Colebrook 2014: 13). For Agamben, 'the fact that we forget our impotentiality' is what maintains those normative drives for change

translated into terms of efficiency and progress (2014: 13). It would take more work than allowed in the space of this chapter for a comprehensive engagement with Agamben's argument and Colebrook's response. Similarly, it would be a curious exercise to dislodge this notion from its seemingly exclusive reference to the human, understood in the sense of a 'principle' of humanity. In any case, it is what impotentiality flags at a base level – the suggestion that 'humanity is not an actuality from which we can draw grounds for action' (2014: 13) – that most interests me here.

References

Ahmed, S. (2008), 'Open Forum Imaginary Prohibitions: Some Preliminary Remarks on the Founding Gestures of the 'New Materialism', *European Journal of Women's Studies*, 15: 1, pp. 23–39.

Barad, K. (2007), *Meeting the Universe Halfway: Quantum Physics and the Entanglement of Matter and Meaning*, Durham, NC: Duke University Press.

Barad, K. (2012a), *What is the Measure of Nothingness? Infinity, Virtuality, Justice*, Documenta 13, Ostfildern, Germany: Hatje Cantz.

Barad, K. (2012b), 'On Touching – The Inhuman That Therefore I Am', *differences: A Journal of Feminist Cultural Studies*, 25: 5, pp. 206–23.

Bennett, J. (2010), *Vibrant Matter: A Political Ecology of Things*, Durham, NC: Duke University Press.

Braidotti, R. (1994), *Nomadic Subjects: Embodiment and Sexual Difference in Contemporary Feminist Theory*, New York: Columbia University Press.

Braidotti, R. (2006), 'The Ethics of Becoming-Imperceptible', in C. V. Boundas (ed.), *Deleuze and Philosophy*, Edinburgh: Edinburgh University Press, pp. 133–59.

Braidotti, R. (2010), 'The Politics of "Life Itself" and New Ways of Dying', in D. Coole and S. Frost (eds), *New Materialisms: Ontology, Agency, and Politics*, Durham, NC: Duke University Press, pp. 201–18.

Braidotti, R. (2013), *The Posthuman*, Cambridge: Polity Press.

Colebrook, C. (2014), *Death of the Posthuman: Essays on Extinction, Volume 1*, Ann Arbor: Michigan Publishing, University of Michigan Library.

Coole, D., and S. Frost (2010), 'Introducing the New Materialisms', in D. Coole and S. Frost (eds), *New Materialisms: Ontology, Agency, and Politics*, Durham, NC: Duke University Press, pp. 1–43.

Davis, N. (2009), 'New Materialism and Feminism's Anti-Biologism: A Response to Sara Ahmed', *European Journal of Women's Studies*, 16: 1, pp. 67–80.

Davis, N. (2014), 'Politics Materialized: Rethinking the Materiality of Feminist Political Action Through Epigenetics', *Women: A Cultural Review*, 25: 1, Spring, pp. 62–77.

Dolphijn, R., and I. van der Tuin (2012), *New Materialism: Interviews & Cartographies*, Open Humanities Press. An imprint of MPublishing, Ann Arbor: University of Michigan Library.

Geerts, E., and I. van der Tuin (2016), 'The Feminist Futures of Reading Diffractively: How Barad's Methodology Replaces Conflict-based Readings of Beauvoir and Irigaray', *rhizomes: Cultural Studies in Emerging Knowledge*, 30, available at <http://DOI:10.20415/rhiz/030.e02/ > (last accessed 9 August 2016).

Irni, S. (2013), 'Sex, Power, and Ontology: Exploring the Performativity of Hormones', *NORA-Nordic Journal of Feminist and Gender Research*, 21: 1, pp. 41–56.

Kirby, V. (1999), 'Human Nature', *Australian Feminist Studies*, 14: 29, pp. 19–29.

Kirby, V. (2006), *Judith Butler: Live Theory*, London: Continuum.

Kirby, V. (2009), 'Tracing Life: La Vie La Mort', *CR: The New Centennial Review*, 9: 1, Spring, pp. 107–26.

Schwartz, M. (2013), 'An Iconography of the Flesh: How Corpses Mean as Matter', *Communication +1*, 2, pp. 1–16, available at <http://scholarworks.umass.edu/cpo/vol2/iss1/1/> (last accessed 15 September 2013).

Thiele, K. (2014), 'Pushing Dualisms and Differences: From "Equality *versus* Difference" To "Nonmimetic Sharing *and* Staying With the Trouble"', *Women: A Cultural Review*, 25: 1, Spring, pp. 9–26.

van der Tuin, I., and R. Dolphijn (2010), 'The Transversality of New Materialism', *Women: A Cultural Review*, 21: 2, pp. 153–71.

Wolfe, C. (2010), *What is Posthumanism?*, Minneapolis: University of Minnesota Press.

Ziarek, K. (2011), 'The Limits of Life: a non-anthropocentric view of world and finitude', *Angelaki: Journal of the Theoretical Humanities*, 16: 4, pp. 19–30.

Notes on Contributors

Vicki Kirby is Professor of Sociology in the School of Social Sciences, The University of New South Wales in Sydney. She is a prominent figure in new materialist debates and in recent attempts to review the work of Jacques Derrida through a more scientific lens. Books include *Quantum Anthropologies: Life at Large* (Duke 2011), *Judith Butler: Live Theory* (Continuum 2006) and *Telling Flesh: the substance of the corporeal* (Routledge 1997). She has articles forthcoming in *Derrida Today; Parallax, PhiloSophia, Journal for the Theory of Social Behaviour*, and a chapter in David Woods et al. (eds), *Eco-Deconstruction* (Fordham University Press).

Ashley Barnwell is the Ashworth Lecturer in Sociology in the School of Social and Political Sciences, University of Melbourne. Her research is based in cultural sociology and social theory, and focuses on the ethics and politics of truth-telling and sharing stories in public life. She has published interdisciplinary research in journals such as *Cultural Sociology, Cultural Studies, Life Writing*, and *Continuum: Journal of Media and Cultural Studies* and is currently working on a book manuscript about methodological debates in social theory, *Living Truth: Critique, Affect, and the Politics of Method*.

Florence Chiew is Head of Higher Degree Research Learning for Social Science at Macquarie University, Sydney. She has published in *Theory, Culture & Society, Journal of Consciousness Studies, Critical Studies in Education* and has contributed to *Anthropocene: Critical Perspectives on Non-Human Futures* (Sydney University Press 2015) and *Relational Concepts in Medicine* (2010, papers from Oriel College Oxford). Her current book project, *Social Physics: Classical and Contemporary* addresses sociology's relevance for a more recent set of debates around ecological ethics, the plasticity of volition and predictive models of human behaviour.

Michelle Jamieson holds a PhD in Sociology and is a Lecturer at Macquarie University, Sydney. Moving between sociology, feminist science studies and the medical humanities, her research critically engages the division between sociality and biology, especially in relation to illness and medicine. Articles include 'The Politics of Immunity' (2015), *Body and Society*, and 'Imagining Reactivity: Allergy Within the History of Immunology' (2010), *Studies in History and Philosophy of Biological and Biomedical Sciences*. She is currently co-editing a special issue of the philosophy journal *Parallax* on the theme 'autoimmunities'.

Rebecca Oxley received her PhD in the Social Sciences from The University of New South Wales, Sydney. She currently holds a three-year Postdoctoral Research Fellowship in the Centre for Medical Humanities at Durham University. Funded by the Wellcome Trust, the project investigates 'The Life of Breath' by drawing on biomedical information and cultural, literary, historical and phenomenological research. Rebecca is intrigued by how and what empirical and theoretical explorations of biology can tell us about being-in-the-world, and what hidden and unexpected complexities comprise lived experience, embodiment and patterns of phenomena.

Noela Davis is an independent scholar who teaches regularly in the School of Social Sciences, The University of New South Wales, where she received her PhD in Sociology. Her research interests range across disciplinary boundaries to encompass new materialisms, Foucault on power and bio-politics, and the implications of epigenetics and social genetics for our social lives. Her work has been published in the *European Journal of Women's Studies*, *Hypatia* and *Nutrition, Epigenetics and Health*, edited by Graham Burdge and Karen Lillycrop.

Xin Liu is a postdoctoral researcher at the School of Social Sciences and Humanities, University of Tampere. Her doctoral dissertation, published by Åbo Akademi University Press, explores perceptions of race. She is a board member of Gendering Asia Network, based at the Nordic Institute of Asian Studies at the University of Copenhagen, and is involved in the management committee of COST Action New Materialism Network (European Cooperation in Science and Technology). Her research interests include feminist science studies, feminist theory and critical race theory. She has a recent publication in *Australian Feminist Studies*.

Jacqueline Dalziell is completing a PhD in Sociology at The University of New South Wales in Sydney and lectures in Environmental Humanities. She is the recipient of several academic scholarships and awards, and was Campaigns Manager at *Animal Liberation* 2008–12 where she spearheaded several national animal rights campaigns and worked extensively with print and visual media. Her work lies at the intersection of feminist theory, continental philosophy, posthumanism and animal studies.

Astrida Neimanis is a lecturer in Gender and Cultural Studies at the University of Sydney. She has published widely on water, weather and other environmental matters in journals that include *Hypatia*, *Somatechnics* and *Feminist Review*. Her monograph, *Bodies of Water*, is forthcoming in 2016 (Bloomsbury Environmental Cultures Series), while *Thinking with Water*, her co-edited collection of cultural theory, was published in 2013 (McGill-Queen's). She is a Key Researcher with Sydney Environment Institute, and co-founder of

The Seed Box: Environmental Humanities Collaboratory – an international research consortium based at Linkoping University, Sweden.

Will Johncock currently teaches in the School of Social Sciences at The University of New South Wales where he received his PhD in Sociology. Publications include *Journal for the Theory of Social Behaviour, Phenomenology and Practice*, and chapters in A. S. Wilson (ed.) *Fly Rhythm,* K. Buccieri (ed.) *Body Tensions: Beyond Corporeality in Time and Space*, and L. McLean, L. Stafford and M. Weeks (eds), *Exploring Bodies in Time and Space*. Will's work is interdisciplinary, however his main research focus concerns questions of time and phenomenology.

Peta Hinton is a feminist new materialist scholar who has held several post-doctoral fellowships; an Erasmus Mundus Scholar (Utrecht University), a Fellow at the Institute for Cultural Inquiry, Berlin, and currently an Honorary Scholar with the University of New South Wales, Sydney. She is published in *Hypatia, Somatechnics, Women: A Cultural Review*, and *Australian Feminist Studies*. She is co-editor of 'Feminist Matters: The Politics of New Materialism' (*Women: A Cultural Review* special issue, 2014), a volume in the AtGender series, *Teaching With Feminist Materialisms*, 2015, and has edited a recent issue of *rhizomes* with Karin Sellberg (Issue 30, 2016).

Index

EU representative:
Easy Access System Europe
Mustamäe tee 50, 10621 Tallinn, Estonia
Gpsr.requests@easproject.com

www.ingramcontent.com/pod-product-compliance
Lightning Source LLC
Chambersburg PA
CBHW081737270326
41932CB00020B/3301